HONOR BRIGHT

A CENTURY OF SCOUTING
IN NORTHERN STAR COUNCIL

DAVE KENNEY

NORTHERN STAR COUNCIL
BOY SCOUTS OF AMERICA

PUBLISHED BY
Northern Star Council, Boy Scouts of America
St. Paul and Minneapolis, Minnesota

IN PARTNERSHIP WITH
North Star Museum of Boy Scouting and Girl Scouting

PROJECT DIRECTION
Peg Guilfoyle, Peg Projects, Inc.

DESIGN
Cathy Spengler Design

ISBN 978-0-9824467-2-0 (cloth)
ISBN 978-0-615-32452-4 (paper)

ABOUT THE COVER

James "Dad" Drew was the first Scoutmaster of what now ranks as the Northern Star Council's second oldest troop, St. Anthony Park Troop 17. He was renowned in Scouting circles for his skills with rope and could tie more than 100 different knots. For many years, the knot-tying section of Scouting's Handbook for Boys featured illustrations of "Dad" Drew's hands.

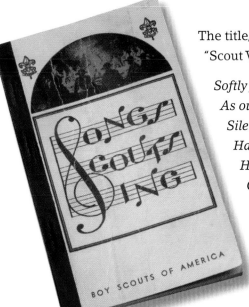

The title, "Honor Bright," was inspired by the first verse of the song, "Scout Vesper," which appeared in midcentury Boy Scout songbooks:

Softly falls the light of day,
As our camp fire fades away;
Silently each Scout should ask,
Have I done my daily task?
Have I kept my honor bright?
Can I guiltless sleep tonight?
Have I done and have I dared
Everything to Be Prepared?

Centennial Commission Membership > vi

Foreword > viii

Preface > ix

Acknowledgments > x

Introduction > 1

1910s

5

NOW+THEN

TROOP

15

1920s

27

NOW+THEN

ACHIEVEMENT

37

1930s

49

1960s

115

NOW+THEN

GATHERING

125

1970s

137

NOW+THEN

JAMBOREE

147

1980s

159

NOW+THEN

OUTING

59

1940s

71

NOW+THEN

CAMP PART 1

81

1950s

93

NOW+THEN

CAMP PART 2

103

NOW+THEN

SERVICE

169

1990s

181

NOW+THEN

SCOUTER

191

2000s

203

Conclusion > 214

Key Three Leadership > 216

Council Names, Territories, and Office Locations > 218

Northern Star Council Silver Beavers > 220

Camps of the Northern Star Council and Predecessors > 224

Table of Contents for Centennial History DVD > 225

Notes > 226

Illustration Credits > 230

Index > 231

CENTENNIAL COMMISSION MEMBERSHIP

As of October 13, 2009

The publication of this Centennial History of Scouting in the Northern Star Council was one of the many important projects made possible by the Scouters and Friends of the Centennial Commission. Their mission was to provide leadership and funding to fully prepare for and celebrate the 100th Anniversary of the Boy Scouts of America within our communities.

Daniel B. Ahlberg, M.D.
Thomas H. Alt, M.D.
Clint Andera
Tim & Amy Anders
Faith G. Anderson
Terri L. Anderson
John & Cheryl Andrews
David & Peggy Arola
Norman W. Baer
Brad & Mary Bakken
Larry E. Bakken
Vickie Bakken
George & Sandie Baldwin
Greg Ball
Collin Barr
David Barsness
Paul Bartyzal
Jill & Robert Bastyr
Mary & George N. Battis, Jr., M.D.
Alan & Lisa Bernick
Troy & Debbie Billings
Gerald C. Bird
Rolf & Idelle Bjelland
Donald & Carol Blacker
Rachel & Michael Blacker
Cortland Bolles
Marv & Betty Borman
James & Jayne Bradshaw
Steve & Suzanne Braun
C. William Briggs
Bill & Karen Brown
Randall Buffie
William & Shirley Bull
Brian & Cindy Bullock
Thomas & Kristine Burbank
Darrell D. Butterwick
Winslow & Linda Buxton
John T. & Susan M. Capecchi
David Carlsen
Robert & Sandra Cedergren
Brad & Mary Chapin
Ronald & Janet Christenson
Jon & Ann Cieslak

Jeffrey W. & Ayanna Coleman
Norb & Mary Ellen Conzemius
James J. Corniea, Sr.
Fritz & Glenda Corrigan
Dr. & Mrs. Kenneth Crabb
Loren Croone
Patti & Kevin Czech
Nancy Randall Dana
William E. & Kay Davies
Robert S. Davis
Sarah & Andrew Dawson
Scott & Mary Degel
David & Julie Denn
The Devine Family
Rob DeWolfe
Chuck & Dottie Dietz
Rich Dohrmann
John E. Dustman
Robert W. Elliott, Jr.
Don & Nancy Engle
William Falconer
Carol & Jim Forrest
Roland & Beulah Francis
Kay Fredericks & Richard Cisek
Mr. & Mrs. William B. Frels
Eugene & Mary Frey
Lawrence Gagner
Mike & Frances Galvin
Allison Gardiner
Jay & Betsy Garey
David & Nina Garfield
Jim & Mary Gillespie
Chuck Gitzen
Joseph W. Glenski
Dennis & Michelle Goetz
Jerome Gohl
Andrew C. Goke
Philip & Helen Goodrich
Pamela A. Grayson
Howard & Betsy Guthmann
John & Teresa Guthmann
C.R. & Cynthia Hackworthy
Richard & Kathleen Halverson

Harry Hammerly
Mr. & Mrs. Robert J. Hannah, Sr.
John J. Hanson, III
John J. Hanson, IV
Susan Harrison
Charles L. Hawley, Jr.
Bruce Herbst
Barbara Corti Herrmann
Chris Holm
Charles & Cynthia Huntley
Melinda Inman
Allen F. Jacobson
Amy & Carter Johnson
Galen & Ann Johnson
Gary C. Johnson
George E. Johnson
Laurie J. Johnson
Monte & Merrick Johnson
Orville Johnson
Paul O. Johnson
Peter Johnson
Philip & Carla Johnson
Michael & Deborah Jonikas
Mark A. Jorgensen
Eileen Mitzi Karl
Jeanne Katz
Paul Kaus
Martin Kellogg
Doug & Katy King
Bob & Sandy Klas
Douglas Kleist
David & Emily Kline
Dan & Joann Knuth
Richard A. Koechlein
Robert S. Koepke
Melissa & Brian Kogler
Jeffrey Kohen, M.D.
James P. Kortz
Skip & Sarah Krawczyk
Stuart Krueger
James & Linda Lee
Stephen Lewis & Judith Frost Lewis
Marshall S. & Katie M. Lichty

Sven, Christine & Hunter Lindquist
Layne Lodmell
Frank Lundberg Post 282
Hugh & Marilyn Madson
John & Sallie March
John A. Martin
Scott & Brenda Martin
Mark & Katey McCabe
Michael R. & Sarah McCarthy
Paul McGinnis, M.D.
Bert J. McKasy
The McKim Family
David & Karyl Mienke
Loren Meinke
Ryan Miske
Eileen Momsen
Thomas G. Morgan
Lawrence E. Moser
G. Douglas & Lynn Nelson
Richard Neuner & Laura Kinkead
Barbara J. Newman
Julie Nitti
Greg & Jill Nonweiler
David R. & Billie Novy
Jennifer Nutter
Scott Oeth
Carol Oldowski

Robert S. Oldowski
Charles Opp
Peggy Opp
Pack 217, Saint Paul
Gregory & Cynthia Page
Robert G. Parent
Carl A. Patow, M.D.
John & Deborah Patterson
Randy & Mary Kay Pearce
Dennis Pederson
Jon & Sophie Pederson
Andrea Pengra
Dale & Jeri Peterson
Robert & Carol Pettitt
The Peyton Family
Ron & Betty Phillippo
Michelle A. Pitheon
Michelle & Steve Pritchard
Don & Peg Qually
Alberto Quintela, Jr.
Linda Rawlings
Joseph A. Reding
Mr. & Mrs. William Reiling
Marie & Jim Rice
W. Patrick & Jeanne Riley
Orem Robbins
Bob & Joyce Rosene
Steve & Shelly Rucks
Jim Rupert
Lawrence P. Sachi
Christopher K. Sandberg
Bill & Martha Saul
Matthew Thomas Schafer
The Schreader Family
Mark Schroeder
Rob Schultz
Jim & Jen Schwieger
LaMonte & Paula Scrabeck
Daniel & Carol Segersin
Richard & Nancy Shaeffer
Richard D. Shank
James & Joanne Simones
Elaine Sinn
The Sit Family
Michael & Julianne Sixel
Craig Calvin Sixta
Lee & Peg Skold
Paul & Marjean Skoog
John & Jeanette Slaughter
Dr. Richard E. Smith
Warren & Mary Lynn Staley
E. Duncan & Marilyn Steinman
Tom & Erin Stober

Bob & Arlene Strom
Jeffrey & Patricia Sulzbach
William L. Sulzbach
Travis & Rebecca Sutten
Nyda Swanson
Lynn Swon
Paul A. Taylor
Jon & Lea Theobald
Troop 17, St. Anthony Park, MN
Troop 303, Chaska MN
Troop 589, Chaska MN
Thomas N. & Virginia Turba
John & Leslie Turner
Brian Uhlenhopp
Roger Vasko
Steve & Monica Weekes
Thomas P. Welna
David & Janet Wettergren
Kim & Helen Whitney
Justin K. Williams
Roland Wilsey
Steven L. & Marjorie A. Wojan
Ken & Nancy Woodrow
Scott & Joyce Woolery
Harold & June Wright
Kathryn Elizabeth Wyatt
Xia C. Yang
Kent & Cindy York
Richard & Janine Zehring
Phil Zoubek

WE ARE SO PROUD, on behalf of the community movement that is the Boy Scouts of America, to present you with this centennial history of Scouting in Northern Star Council's 25-county territory.

Please . . . set aside the quiet moments necessary to read and absorb this entire book. We are confident that you will be entertained, inspired, moved, and called to action.

Your action, then, will make all the difference.

This gathering up of events, people, places and things—all symbols of the largest youth movement the world has ever known—is dedicated to the volunteer: the Scoutmaster, the merit badge counselor, the commissioner, the donor.

Poet Edgar A. Guest wrote of the Scoutmaster:

There isn't any pay for you, you serve without reward,
The boys who tramp the fields with you but little could afford.
And yet your pay is richer far than those who toil for gold,
For in a dozen different ways your service shall be told.

Nay, in a hundred different ways your service shall be told.

On one day in June 2009, while one of our Scouts was being honored in the national media as the BSA's two millionth Eagle Scout at the Base Camp groundbreaking, Judge John Guthmann (chair of the Centennial History Book Committee) was presiding over a trial in which another young man was being convicted of selling heroin.

In *two million* different ways your service shall be told, and . . .

As we celebrate 100 years of making a difference, we are reminded that our work is not done, and never will be. Sir Robert Baden Powell subscribed to the saying that "the boy is the father of the man." Legions of good people have since subscribed to that belief, and in this book are their stories, on behalf of every future man and future woman.

Read this book. Consider what your legacy will be in the second century of Scouting. Go out and make a difference.

Yours in Scouting,

Thomas H. Alt, M.D.
Centennial President

Jon R. Pederson
Centennial Commissioner

John R. Andrews
Centennial Scout Executive

HOW DOES AN INNOVATIVE and forward-looking organization like the Northern Star Council find the time to look back and reflect on 100 years of youth development and community service? And why? At most, the organization keeps moving forward with one eye on where it has been, and, as Pearl Buck said, "If you want to understand today, you have to search yesterday."

The effort to document and commemorate the centennial of Scouting in the Northern Star Council, Boy Scouts of America, began in February 2006 with a small group of interested volunteers facilitated by author and volunteer Scouter Deb Gelbach. Raising more questions than answers, the group considered potential topics, the variety of media available to distribute historical images, stories and data, and how to organize production efforts. The project was difficult to conceptualize and it seemed that putting the Council's first 100 years in one place would be an unattainable task. We certainly wanted to take heed of the warning once issued by author Hannah Farnham Lee, "A mere compilation of facts presents only the skeleton of history." Whatever form our production would take, it would be rich with the stories of Scouting rather than be a repository of lists and numbers.

After nearly four years of meetings, planning, writing and fact checking, you are holding the product of that first meeting in your hands. In the fall of 2007, we embarked in earnest on the Centennial History Book venture when the Northern Star Council and the North Star Museum of Boy Scouting and Girl Scouting entered into a contract to engage Peg Guilfoyle of Peg Projects, Inc., as project director. Peg enlisted her award-winning team of well-known local author Dave Kenney as writer and designer Cathy Spengler to sign on for the duration. The three have collaborated to create published histories of several significant regional institutions including Plymouth Congregational Church and the Minnesota Telecom Alliance. The former project received a national book award. Peg Guilfoyle also produced the award-winning history of the Guthrie Theater. As you enjoy this book, you will appreciate the unique talents of Peg, Dave, and Cathy.

Dave Kenney's vision and the design concepts of Cathy Spengler were certainly enhanced by our partnership with Jostens, Inc. Thanks to the generosity of Jostens, we could afford to reproduce the colorful history of the Northern Star Council in a beautiful full-color volume. We are deeply grateful.

No organizational history is possible without the volunteer efforts of many people. In late 2007 the Centennial History Book Committee was formed to oversee production of the book and to otherwise help out as needed along the way. Each member of the committee gave significant amounts of their time and talents on top of whatever else they contribute as council volunteers or staff. Thank you to committee members John Andrews, Bruce Cary, Deborah Gelbach, Steve Granger, Gary Gorman, Howard Guthmann, Barb Herrmann, Tim Jopek, Kurt Leichtle, Claudia Nicholson, Bob Nelson, Bob Oldowski, Charlie Opp, Rick Schaefer, Jim Schuster, Hank Seifert, Terry Wolkerstorfer, and Kent York. Thanks to Mary Schuster for helping with fact checking.

Our history book is filled with striking original images of Scouting memorabilia and other examples of the Northern Star Council's material culture. Special thanks to Doug Knutson of Knutson Photography, who donated his time and talents to make inclusion of these images possible. Another thank you goes to staff member Clint Andera, whose cartography skills produced the maps you see in the book.

David Thelen once wrote that the "challenge of history is to recover the past and introduce it to the present." Dave Kenney has more than met the challenge. As you read this book, you will recognize the timelessness of Scouting. You will see a piece of yourself on every page regardless of the era or the topic. Enjoy this book for the past it brings to life and for the future generations it will inform.

Judge John H. Guthmann
Chair, Centennial History Book Committee,
Northern Star Council

ACKNOWLEDGMENTS

I SHOULD HAVE KNOWN that people in the local Scouting community, upon hearing that I was writing a history of the Northern Star Council, would almost invariably ask me the same simple question: "Are you a Scout?" After initially fumbling for a suitable response, I finally came up with a stock answer: "Actually, I was a Cub Scout for only one year," I responded, pausing for effect. "But my father is an Eagle Scout!"

So, Dad, thanks for bequeathing to me a semblance of Scouting legitimacy.

To be sure, the Northern Star Council took a leap of faith when it decided to trust its history to a writer with such a skimpy Scouting résumé. Thankfully, though, I've received guidance throughout the research and writing process from a wealth of Scouting professionals and volunteers who graciously put up with my ignorance of such things as the intricacies of Cub Scout advancement. The list of those who deserve thanks necessarily begins with the members of the Centennial History Book Committee, all of whom were properly acknowledged in John Guthmann's preface. I would, however, like to single out several members of the committee for special mention: John Guthmann, John Andrews, and Kent York, for putting in much extra time with me outside the regular committee schedule; Claudia Nicholson, for granting me broad access to the collections of the North Star Museum of Boy Scouting and Girl Scouting (which, by the way, you should make a point of visiting); and Terry Wolkerstorfer for serving as my copy editor—a thankless job if there ever was one.

The information and images found in this book come from multiple sources, and I'm very grateful to the following people for making those sources available to me: George Battis, Jr.; Reid Christopherson; Jim Frost; Bill Hoffman: Mike Hughes; Kevin James; Matt Mamura; David Pearson; Jon Pederson; David Pettiford; Dave Roberts; Mike Smith; Norma Spicer; Travis Sutten; Mike Worcester; and Steve Young. An extra round of applause goes to Bob Hannah, owner and operator of the fascinating Scouting Memories Museum in Savage, for letting us include in this book several rare items from his marvelous collection.

As you soon will discover, a substantial portion of this book is devoted to stories of current-day Scouts and Scouters. I never could have told those stories without the cooperation of the people I wrote about. Special thanks, then, to Mark Marrone, Joel Ohman, Jacob Olson, Joshua Olson, Steve Olson, Corwin Diamond, Matt Swallow, Jim Schuster, Gary Zielinski, Dan Bennett, Bryce Palmer, Bob Nelson, and dozens of others for letting me invade their space.

Finally, I extend my deepest gratitude to the production team that turned my words into the handsome volume you are now reading: to Doug Knutson, who volunteered hours of his valuable time to photograph the many colorful objects that populate these pages; to my frequent collaborator, Cathy Spengler, who once again delighted me with her creativity and unexpected designs; and to my friend and colleague, Peg Guilfoyle, who kept me on task and did all that essential work that I'm incapable of doing on my own. You all make writing history fun.

—D.K.

IT WASN'T UNTIL THE LAST WEEK of August 1910, during the annual run of the Minnesota State Fair, that the people of the Upper Midwest first began taking notice of a new boys' "movement" that was spreading across the globe. The publisher and editors of the *St. Paul Pioneer Press*—always on the look-out for stories that might boost their readership—devoted most of the "Boys and Girls Section" in that week's Sunday edition to "a very interesting story [that] every boy and girl will want to read." It was the still-developing saga of the Boy Scouts of America.[1]

As the newspaper noted, the Boy Scout movement had taken root a few years earlier in England. Its founder was British military officer Robert S. S. Baden-Powell, a celebrated national hero of the Boer War in South Africa. Baden-Powell's 1908 Boy Scout manual, *Scouting for Boys* (a revision of his well-received military training manual, *Aids to Scouting*), had inspired thousands of boys throughout England and the British colonies to form their own Scouting patrols and troops, and to rediscover the joys of outdoor life. By 1910, *Scouting for Boys* was a bestseller in the United States as well, and American boys were clamoring to join the fun.

At first, the American version of the Boy Scout movement was a jumble of good intentions and unfocused enthusiasm. Boys and adults who desired to form patrols and troops had to do so on their own. There was no national organization to guide them. But in June 1910, the pieces of America's fragmented Boy Scout movement began coming together. At a meeting spearheaded by a YMCA executive named Edgar Robinson, leaders representing about two dozen national youth and social work groups set in motion the creation of a permanent Boy Scout organization in the United States. The participants included several men whose names would forever be associated with America's early Boy Scout movement.

Topping the list was William Dickson Boyce, a millionaire Chicago publisher who had incorporated the Boy Scouts of America on February 8, 1910. Boyce traced his interest in the Boy Scouts back to a memorable encounter on the foggy streets of London. He had lost his way in the pea-soup murk and had just about given up hope of arriving at his destination when a boy, about 12 years old, approached him and offered to help. When Boyce tried to give the boy a shilling for his trouble, the youngster declined, explaining that he was one of Baden-Powell's Scouts and that Scouts did not accept tips for good turns. Boyce was so impressed that he set out to introduce Scouting to the United States.

Also at the meeting was Ernest Thompson Seton, a well-known naturalist, wildlife artist, author, and lecturer. Seton was the founder of the Woodcraft

BOY SCOUT AND JUVENILE SECTION

St. Paul Sunday Pioneer Press
and St. Paul Sunday Dispatch

ST. PAUL, MINN., SUNDAY, MARCH 24, 1912.

COLLEGE PROFESSOR AND STUDENTS ACT AS SCOUT MASTER'S ASSISTANTS.

REV. EDWIN B. DEAN,
Scout Master.

DR. FRANZ F. EXNER,
Leader Mustang Patrol.

ARTHUR PERSONS,
Leader Wolf Patrol.

DAVID REMPEL,
Leader Owl Patrol.

Northfield Boys Become Scouts, Having Adequate Leadership and Unusually Favorable Facilities

Pastor Who Is Very Popular With Boys Is Scout Master—Carleton Professor and Students Act as Patrol Leaders

Special to the Pioneer Press.

NORTHFIELD, Minn., March 23.— The Boy Scout movement has just begun to receive recognition in this city, but there is now in the process of formation a troop which should become one of the strongest in the Northwest.

Boy Scouting has been on probation here, so to speak, since it first reached the city about a year ago. The people and the boys, too, have been sitting back studying the movement and watching carefully to see if it really measured up to all that was claimed for it, and there has been a steadily increasing favorable sentiment, which is now culminating in organizing the work on a firm and lasting basis.

How the Boys Were Introduced to It.

The movement first took root here about a year ago, when the Rev. Edwin B. Dean, pastor of the Congregational church and a man who has done wonders for the boys of this city, became convinced of the merits of the organization. He obtained a Scout Master's certificate and began work with the officers of the Boys' Brigade, teaching them the Scout oath, the laws and other fundamentals of the work. Then, at the summer encampment of the Boys' Brigade, he taught these principles to every boy in camp. Each day a certain part of the Scout law was assigned to be learned and no boy was allowed to take his morning swim until he had mastered his lesson.

Three Patrols Organized Last September.

As he had plenty of adult assistants and the boys were eager to become real, full-fledged Scouts, three patrols were organized last September. One patrol, the Mustang, was placed in charge of Dr. Franz F. Exner, who has charge of the chemical department of Carleton college; another patrol, the Owl, was placed in charge of David Rempel, a junior student at Carleton, while the third, the Wolf, was taken charge of by Arthur Persons, a freshman at Carleton.

Leaders Came to the Scout Rally Here.

These three patrols have been working steadily all winter and their membership has been increasing. Just before the time of the visit of Sir Robert at the time of the visit of Sir Robert Baden-Powell, interest in Scouting increased rapidly. Mr. and Mrs. Persons, accompanied by one Scout, attended the rally and made a complete report to the boys at their return.

What the Olivet Boys Did.

On Friday evening, March 15, the annual boys' banquet was held at the Congregational church and the main feature of the program was an exhibition of Scout work by eight Boy Scouts from Olivet Troop, St. Paul. This exhibition made such an impression that within two days following, enough boys to form two full patrols and part of a third signified their intention of becoming Scouts. They will be enrolled in the troop immediately.

Unusual Facilities for Work With Boys.

It is unlikely that there is any city in the Northwest which has such facilities for working with boys as has Northfield. Through the excellent work of Mr. Dean with the Boys' Brigade and other organizations the people have come to be heartily in sympathy with boys' work and willing to support it well. While the center of the boys' activities is the Congregational church, denominational prejudices are so slight that all the boys in the city are able to enjoy the excellent facilities provided for them by this church.

Among these facilities the most important is a big gymnasium completely equipped with apparatus and hot and cold shower baths. There is also a three-acre tract of land on the shore of Union lake, eight miles from town, improved with five cottages, a big dining room and a kitchen.

On the Canon river, which flows through the center of town, is a steel boat named the "Scout" which is big enough to hold a whole patrol and which is at the disposal of the boys during the summer months.

Every spring the boys give an exhibition to earn money to pay the expenses of a summer camp which gives them a two weeks' outing at their Union lake home.

Scout Master Problem Easily Solved There.

These are some of the advantages the Boy Scouts of Northfield will enjoy from the very start. But an even greater advantage is the fact that there are plenty of men willing to work with the boys. The Scout Master problem is one easy of solution. Every patrol will be in charge of an adult while the affairs of the troop as a whole will be looked after by Mr. Dean.

With such advantages, coupled with the fact that the ground has been so carefully prepared and the plans for organization so well worked out, the Northfield Scouts will undoubtedly develop into a most efficient organization. The members of the three patrols which have been organized are:

MUSTANG.
Dr. Franz Exner, leader; Hill, Hunt, Exner, Gilbert, Street, Bundy, Rempel, Wilson.

OWL.
David Rempel, leader; Dayton, Large, Bonne, Bue, Fuller, Peterson, Offerdal.

WOLF.
Arthur Persons, leader; Lyme, Armstrong, Bertrand, Lee, Suseman, Harold Healy, George Healy, Rigs.

Nibowka Troop Leads in Trophy Contest

Twilight troop, which now holds the trophy shield, will have to keep on hustling if it means to keep possession of it.

Last Sunday the published record allowed the Twilights to be ahead in the present contest, but the Nibowkas have been "digging in their toes" since then, with the result that they have forged ahead of the St. Anthony Park boys. Their lead, however, is only a little more than a hundred points, and now that Twilight has carried out its successful entertainment (preparations for which took a lot of time) the troop probably will be getting back to those things which count for more on the contest score card. So the First Baptist church fellows will have to keep on hustling to retain their lead.

But maybe the Morning Stars or the Arlingtons or the Dayton's Bluff Indiana will spring a surprise on everybody else by leaping to the top! Who knows?

TROOP STANDINGS.

Troop	Points
Nibowka troop, First Baptist church	12,372
Twilight troop, F. A. Cone	12,245
Morning Star troop, George Winge	11,507
Arlington troop, C. D. Loudin	10,552
Dayton's Bluff Indian troop, C. W. Eddy	8,810
Sibley troop, J. H. Wheeler	5,066
Australian troop, C. B. Fosbroke	5,244
Baden-Powell troop, W. Freljsen	6,090
Olivet troop, W. A. Buchanan and J. H. Sowerby	5,500
Curley troop, William Phillips	4,956
Roy Roy troop, F. S. Heron	3,300
Tukanwadel troop, L. M. Burs	3,305
Troop M., D. Lange	2,741
Troop B, Frank Lund	744

Good Turns Begin At Home, Says B.-P.

Sir Robert S. S. Baden-Powell says that good turns like charity should begin at home.

"I have often heard," he says, "of a Scout going about looking for someone he could find to help, and complaining that he could not find a chance of doing his good turn. All the time he had a mother at home working away at getting dinner ready, or getting flowers from the garden, or looking after the children. He might very well have given her a helping hand, but he had not thought of looking so near to do his act of helpfulness. A good turn is quite easy if you begin it at home."

Five on the Scout Honor Roll Today

Still the Honor Roll grows. There are not twenty-one names on it this week as there were last, but the five show that the long roll published on March 17 did not exhaust the entire bunch of young fellows who are working to get into higher grades. It is predicted that the promotions will come along even more rapidly when spring opens up, for there are some tests which can be taken best in warm weather out of doors.

Anyhow, just watch the list from Sunday to Sunday and you'll know that the St. Paul Scouts are not idlers.

THE HONOR ROLL.

FIRST CLASS SCOUTS.
Robert West, Olivet Troop.
Lloyd Woods, Olivet Troop.

SECOND CLASS SCOUTS.
Paul Archer, Twilight Troop.
Eugene Green, Nibowaka Troop.
Charles Davies, Nibowaka Troop.

Famous Sculptor Organizes Troop.
Solon H. Borglum, famous sculptor, whose statues of cowboys, Indians and bronchos have attracted great attention throughout the world, has organized a troop of Boy Scouts in South Norfolk, Conn. He has the co-operation of Alfred Aitken and Arthur Sylvester.

Indians, an eight-year-old boys' organization that emphasized hiking, camping, woodcraft, nature lore, and an appreciation of American Indian culture.

Finally there was Daniel Carter Beard, a distinguished illustrator and author, best known for illustrating the first edition of Mark Twain's *A Connecticut Yankee in King Arthur's Court*. Beard's national boys' groups, the Sons of Daniel Boone and the Boy Pioneers were rooted in the ways of America's old-time frontiersmen.[2]

The June 1910 meeting led to a swift consolidation of America's Boy Scout movement. Boyce transferred legal title to the name "Boy Scouts of America" to a new executive board. Many competing boys' groups, including the Woodcraft Indians and the Sons of Daniel Boone, were absorbed into the new BSA. Seton assumed the official title of chief Scout and hastily wrote the first American Scouting handbook, *Boy Scouts of America: A Handbook of Woodcraft, Scouting, and Life-craft*. Beard took on a succession of positions within the new organization including national commissioner and chairman of the National Court of Honor.[3] The YMCA's Edgar Robinson served as the BSA's unofficial chief Scout executive until late 1910, when he was succeeded by James E. West. West would continue to lead the organization for 33 years.

The establishment of a new national organization encouraged the formation of Boy Scout units throughout the country, including the Upper Midwest. In some cases, boys who belonged to other national groups simply turned themselves into Boy Scouts. Such was the case in Northfield, Minnesota, where the first Boy Scout patrols apparently grew out of a paramilitary organization called the Boys' Brigade. Newspaper reports from the time indicate that the adult leader of the local Boys' Brigade unit, the Rev. Edwin B. Dean of Northfield's First Congregational Church, obtained a BSA Scoutmaster's certificate and formed three Boy Scout patrols in the fall of 1911.[4] While the 1911 date is well documented, it's possible that Scouting's presence in the city dates back even further. Fredrick Heiberg, one of the first members of Northfield's "Mustang Patrol," traced the beginning of the local Scouting movement back to 1908—two years before the formation of the BSA—when he and two friends obtained a copy of Baden-Powell's *Scouting for Boys*.[5]

Big news: Scouting arrives in Northfield.

Although the exact date of Scouting's arrival in Northfield and other Upper Midwest communities may forever remain shrouded in historical fog, it's clear that Boy Scout units were forming in Minnesota and Wisconsin by the early fall of 1910. Within weeks, the two local councils that would eventually combine to become today's Northern Star Council were officially established. It was an exhilarating time, full of possibilities. "The Scouts are boys banded together in their different cities, towns or neighborhoods to learn how to have a good time and to learn other things that every boy should know," the *St. Paul Pioneer Press* explained in its first account of the Boy Scout movement back in August of 1910. "Do you think you know how to have a good time? Perhaps you do: but just wait until you learn what a Boy Scout has to learn and you will know how to enjoy yourself more than ever before."[6]

1910s >

DURING THE LAST WEEK of August 1910, 86 boys from the city of St. Paul took part in a grand experiment. They gathered at YMCA's new Camp St. Croix—just south of Hudson, Wisconsin, and across the St. Croix River from Lakeland, Minnesota—to find out what it meant to be a Boy Scout.

The Boy Scout movement—inspired by the work of Robert S. S. Baden-Powell—had only recently taken root in the United States. A few pioneering troops had formed in communities around the country, but they existed in isolation. There was no national Scout organization capable of providing effective leadership. Scouting remained a mystery to most American boys, and even those who knew something about it often had no idea how to form their own troops.

But now, along the banks of the St. Croix, Scouting was about to get a big boost.

The man in charge of the Minnesota experiment was Ernest Fagenstrom, an employee of the St. Paul YMCA who held the title, "boys' work director." Working with the blessing of executives from the national YMCA, Fagenstrom and several assistants planned to turn their summer camp on the St. Croix into one of the nation's first Boy Scout camps. (The first such camp, operated by the YMCA in upstate New York, had opened just two weeks earlier and was about to wrap up.)[1] For guidance, Fagenstrom intended to rely heavily on the recently published *Boy Scouts of America: A Handbook of Woodcraft, Scouting, and Life-craft*—an Americanized version of Baden-Powell's *Scouting for Boys*.

When the boys arrived at camp, Fagenstrom and his assistants split them into patrols. Each patrol was assigned a name—Eagle, Owl, Moose, and in

< Minneapolis Scouts build a "live signal tower."

5

THE SAINT PAUL PIONEER PRESS, SUNDAY, SEPTEMBER 4, 1910.

THE FIRST BOY SCOUTS IN THE NORTHWEST

ORGANIZED TEMPORARILY

Y. M. C. A. Boys in Camp Enthusiastic Over Scout Plan.

OTHER PATROLS TO BE FORMED

L AST WEEK you read in the boys' and girls' section of the general scheme of the Boy Scouts' organizations. Now we are going to tell you about the tent that was made by St. Paul recently.

The camp just closed of the boys of the Y. M. C. A. at the Anchorage, on the St. Croix, was divided into "patrols" and run on the scout system as devised by Ernest Thompson Seton and Lieutenant General Sir Robert S. S. Baden-Powell for the boys of England, and revised in a later hand-book for the youth of America.

Each Patrol Named After an Animal

There were eighty-six boys at the summer camp, ranging in ages from 12 to 15 years. Ernest Fagenstrom, boys' work director at the "Y," and his assistant ...

The St. Paul Y. M. C. A. campers as Boy Scouts. This picture was taken when the patrols were in line in front of their separate tents. Each patrol was named after some animal.

More Scout Patrols to be Formed in St. Paul

the followers studied the soles of their shoes or moccasins for betraying marks. Then Patrols 3 and 4 went to the beach, where the sand showed their trails, and started in opposite directions, the start being made out of sight of the followers. Fifteen minutes later the other two patrols went down to the beach and took up the hunt.

First of all, each following patrol had to decide in which of the two directions the group of boys it was to follow went. Here their memory of the way the bottoms of the shoes looked came into play. The patrols that had gone out ahead were required to go not more than a mile away, were to stop and conceal themselves as well as they could at the end of half an hour, and could use any means they liked to conceal their tracks or lead their trackers astray.

If, at the end of the half hour, Patrol No. 1 had discovered Patrol No. 3, it won the credits for this test. If not, Patrol No. 2 took the credits. And so also, with Patrols No. 2 and 4.

In this test the boys showed what they knew about following a trail through the underbrush, under water, over grass, or across rocks.

How to Become Scouts

As we announced last week, the Boys' and Girls' Section of the Sunday Pioneer Press and Dispatch will publish "THE OFFICIAL HANDBOOK OF THE BOY SCOUTS OF AMERICA." This will tell the boys precisely how they should go about it to become scouts, help them to organize troops, and give instruction. They may advance from through the various Scouts and win honors.

It Starts

All boy the Boy

one case of whimsy, Kangaroo—and was told to choose a leader. Then it was time to put Baden-Powell's Scouting theories to the test.

Much of the boys' time in camp was spent in pursuit of the ultimate reward: an emblem signifying the achievement of certain goals and standards. They were tested on their abilities to judge distances, start a campfire, tie knots, and identify birdcalls. They tracked each other using only footprints as clues. They spent the night alone in the woods and tried not to let on that they were scared out of their wits. "If any of the Scouts got 'cold feet' when the branches began making funny noises in the darkness," one reporter observed, "they kept their mouths shut and nobody knew anything about it."[2]

Thirty-two of the 86 boys who attended Fagenstrom's camp went home with St. Croix emblems. They were, in essence, among the first American Boy Scouts to receive recognition for advancing from one level to another. In the words of the *St. Paul Pioneer Press,* they were "the cocks of the walk."[3] The other 54 boys would have to wait until the next summer—if someone didn't get around to starting a real Scout organization before then.

Ernest Fagenstrom considered his experiment on the St. Croix a great success, and over the next few weeks, he embarked on a one-man crusade to spread the word of Scouting's potential. He spoke at a succession of local churches about what he called "the boy problem" in the Twin Cities. He told his audiences that city boys needed outlets for their natural impulses.

> *The boy likes to live close to nature. We have trees in the city, but he mustn't climb them. We have birds and small animals in the trees, but he mustn't hunt them. We have plenty of bodies of water, but the boy mustn't swim in them. We have lots of stones, but the boy mustn't throw them. It seems that there are very few things a healthy American boy can do. His world is limited by a great big "Don't," spelled with capital letters and underlined with red ink.[4]*

Scouting was the antidote to the "boy problem," Fagenstrom said, and he encouraged church leaders to organize troops of their own. Several churches, including Olivet Congregational and Trinity Episcopal in St. Paul, did just that. But they had little support. The Twin Cities still had no organization capable of coordinating the budding Scout movement.

St. Paul Pioneer Press, September 4, 1910.

Then, on the afternoon of October 1, 1910, Scouting in the Twin Cities advanced to a new stage. Fagenstrom and a group of some of St. Paul's most distinguished civic leaders gathered at the Commercial Club to officially incorporate Ramsey Council No. 1 of the Boy Scouts of America. The highlight of the meeting was an address by C. J. Proctor, a British Scouting official and contemporary of Baden-Powell, who was promoting Scouting in the United States. "We tried the [Scouting] scheme on 1,000 [British] boys first and since then it has never looked back," Proctor told the St. Paul group. "It has changed the spirit of the boys from one of mischief to a spirit of good citizenship."[5]

The parlor of the St. Paul Commercial Club, where Scouting in the Upper Midwest was first incorporated.

But St. Paul was not alone. Later that same day, a group of like-minded civic leaders met at the Commercial Club in Minneapolis to make plans for a new Scout council in Hennepin County. Once again, C. J. Proctor was the guest of honor. Inspired by Proctor's pep talk, the Minneapolis men met again two weeks later, on October 15, to draw up a constitution and bylaws for the newly formed Hennepin Council of the Boy Scouts of America. Like their counterparts across the river, the men from Minneapolis believed that Scouting had the potential to cure some of society's most pressing ills. "The boyhood of Minneapolis must be helped to build his character," they declared.[6]

The local councils operated with little guidance for the first month or so as the newly consolidated Boy Scouts of America developed a standardized program for use nationwide. In the words of one of St. Paul's earliest Scouting supporters, leaders were "groping in the darkness for a program to hold boys' attention."[7] But the lack of national oversight did not hinder the growth of the Scout movement in the Twin Cities. By the end of November, St. Paul had 15 recognized troops and ten unofficial units known as "Monkey Patrols."[8] Within six

Original constitution and by-laws of the Hennepin Council, BSA.

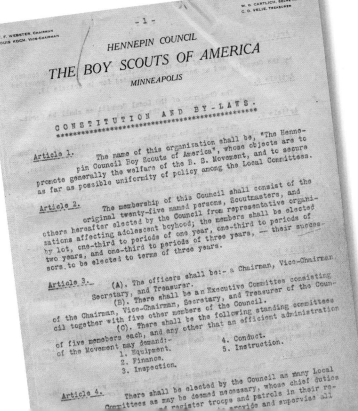

months, 30 troops had organized in the Minneapolis area and more were in the process of forming.[9]

Scouting was slower to catch on in communities outside the Twin Cities, but by the spring of 1911, new troops were proliferating in small cities and towns throughout the state. Much of the credit for the spread of Scouting in Minnesota and beyond belonged to the BSA's regional organizer, Ludwig Dale. Dale traveled from town to town, organizing dozens of troops in Minnesota, Wisconsin, and the Dakotas. Along the way, he was instrumental in the formation of what was billed as the nation's first American Indian troop (on the Fond du Lac Reservation near Cloquet)[10] and the nation's first troop of hearing impaired Scouts (in Faribault).[11]

In the first months after the formation of the St. Paul and Minneapolis councils, Scouts and Scoutmasters had to think creatively to come up with fun and worthwhile activities that seemed appropriate to Scouting. (Early *in*appropriate behavior included "lighting fires near the target range" at Fort Snelling, an activity that the fort's adjutant feared would "endanger public buildings and property.")[12] Hiking was by far the most popular activity. Some troops made only short forays out of the cities. Others went on long hikes that began early in the morning and ended well past sundown. Some Scouts knew how to pack for long outings, but as the *Pioneer Press*'s Scouting columnist noted, many did not.

Three of Minnesota's earliest Boy Scouts: Leigh, Arthur, and Dwight Caswell of Anoka, 1910.

Many St. Paul Scouts have gone on their first hike with their knapsacks filled with fancy cookies, chicken sandwiches, potato salad, and chocolate creams. Just think how foolish one of these Scouts would have felt if he had met an old frontiersman or Indian hunter who wanted to have a "peek into his warsack."...

On those first hikes, too many Scouts were seen on the line of march, cracking peanuts and munching apples. That is not good Scouting, for it not only leaves a trail that could easily be followed, but it takes the Scout's mind off his work so he will fail to observe the things a Scout is supposed to see, and spoil his appetite for the fine meal that is to be prepared over the campfire.[13]

During the first few years of Scouting in the Twin Cities area, Scouts, Scoutmasters, and council leaders looked forward to those rare opportunities when they got a chance to connect with the larger Scouting movement. In the spring of 1911, Scouts in Minneapolis and St. Paul flocked to see the BSA's chief Scout, Ernest Thompson Seton. Seton spoke to big crowds in

Floppy-hatted Minnesota Scouts picking wild grapes, about 1915.

both cities, regaling them with wilderness stories and demonstrations of fire-building prowess.[14]

The following February, local Scouts welcomed the founder of the Scouting movement, Robert S. S. Baden-Powell, and the BSA's chief executive, James West, to the Twin Cities. Scouts turned out for big rallies in both Minneapolis and St. Paul, hoping to show their leader that they were living up to his ideals. Afterward, Baden-Powell—not known for long-windedness—issued a brief assessment that made it clear he appreciated Midwestern efficiency. "I was very much pleased with the spirit of your Scouts," he said. "While your exhibition was not so long nor so comprehensive as some I have seen in other cities, it went off with a snap and go that I liked."[15]

Although most Minnesotans admired the Boy Scouts for their lofty principles and love of the outdoors, some objected to what they considered the Scouting movement's militaristic tendencies. Since its inception, the BSA had been dogged by accusations of militarism. Some of its early rivals, including the American Boy Scouts, had sown confusion by openly training young men for military service. It didn't help that the first BSA uniforms looked like miniaturized U.S. Army garb. National and local BSA officials denied all allegations of creeping militarism, but concerns continued to linger. When Minneapolis Scouts marched

BADEN-POWELL IN ST. PAUL.

SCOUT GROUT GREETS HIS CHIEF.

The picture on the left shows Sir Robert entering an automobile at the Union depot to be taken to the Minnesota club. That on the right shows Scout Edward Grout delivering Mayor Keller's letter of welcome to the distinguished Englishman. The small picture is of young Grout.

Baden-Powell's visit to the Twin Cities in 1912 was front-page news in St. Paul and Minneapolis.

SAINT PAUL ARMORY
February 26th—3:00 P. M.
Robert S. S. Baden-Powell
This Ticket Entitles Holder to Sea

A gathering of Twin Cities Scouts, 1915.

Early photographs of local Boy Scouts often incorporated the Stars and Stripes.

beside army veterans in the city's 1911 Memorial Day parade, critics pounced. "After all these assurances, what is the public to think if on the first Memorial Day after the movement has been introduced into our city, the patrols are called out to march with the veterans and with soldiers from Fort Snelling?" one detractor asked. "If the organization is non-military in its intent, the less it has to do with military spectacles the better."[16] Local officials responded by decreeing that only physical fitness directors, not "military men," be allowed to lead Scouts in military-style drilling exercises.[17]

After an initial flurry of excitement following the establishment of Scouting in the Twin Cities region, the movement hit a sudden and distressing plateau. By late 1912, officials in both cities were openly concerned that Scouting was on the brink of failure. In Minneapolis, for example, a study of membership found that less than half of 1,500 Scouts presumed to be enrolled actually belonged to a troop. One member of the council's executive committee declared bluntly that the situation with "regard to the future of the movement" was "very grave."[18]

The problem was not so much the Scouts as it was their adult leaders. At a meeting of the Minneapolis Council's executive committee, several Scoutmasters admitted that they could not devote enough time to their troops. Others expressed concerns that some of their fellow Scoutmasters were "not the right sort." Council officials agreed to put a new emphasis on finding adult leaders who were truly committed to Scouting.[19]

Still, the Scout movement in the Twin Cities continued to languish. At the end of 1915, the Minneapolis Council reported only 458 registered Scouts on its membership rolls.[20] The numbers from St. Paul were worse: 120.[21] For two years, the Ramsey Council had lurched from crisis to crisis under the leadership of two overwhelmed Scout executives. (When H. S. Sorrels took the job—briefly—in 1915, he noted that the council under his predecessor, Elmer Palmer, had less than a half-dozen troops and not "a cent in the Treasury.")[22] The council's leaders could only hope that a third Scout executive, Frank Neibel, would stop the hemorrhaging. It appeared in both St. Paul and Minneapolis that Scouting might soon fade from existence.

But then the Scouts got a new chance to prove their worth.

Local Scouts proved to be effective salesmen, especially during the second Liberty Loan campaign.

On April 6, 1917, the United States declared war on Germany, formally entering a conflict that had been raging on the European continent for nearly three years. The next day the BSA's national executive board committed the nation's 250,000 Scouts to the war effort. Chief Scout Executive James West sent telegrams to councils around the country—including those in St. Paul and Minneapolis—calling on them to meet their wartime responsibilities. The Scouts would serve their country not as small soldiers, but as indispensable home front volunteers.

In the two years that followed, Boy Scouts in the Minneapolis and St. Paul area mobilized to pitch in wherever and whenever they were needed. Their first big mobilized efforts came in 1917, when they participated in the nation's first two Liberty Loan campaigns. The initial campaign went slowly, prompting James West to name St. Paul as one of four cities where Scouts failed to live up to their obligations.[23] But the second Liberty Loan campaign

First-place medallion awarded to the St. Paul Scouts following the Second Liberty Loan campaign.

was another matter. When the final numbers were tallied, St. Paul Scouts ranked first in the United States, with more than $8.6 million worth of Liberty Bond subscriptions collected.[24] Scout Executive Frank Neibel, accepting an award commemorating the achievement, admitted feeling "quite 'cocky.'"[25]

When they were done hawking Liberty bonds, the Scouts turned their attention to other worthwhile pursuits. They collected salvage goods for the Red Cross.[26] They planted, tended, and harvested more than 1,000 acres of "war gardens."[27] They fanned out throughout the cities in search of barberry bushes ("that friend of the Hun"), which were targeted for eradication because they hosted a fungus capable of devastating wheat crops.[28] They gathered tons of fruit pits and nutshells for conversion into a type of charcoal used in gas masks.[29] They proved to be, in the words of Minneapolis's chief Scout executive, Ludwig Dale, "our richest asset" in the home front war effort.[30]

Local Scouts collected tons of fruit pits and nutshells, which were later converted into charcoal for use in gas masks.

With boys rushing to heed the wartime call to service, the membership declines that had plagued the Twin Cities area councils suddenly reversed themselves. In Minneapolis, for example, the number of registered Scouts more than doubled from 800 to 1,700 during the twelve months between September 1917 and September 1918.[31] By the end of the decade, membership in the St. Paul area had risen to more than 1,100.[32]

Community support for the Scouting movement was growing as well. Service organizations were particularly impressed. In 1918, the Minneapolis Rotary Club donated funds to improve the Minneapolis Area Council's summer camp on Lake Minnetonka, which was promptly renamed Camp Rotary. Not to be outdone, the Minneapolis Elks Club soon began raising money for yet another Lake Minnetonka property—one that would become known as Camp Tonkawa. (The two Minneapolis fundraising efforts set a local precedent of sorts: money raised by the St. Paul Rotary soon paid for the St. Paul Area Council's acquisition of the St. Croix River Camp and many years later the Kiwanis Foundation of St. Paul turned to the Scouts to operate Camp Kiwanis at Marine on St. Croix.) An editorial in the *Minneapolis Tribune* expressed the gratitude that the community felt for the Scouts when the Great War was finally over.

There is nothing in the signs of the times more assuring with regard to the future than the growth of the Boy Scout movement and the high appreciation of its value now generally entertained. It has taken some time in this community, as well as others, to persuade the general public to take this movement seriously and estimate its true value. A good many people

were inclined to think of it in the beginning as something of a fad—just a scheme to give the boys a good time, and not much else. But there were good people in most communities, as there were in this one, to get the right perspective on this institution, to discover its unique character and realize that whoever initiated it had started something of which every American boy ought to have the benefit.

The growth of the movement in the past year or two has been phenomenal. The war has contributed to this in some measure because the boys have helped to win the war. But it is not a military or a wartime organization primarily. Rather is it a movement for peace times when, quite as much as in wartimes, boy energies need wise direction; and when you have got to the heart of the Scout movement, you will find that this is just what it is. The boy who doesn't wish to be decent is a mighty rare specimen. The trouble is, or has been, that under the handicap of daily contact with those things which mislead, he has not always had a fair chance.

The Scout movement seeks to give him that chance.[33]

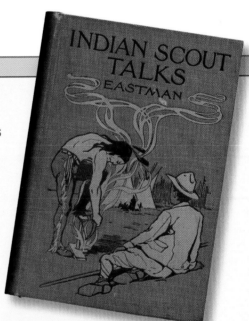

Ohiyesa (Charles Eastman)

Among the many largely unheralded proponents of the early Boy Scout movement in America was a highly accomplished Dakota man with strong Minnesota ties—Ohiyesa. Born in 1858, Ohiyesa was the great-grandson of a Mdewakanton Dakota chief and the grandson of Seth Eastman, a United States soldier and artist who once commanded Fort Snelling. Ohiyesa spent his early childhood among the Dakota, but when he was a teenager, his father took him to live among white people and gave him a new name—Charles Eastman. He later attended college, received a medical degree, and became a respected doctor.[34]

Ohiyesa spent much of his life trying to bridge the gaps between Indian and white cultures. For many years beginning in the mid-1890s he worked to establish YMCA chapters on Indian reservations throughout the western United States. Later he became a prolific chronicler of the traditions of the Dakota people. His stories—heavily shaped by his childhood memories—helped form white society's understanding of American Indian culture. They also found their way into Ernest Thompson Seton's *The Birch Bark Roll,* an early outdoors manual that played a key roll in Scouting's origins. For much of the 1910s, Ohiyesa worked as an unofficial advisor to the Boy Scouts of America, sharing his knowledge of the outdoors through lectures and articles in *Boys' Life.* Although some critics accused the early BSA of stereotyping indigenous peoples, Ohiyesa believed the Boy Scouts (as well as the developing Camp Fire Girls movement) had much to learn from native cultures. In 1914 he wrote *Indian Scout Talks: A Guide for Boy Scouts and Camp Fire Girls.* He began the book with a short dedication:

These chapters represent the actual experiences and first-hand knowledge of the author. His training was along these lines, until he was nearly sixteen years of age. It is with the earnest hope that they may prove useful to all who venture into the wilderness in pursuit of wisdom, health, and pleasure, that they are dedicated to the Boy Scouts of America and The Camp Fire Girls of America.

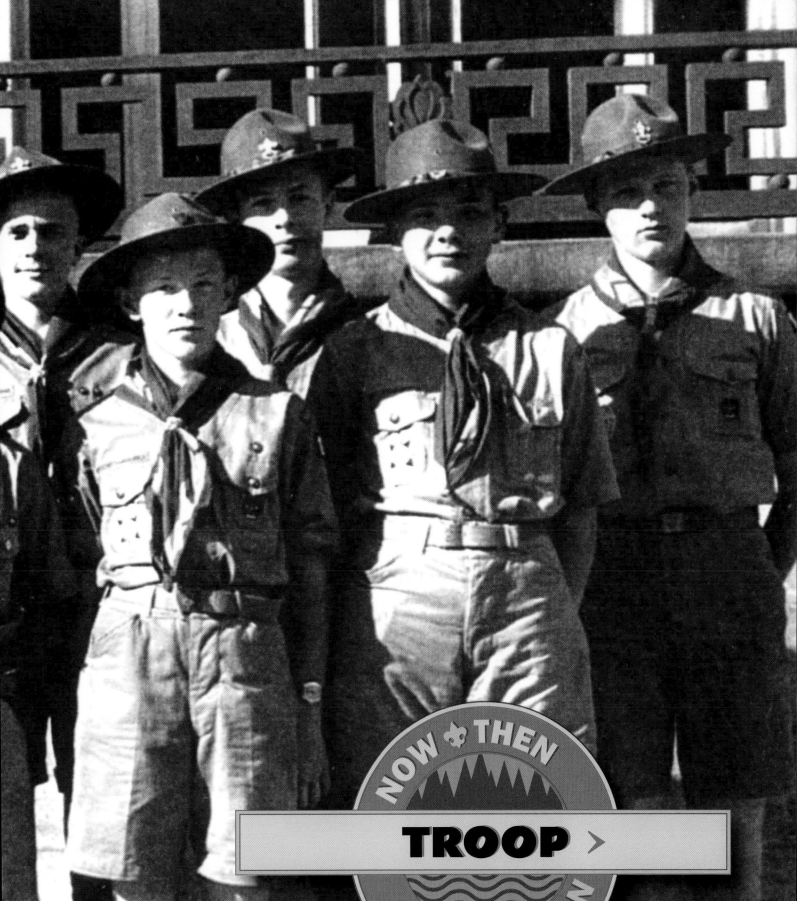

THE "BAND ROOM" AT ST. MARK'S SCHOOL has the look of a decades-old classroom, last updated sometime in the 1960s. The floor tiles are pink. The walls are whitish, not white. Several of the acoustic ceiling tiles show stains left behind by long forgotten water leaks. There's an old wooden loudspeaker above the door that may or may not work. The blackboard is dusty with chalk. The room definitely shows its age. But this evening, as it is on most Monday evenings, it's the home of St. Paul Troop 1.

Previous pages: Anoka Troop 124, 1937.

St. Mark's—or more accurately, the Church of St. Mark, which includes the school—has a long history with the Boy Scouts. BSA records indicate that in 1910, St. Mark's chartered the first Boy Scout Troop in St. Paul, a unit known as George Washington Troop 1. The church itself claims that the original Troop 1 was also the first Catholic-sponsored troop in the United States. Troop 1 disappeared a few years after its formation, but in the 1920s and 1930s St. Mark's organized two new units, troops 68 and 69. The current Troop 1, which is meeting here tonight, is the renumbered successor of the old Troop 69.

St. Paul Troop 1 through the years: 1910 . . .

Through it all, St. Mark's has been the one constant. "We really do hold a lot of pride in being the first Catholic troop," Scoutmaster Mark Marrone says, scanning his roomful of Scouts. "We really do want these guys to appreciate it."

Marrone has brought out a few old photographs that he keeps in the troop's storage cabinet. One of them, taken in 1910, shows the original Troop 1—about 60 boys strong—lined up in neat rows outside St. Mark's. Another, taken about a half-century later, depicts the well-provisioned and well-uniformed Scouts of Troop 69 posing with St. Mark's pastor, Monsignor F. J. Gilligan, in the church gymnasium. Looking at the 1950s photo, Marrone can't help but marvel at how times have changed. "We used to sweat the guys on their uniforms," he says almost apologetically, "but we've relaxed the rules a bit."

Two of Marrone's more relaxed looking Scouts approach as if on a low priority mission. James (wearing a t-shirt) and Chris (in a gray hooded sweatshirt) have teamed up to compete in the evening's designated activity— "Scout book scavenger hunt." The six pairs of boys who've shown up here tonight are trying to prove to Marrone and his five assistant Scoutmasters that they have mastered certain facts and skills spelled out in the Scout Handbook. James and Chris insist they're ready to demonstrate their grasp of a basic Scouting concept, although they don't seem particularly focused on the task.

"Outdoor essentials," Marrone says, announcing the topic.

James chimes in. "You want to bring a pocketknife, rain gear, water bottle, extra clothes." His voice trails off as he tries unsuccessfully to come up with another item for his list.

Marrone offers a hint. "Can't find my way," he says. "Which way is north?"

"Compass!" both boys shout.

"I like the rain gear being near the top of the list, guys," Marrone says. Then he throws out another question to keep them going. "What about if you cut yourself?"

"First aid kit?" Chris answers.

"Thank you." Marrone gives them a score of three out of a possible four and sends them off to work on another assignment.

Marrone was a student at St. Mark's during the 1970s, and although he never joined the troop, he's well aware of the important role the church has played in

1950s . . .

nurturing the Boy Scout movement here in St. Paul's Merriam Park neighborhood. "You don't need to be Catholic to join the troop, but we do ask that the boys respect our ties to the Catholic faith," he says. "All of our Eagle Scout Courts of Honor are done in the church. It's kind of an assumption that it's going to happen here. If we had someone who came along and said we really don't want to do it in the church, we're not Catholic, that's something we definitely would look at, to do it outside the church. But our last 20-some Eagle Courts of Honor have all been in the church and involved the pastor of the church."

Two more Scouts—Vince and Jack—approach Marrone, intent on crossing off another item from their scavenger hunt list. These two look like they mean business. Vince (who happens to be the twin brother of hoodie-wearing Chris) could be a Scouting catalog model with his black neckerchief and green pants rolled up to his calves. "He is a Scout's Scout," Marrone whispers. "He will definitely be leading this troop someday." Vince and Jack have come to sing a campfire song.

"What are you going to sing?" Marrone asks.

"Johnny Appleseed."

"Ah, I've already heard that. How about my second-favorite?" Marrone makes a motion with his arms. The boys cringe and reluctantly break into half-hearted rendition of "I'm a Little Teapot."

"Perfect!"

By eight o'clock, parents have begun arriving and the time has come to announce the winner's of tonight's competition. To no one's surprise, Vince and Jack grab first place. James and Chris come in third. Although winning affords bragging rights, its real significance lies in the fact that Vince and Jack receive more candy—Dots, Tootsie Rolls, and Kit Kats—than everyone else.

The Scouts, adult leaders, and parents of Troop 1 arrange themselves in a circle for their closing ritual. As they do this, they leave a space to honor the memory of Scout Mike Pringle, who drowned a few years earlier during a family outing. The ritual begins with the recitation of the "Our Father" prayer and the sign of the cross. Then comes the retreat of the colors. The meeting closes with a blessing from the troop's chaplain aide, Tom Nieszner.

"May the great Scoutmaster in heaven be with us until we meet again," he says.

"Good night, Scouts."

1980s.

DETERMINING WHICH TROOPS rank as the oldest in the council has always been as much an art as a science. Early registration records were often incomplete and confusing. Many documents later disappeared or were destroyed. Definitions varied. Does a troop's age depend only on when it was originally chartered? What if a troop lets its charter lapse for a year or more? And what if it's had more than one chartered partner? The Northern Star Council has chosen to identify its oldest troops as those that hold the longest continuous registration, regardless of chartered partner. Under that definition, Troop 283, chartered by Wayzata Congregational Church (now Wayzata Community Church) in 1915 ranks as the council's oldest. Troop 17, chartered in 1916 by St. Anthony Park Congregational Church (now St. Anthony Park United Church of Christ) comes in a close second.

Chartered partners have, from the beginning, provided essential links to the communities in which Scouting operates. The partnerships they forge with packs, troops, crews, and posts help ensure that Scouting—a national and international movement—maintains its local focus. Over the years, local houses of worship have constituted the bulk of Scouting's chartered partners in the Twin Cities region. Many schools, clubs, and civic organizations have also served as chartered partners.

During the past half-century, the Northern Star Council and its predecessors have tried to strengthen themselves by encouraging the establishment of packs and troops in communities that Scouting has often struggled to reach—especially communities of color and among youngsters with special needs. Through it all, the relationships forged between troops and their chartered partners have remained crucial components in Scouting's local and regional growth.

The Scouts of Maplewood Troop 197 replace a tattered American flag belonging to the troop's chartered partner, Gethsemane Lutheran Church and School, 2008. Many troops perform frequent service projects for their chartered partners.

One of the oldest surviving photographs of a Minnesota Boy Scout troop (community and number unknown), taken in 1912.

There are a few troops in the city which have fallen apart because of losing their Scoutmasters, or for some other reason, and Commissioner Wauchope is particularly anxious to help them get started again. Any boys who belonged to such an organization are requested to call at his office and explain the situation so he can tell what to do to help them out.

— *St. Paul Pioneer Press,* April 30, 1911

Minneapolis "Troop K," consisting of Scouts from the Sumner Branch Library, Plymouth Congregational Church, and the Pillsbury Settlement House, 1914.

St. Anthony Park Troop 17, shown here during the 1932 Boy Scout Roundup at the State Fair Hippodrome, is the council's second oldest troop.

St. Paul Troop 18 had the distinction of producing two U.S. Supreme Court justices—Chief Justice Warren Burger and Associate Justice Harry Blackmun—who were members of the troop at the same time. Researchers have been unable to determine whether either of the two future justices appears in this photo, which was taken in about 1920.

From [my] personal contact with Scouts and Scoutmasters in St. Paul, [I have] come to the conclusion that it is not the best policy to allow the troop to develop irregularly. If one Scout has a particular liking for knots, and another for signaling, let them go ahead and learn all they can about it, but make them come up to the other standards. If their tests for Second and First Class keep them about even, then you will have a symmetrical, well-balanced troop, and you will be able to call on any member of it for any particular stunt.

— The Pioneer Scout (anonymous columnist), *St. Paul Pioneer Press,* August 6, 1911

I wish to express my appreciation to the pastors who have co-operated with the Diocesan Committee on Scouting in laying the foundation for the development of an unselfish and devoted type of boyhood . . . through the Scouting program which in its supernatural application under the auspices of parish life is designed to build a high type of Christian manhood. . . .

— John G. Murray,
Archbishop of St. Paul, 1941[1]

Troops often reflected the ethnic makeup of their chartered partners. St. Paul Troop 87 was chartered to Holy Redeemer Catholic Church, which served the Italian American community on the city's east side.

Beth El Synagogue was the chartered partner of St. Louis Park Troop 86, a unit of Jewish Scouts.

The Boy Scouts of America, as an organized body, recognizes the religious element in the training of a boy, but is absolutely non-sectarian in its attitude toward that religious training. Its policy is that the religious organization or institution with which the Boy Scout is connected shall give definite attention to his religious life. If he be a Catholic Boy Scout, the Catholic church of which he is a member is the best channel for his training. If he is a Hebrew boy, then the synagogue will train him in the faith of his fathers. If he be a Protestant, no matter to what denomination of Protestantism he may belong, the church of which he is an adherent or member should be the proper organization to give him an education in the things that pertain to his allegiance to God.

— Ramsey (County) Council, "Information Concerning Scouting in St. Paul," 1917[2]

Houses of worship have long constituted the bulk of local Scouting's chartered partners. In the photo above, taken in 2008, Scouts of Afton Troop 226 clean the parking lot of the troop's chartered partner, Memorial Lutheran Church.

Many chartered partners work with Cub packs as well as Scout troops. During the early 1960s, St. Casmir's Catholic Church in St. Paul partnered with Cub Scout Pack 44, which had its own drum and bugle corps.

Every pastor is concerned about the needs of his parish. . . . When a program can engage young people and get them to develop a real sense of values, that's the best thing we can do for them to prepare them to deal with the less pleasant realities of life. I think Scouting does that for boys.

— Father Robert E. Zasacki, St. Peter's Catholic Church, Forest Lake, in *Council Close-ups* (Indianhead Council newsletter), June/July 1988

During the 1950s, many units, including Pack 181 from St. Paul's Homecroft Elementary School, were chartered to the school PTA.

Cokato Troop 249, 1942. Beginning in the 1920s, the Boy Scouts of rural Cokato went through a series of chartered part-ners including the local American Legion post and "A Group of Citizens."

During the polio epidemic of the 1940s, the Elizabeth Kenny Polio Institute of Minneapolis partnered with a new Cub pack made up exclusively of boys who had contracted the disease.

The Lake Elmo Lions Club serves as the chartered partner of Lake Elmo Troop 224.

This homemade drum, used by a local Cub den, is among the many Scouting unit artifacts in the collections of the North Star Museum of Boy Scouting and Girl Scouting.

Eagan Troop 345, chartered to the Eagan Rotary Club. Service clubs and fraternal organizations have long been among Scouting's most reliable chartered partners.

1920s >

BY THE END OF WORLD WAR I, the Twin Cities area was home to about 3,000 Boy Scouts. The St. Paul and Minneapolis councils had experienced impressive growth during the war years, and local leaders hoped that the momentum would carry through into the new decade. But the patriotic fervor that helped boost interest in Scouting during the war subsided once the fighting was over and the soldiers came home. Scouting's growth spurt stalled. The number of Scouts in the Twin Cities area continued to hover around the 3,000 mark throughout the first four years of the 1920s. As they had during the previous decade, local and national officials fretted that Scouting might turn out to be nothing more than a fad.

Part of the problem was that Scouting remained a largely urban phenomenon. Sixty percent of the nation's villages and towns still had no Scout troop.[1] The numbers in Minnesota were typical. The St. Paul and Minneapolis councils encompassed Minnesota's two most populous counties—Ramsey and Hennepin—but accounted for only a fraction of the state's geographic territory. Fifty-five percent of Minnesota's Scouting-age boys lived on farms, beyond the reach of the Twin Cities councils.[2] If Scouting were to continue growing in Minnesota, it would have to expand outside its urban strongholds.

In 1924, the BSA began actively recruiting boys in rural areas throughout the country, including Minnesota. In a move that immediately added as many as 100,000 boys to its membership rolls, the national organization absorbed the Lone Scouts of America, a separate group founded by BSA incorporator William D. Boyce. Boyce's Lone Scouts organization catered to boys from farms and small towns who couldn't find a troop to join. With the merger, the BSA hoped to build on the Lone Scouts' success. In Minnesota, boys from rural areas could now become Scouts simply by registering through the mail with one of the Twin Cities councils. "Rural Scouting will be distinct from

< Boy Scout exhibition, Minnesota State Fairgrounds, 1921.

27

John Salt, Frank Kammerlohr, Adolph Kodletz, Renne Carlson, and Daniel Pickett of Minneapolis "Pine Tree" Troop 9, 1925.

"Bean Feeds" ranked among the most popular Scout gatherings during the 1920s.

SCOUT - O - E'EN
[Boy Scout Night in Southeast Minneapolis]
ADMIT ONE TO
The Big Bean Feed
FIRST M. E. CHURCH, 12th Ave. S.E. and 4th St.
Monday, December 29th
Mark Hamilton Troop No. 9,
Boy Scouts of America
Mark Hamilton Post No. 232
The American Legion

city work in that no emphasis will be placed on hiking and other forms of outdoor life," the BSA's Lone Scout coordinator, O. H. Benson, explained during a visit to the Twin Cities. "Instead we will emphasize the Scout oath, and the parts of the Scout program which train boys in unselfish service. Chores around the farm will be considered the daily 'good turns.'"[3]

The "ruralizing" of Scouting included an expanded list of merit badges, many of which were designed to appeal directly to farm boys. Scouts became eligible to earn badges in such new fields as animal husbandry, beef production, beekeeping, blacksmithing, corn farming, dairying, gardening, hog and pork production, horsemanship, poultry keeping, sheep farming, and soil management. In addition, the Second Class requirements were revised

Minneapolis Scouts with wireless radios, 1921.

to let Scouts demonstrate their first aid skills on animals instead of humans.[4] In a letter to the Minneapolis Council, an Anoka County farm boy named Frankie Spohn expressed the eagerness with which many rural youngsters greeted the new Scouting opportunity.

Lone Scouts depended heavily on the mail to maintain connections with like-minded boys in other rural areas.

I am 13 years old now, but will be 14 in January. There are two other boys who live near me and go to the same school as I do. I was reading the Farmer *when I saw the Boy Scout article. When I was at school, I asked the boys if they wanted to join. There are Boy Scouts in Anoka, but it is four miles away. I would like to join but couldn't get down to the meetings. I live on a farm and can ride horseback—not very good with a saddle. I can do agriculture work, a little poultry raising, but I wouldn't want to try beekeeping. My father had bees last year and they all died in the winter.[5]*

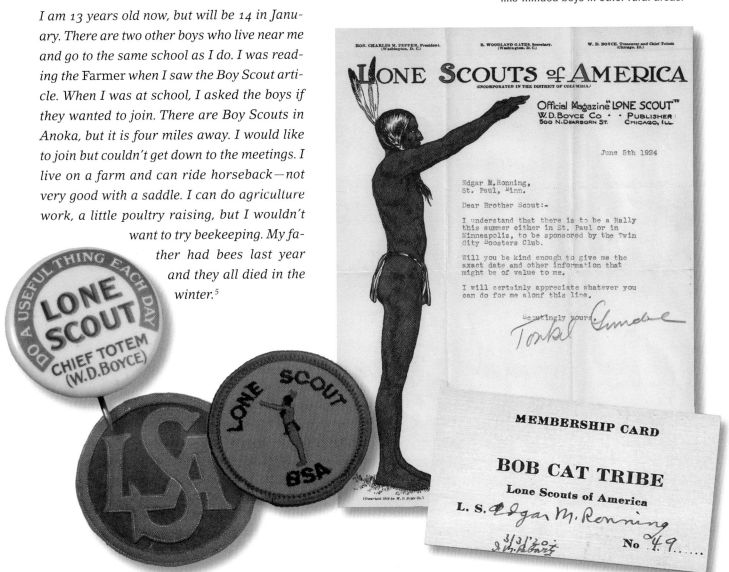

Gatherings of Scouts from farming communities at the 1929 Minnesota State Fair.

The Lone Scout program helped rejuvenate Scouting in the Twin Cities area. In 1924, after several years of nearly stagnant growth, the combined membership of the St. Paul and Minneapolis councils jumped 15 percent. The number of Scouts continued to grow at a similar rate throughout the rest of the decade.

Although the addition of the Lone Scouts was an important factor in Scouting's rebound during the middle years of the 1920s, the territorial expansion that occurred during the last half of the decade was even more significant. In 1927, the Minneapolis Council, which had previously been confined to Hennepin County, began spreading westward, adding the counties of Isanti, Anoka, Meeker, McLeod, Carver, Wright, Chippewa, Renville, and Yellow Medicine. The following year, the St. Paul Council, which encompassed Ramsey, Washington, and Dakota counties, added Chisago County in Minnesota and Polk and St. Croix counties in western Wisconsin. With their territory greatly expanded, the councils launched new recruiting campaigns that dwarfed the Lone Scout program. By the summer of 1928, the Minneapolis Council counted 38 new troops and 700 new Scouts in the western counties known collectively as the "area." Scout Executive George Wyckoff called the region west of the city "a vast empire" of which "the surface has just been scratched."[6]

The addition of territory outside the cities forced the two councils to expand their offices and admin-

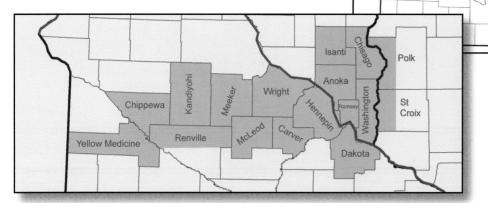

By 1927 the combined territory of the Minneapolis and St. Paul councils stretched from Chippewa and Yellow Medicine counties in Western Minnesota to Polk and St. Croix counties in western Wisconsin.

istrative staffs to accommodate the diverse needs of their growing memberships. Each council hired a new "area field executive" to work directly with local leaders and build a network of district committees based in communities as far east as Hudson and New Richmond, Wisconsin, and as far west as Willmar, Montevideo, and Granite Falls. The Minneapolis Council was especially aggressive in its expansion and reorganization, and its efforts soon caught the attention of BSA Chief Scout Executive James West. During a visit to the Twin Cities, West suggested that other councils around the country could learn much from the Minneapolis approach. "Minneapolis and its unique and effective scheme of organization has been a great relief and of much assistance to us nationally," he said.[7]

One of the towns that came under the Minneapolis Council's expanding umbrella was Cokato, in south central Minnesota. Cokato's American Legion post had chartered a Boy Scout troop earlier in the decade (the local newspaper hailed the troop's installation as "a new and important epoch in Cokato boy life"),[8] but without support from a centralized council, the troop soon faded from existence. In 1928, Cokato tried again, this time under the guidance of the Minneapolis Council's area field executive. The newspaper article announcing the new effort alluded to the failure of the previous attempt to introduce Scouting to Cokato, and assured skeptical rural families that they had nothing to fear.

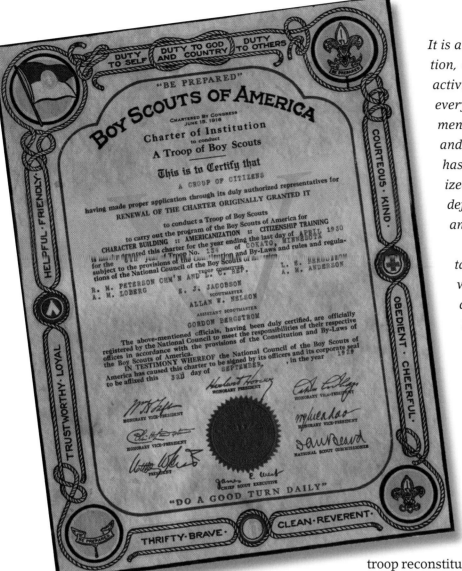

It is a program of fun, of information, of adventure, of worthwhile activities, that appeals to boys of every country, of every environment, on the farm, in the town and village, and in the city, and has the support of every organized body in America that has a definite interest in boy activities and boy welfare.

Scouting is not intended to take the place of or conflict with other work for boys. It is a supplementary program of leisure time activities, cooperating in every way with the home, the church, and school to give the boy the best that may be possible in the way of outside activities.[9]

Cokato Troop 134 was officially chartered in the fall of 1929 in partnership with "a group of citizens." After a few stops and starts, the troop reconstituted as Troop 249, and went on to enjoy considerable success and popularity in the decades that followed.[10]

The charter issued to Cokato Troop 134 in the fall of 1929.

Peeling potatoes at the 1928 State Fair encampment.

Even with the new focus on boys from farms and small towns, most Scouts in the expanded councils were city boys, and they continued to enjoy the camaraderie and sense of purpose that Scouting provided. The 1920s saw the introduction of council-wide get-togethers called Wali-Ga-Zhus (in Minneapolis) and Roundups (in St. Paul) featuring exhibitions and troop-versus-troop Scoutcraft competitions. Every February, Twin Cities-area Scouts joined their counterparts around the country in a weeklong series of events marking the anniversary of the founding of the Boy Scouts of America. The commemorations usually began with "Scouting in the Church" Sundays, during which Scouts attended worship services in uniform, and went on to include banquets, school assemblies, and city-wide public service projects.

Minneapolis drum and bugle corps in front of the city courthouse, 1923.

Musically minded Scouts in both cities joined drum and bugle corps that, in the words of the St. Paul Council's newsletter, produced "the peppiest music ever heard."[11] Drummers and buglers performed at public events around the Twin Cities and served as effective recruiters for the two councils. In at least one case, however, an overly enthusiastic would-be musician triggered a public relations headache for the Minneapolis Council. The *Minneapolis Journal* reported that a letter published previously on its editorial page had prompted Scout Executive George Wyckoff to call for an immediate moratorium on "discordant bugle blasts."

The published letter concerned a complaint in the vicinity of 47th Street and Colfax Avenue South, where a boy was reported blowing discords early in the morning and late at night. Troops 48 and 148, St. Luke's Episcopal Church, were asked to stop this complaint in a personal appeal by Mr. Wyckoff. . . .

In his order to the entire Scouting field, Chief Wyckoff called on all Scouts in the city to cooperate to respect neighbors and assume responsibility for younger boys . . . who thoughtlessly are disturbing citizens. These boys, Mr. Wyckoff said, are imitators of Scouts and do not realize the nuisances their bugles become. Few of them can play any regular bugle notes and the result is disturbing.[12]

The rogue bugler apparently was never apprehended.

The two councils and their Scouts received regular invitations to participate in civic events, and while they accepted many requests, they turned down others. In 1925, the Minneapolis Council declined an invitation to take part in a parade supporting efforts to keep open the city's aging armory. Council officers wanted to avoid negative reaction from critics who continued to believe that Scouting was a "military movement."[13]

After a membership lull during the first few years of the decade, Scouting was once again on an upward trajectory in St. Paul, Minneapolis, and the surrounding region. By the end of the 1920s, the combined membership of the two councils approached 6,000, about twice what it had been at the start of the decade. Scouting

One September evening in 1928, a group of Scout leaders met around a campfire on the grounds of the new St. Croix River Camp. When a skunk wandered into their campsite, the men scattered. From that moment on, the men called themselves the Order of the Odor. The order held annual meetings at the River Camp's Good Medicine Lodge and initiated a new member each year until the onset of World War II. In 1947, the *Dakota County Tribune* reported that the Order of the Odor had 14 living members, and that all of them greeted each other with the salutation, "Hi, Stinky."

All are former Scoutmasters in the St. Paul Boy Scout area who have had experiences, both happy and sad, with little striped kitties. Some of them collect skunk replicas in all manner of materials and sizes. The head of the Order is the Most Delectable Odor and the single annual neophyte is dubbed the Common Stinker. Unquestionably a snooty outfit.[15]

For many years, the members of the Order of the Odor served as the unofficial keepers of Scouting history in the St. Paul region. They eventually founded North Star Scouting Memorabilia, Inc., to assume their history-keeping responsibilities and oversee the North Star Museum of Boy Scouting and Girl Scouting.

Members of the Order or the Odor identified themselves with an appropriate insignia.

More 1920s-style competition at the State Fairgrounds.

was spreading well beyond the city limits and was weaving itself securely into the area's social fabric.

On a winter evening in January 1924, at the annual meeting of the Minneapolis Council, a visiting Scoutmaster demonstrated through words and deeds what a difference Scouting could make in the life of a boy. Rev. Frederick May Eliot of Unity Church in St. Paul had come to the downtown Minneapolis YMCA to deliver an address titled "My Adventures in Scouting." Shortly after beginning his remarks, a "rather questionable appearing boy" burst into the room, pursued by a Minneapolis police officer. Eliot, seemingly unperturbed by the interruption, asked the officer what was going on. The officer accused the boy of stealing a tire. Eliot interceded on the boy's behalf, promising to keep the boy out of further trouble. The officer agreed to drop the matter. Then Eliot asked a Scout in the audience to take the young thief under his wing and introduce him to the other members of his troop. The Scout complied and escorted the boy from the room. When the two youngsters had left, Eliot turned back to his audience and flashed a wide grin. He concluded his remarks, extolling "in a very happy way the great adventure that Scouting offered to men who had the privilege of leadership."[14]

ACHIEVEMENT >

THE TABLE AT THE BACK OF THE FELLOWSHIP HALL at Forest Lake's Hosanna Lutheran Church is decked out as a tribute to three boys' accomplishments. This morning three Scouts from Troop 733—Joel Ohman and his younger counterparts, twins Jacob and Joshua Olson—will be publicly recognized as Eagle Scouts—an honor that only about 5 percent of all boys who join Scouting ever earn. Display boards and scrapbooks strewn across the table chronicle the boys' life in Scouting, from their earliest days as Tiger Cubs to the completion of their Eagle projects. The photos compress time, prompting each viewer to marvel at how quickly little boys turn into young men.

The large room, suffused in natural light, teems with Scouts and Cubs and adult leaders in uniform. About 75 visitors—friends and relatives mostly—have joined the throng. They mill around the display table, paging through scrapbooks, and cluster in small groups, engaging in animated conversation. The soon-to-be Eagles make the rounds, trying not to look nervous. Joel repeatedly runs a comb through nonexistent tangles in his longish hair. The Olson boys are growing impatient. "I've been working on this for most of my life," Jacob says. "I can't wait to get this done."

The guests begin drifting toward their seats. Rows of chairs are arranged neatly in front of a wall of picture windows. A large wooden cross hangs between the central panes. Outside, denuded trees shed clumps of snow.

A Scout color guard assembles in back. A young bugler launches into "When the Saints Go Marching In." As the music plays, about two dozen Cubs, Scouts, and Scouters stride up the center aisle and take their places for the ceremony. The flag bearers plant their banners in the appropriate stands—the American flag on left and the Troop 733 flag on the right.

Most Eagle Scout Courts of Honor follow the same basic script, and this one is no different. The ceremony begins with a welcome from the Scoutmaster (in this case, Jacob and Joshua's father, Steve Olson) and an opening prayer by the church's pastor. Then six younger Scouts take their places beside an arrangement of six candles. It's time for the segment of the ceremony known as the "Eagle Trail." As Assistant Scoutmaster Ted Henrichs narrates, each of the six Scouts steps forward to light a candle.

"The Eagle trailhead is the crossing-over where a Cub joins the Scout troop," Henrichs begins.

Webelos Dominic Christen lights his candle.

"The first Scouting rank is Tenderfoot," Henrichs says.

Tenderfoot Dan Johnson lights his candle.

The ceremony continues until all six candles representing the six ranks from Tenderfoot to Life Scout have been lit. The resulting display is a reminder of all the years and all the effort that go into the making of an Eagle Scout. Henrichs urges the Eagle candidates to keep that symbol in mind. "One who achieves Eagle Scout should never forget the rigors of training you endured," he says.

More candles are lit: twelve representing the twelve points of the Scout Law, and three final ones—one each for the three promises of the Scout Oath. Northern Star Council Scout Executive John Andrews steps forward to

Previous pages:
1930 Court of Honor, probably at the State Fairgrounds Hippodrome.

administer the Eagle Pledge. "Once you're an Eagle, you're always an Eagle," he says.

After the three Scouts recite the pledge, they walk into the audience, handing out pennies minted in 1910, the founding year of the Boy Scouts of America and the predecessors of the Northern Star Council. "This could perhaps be a 'challenge coin,'" Andrews tells them as they return to the front. "You will be among the last Eagle Scouts of our first century. What do you think the second century of Boy Scouting will look like?"

A representative from the local Lions Club, the troop's charter organization, presents blue Eagle neckerchiefs to the three candidates. Then each boy steps forward to say a few words. All three thank their parents for supporting them in their quest to become Eagles. Joel ends with a message for the younger members of the troop. "Scouts, stick with it," he says. "Pace yourself. It's possible."

Newly minted Eagles Joel Ohman, Joshua Olson, and Jacob Olson of Forest Lake Troop 733.

Several adults approach the podium to share a few thoughts about the boys. "Most of my memories are from when they were younger, shorter, and cuter," Ted Henrichs laughs. He recalls the Olson twins' first year with the troop, when he couldn't tell them apart, and praises Joel for sticking with Scouting after the rest of his patrol dropped out. "It's quite the challenge when you don't have buddies to do things with," he says.

For Jacob and Joshua's father, Scoutmaster Steve Olson, it's a bittersweet moment. "It's been a long road from Tigers until now," he says. "They've gone from fine boys to fine young gentlemen."

It's taken Joel, Joshua, and Jacob the better part of a decade to reach this point. The pictures at the back of the room and the words contributed by their parents, friends, and mentors attest to their growth and accomplishments over the years. Now it's time for their reward. Each boy's mother comes forward to pin the hard-earned Eagle badge on her son's uniform.

The reception afterwards is a swarm of hugs, congratulations, and shared memories. The sheet cake with the Eagle insignia on top is soon reduced to crumbs. As the three new Eagles shake hand after hand, it's clear that they share a mighty sense of relief. For Joshua and Jacob, their quest to become Eagles had always carried an air of inevitability. They finished their Eagle projects—both focused on helping a local assisted living home—early, during their sophomore year in high school. It didn't hurt that their father was the Scoutmaster. Joel, on the other hand, had taken more time. He didn't finish his project—the construction of two horseshoe pits in a public park—until three weeks before his eighteenth birthday. Like many other potential Eagles, he had been forced to overcome a series of obstacles that almost any teenage boy could appreciate. "Our Scoutmaster calls them the three Ws," he explains. "Work, women, and wheels. Those are the things that keep you from getting your Eagle."

The oldest of the three new Eagles flashes a wry smile. "It's a good thing my mom kept pushing me."

IT DIDN'T TAKE LONG for Twin Cities area Scouts to begin earning a national reputation for quickly moving up the ranks. In the spring of 1911, all nine Scouts from a troop in Forest Lake achieved First Class rank, prompting Ramsey Council No. 1 Field Secretary Preston G. Orwig to boast that they constituted "the first full patrol of First Class Scouts in the country." About a year later, the *St. Paul Pioneer Press* reported that Roy Young of the "Twilight Troop" in St. Anthony Park had earned the 21 merit badges necessary to make him "the first 'Eagle Scout' in the country."[1] (A "misunderstanding" on the part of Council officials delayed Roy's merit badge application, allowing two Scouts from out east to slip ahead of him on the Eagle list.)[2]

The merit badge program and the system of advancement (Tenderfoot, Second Class, First Class, Star, Life, and Eagle) have remained remarkably stable since those early years, although some changes have occurred. The establishment of Cub Scouting in the 1930s introduced new ranks to the advancement process. (The Arrow of Light is the only badge of Cub Scouting rank that may be worn on the Boy Scout uniform.) Programs designed for older boys and girls—including today's Exploring and Venturing programs—have added even more achievement awards. In 1939, Roman Catholic Scouts in the Archdiocese of St. Paul and Minneapolis began earning the Ad Altare Dei, the first religious emblem approved by Scouting. Over time, houses of worship from other Christian denominations and other religions initiated similar programs.

For more than eight decades, select Scouts from the Twin Cities-based councils also have been invited to join the BSA's camping honor society, the Order of the Arrow. In 1925, Minneapolis became home to Tonkawampus Lodge, the nation's sixteenth recognized OA chapter. St. Paul's OA chapter, Agaming Lodge, was established 19 years later. Tonkawampus and Agaming combined to form a new lodge—Totanhan Nakaha—following the consolidation of the Viking and Indianhead councils in 2005.

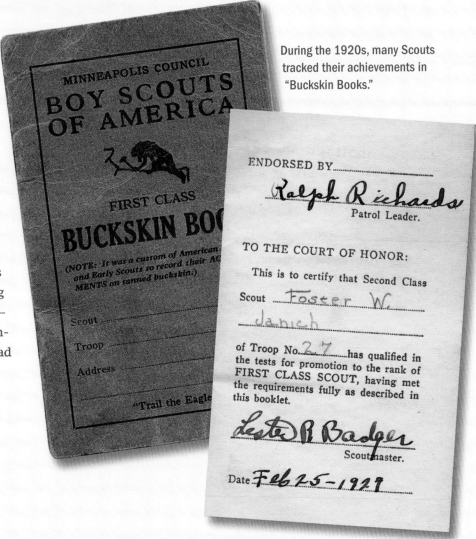

During the 1920s, many Scouts tracked their achievements in "Buckskin Books."

SCOUT ROY YOUNG.

"The presentation of the Eagle Scout badges made a very impressive ceremony, the mothers of the three boys being escorted to the front by Sea Scouts where each mother pinned the coveted badge on her boy and the Eagle Scouts then each pinned a rose on their mothers. A musical background added to the effect of the ceremony."

— *Dakota County Tribune,*
December 6, 1940

Forty-six merit badges have been earned by St. Paul Boy Scouts whose applications have been approved by the Court of Honor of Ramsey Council No. 1, Boy Scouts of America. . . . It is interesting and remarkable that of the forty-six badges, twenty-three have been earned by ONE Scout— Roy D. Young of Twilight Troop. This means that Scout Young is "Eagle Scout," and it is probable that he is the first "Eagle Scout" in the country, for no report has been received at the St. Paul headquarters of any other boy who has won that great honor.
— *St. Paul Pioneer Press,*
March 10, 1912

Nine First Class Scouts in Minnesota! Think of it boys! Nine young fellows [from a Forest Lake troop] already have passed all of the tests . . . and Boy Scouts have been organized in this state less than a year. . . .

Buck up, Scouts! Don't let other boys get ahead of you. Keep on studying and practicing until you can pass every test. Then you will be in the First Class. It will mean a great deal to your patrol and troop.
— *St. Paul Pioneer Press,* June 4, 1911

What a fine thing it would be to have every member of the Black-foot Troop a First Class Scout! "Yes, but that is not possible." Well, now, why not? A Scout needs to be a Tenderfoot but one month, and a Second Class Scout only sixty days. How many of the boys in the troop have been members longer than the time necessary to become a First Class Scout? Or even a Second Class Scout?

— *Blackfeet Prints* (St. Paul Troop 17 newsletter),
December 10, 1918

A sampling from the Minneapolis Area Council's "Eagles Nest" display: Hamilton Craig, Troop 7 (Eagle #3); Leland Hewitt, Troop 88 (Eagle #22); Neal Crocker, Troop 110 (Eagle #27); Kenneth Lucas, Troop 98 (Eagle #31); Chester Solomson, Troop 88, (Eagle #50); and Robert Lee, Troop 72 (Eagle #53).

At the Minneapolis headquarters, the picture gallery of the Eagle Scouts, known as the "Eagle's Nest," is assuming striking proportions. Twenty-two portraits are now framed and displayed. Twelve others are being made ready and seventeen Eagles are arranging for appointments with the photographer, so that the nest will soon be complete. "A place in this gallery is one of the greatest honors that a Minneapolis Boy Scout can attain," says the local Scout monthly. "The ever-growing display will go down through the years as a lasting recognition of the high Scouthood of each Eagle who has merited a place in it."

— *New York Times*, January 7, 1923

In 2008 seven Scouts from Troop 96 (St. Peter Claver Church, St. Paul) achieved Eagle rank, setting a council record for the number of African American Eagle Scouts in a single troop.

Proof that Cokato Scout Kenneth Eastlund earned his cooking merit badge in 1944.

Counselor Devin Tunseth helps a Scout earn his Environmental Science Merit Badge during a 2009 workshop at the North Star Museum of Boy Scouting and Girl Scouting. Council-sponsored hands-on merit badge training has been a local Scouting tradition since mid-1980s, when the Indianhead Council introduced its "Meriting With the Experts" program.

The 2,033 merit badges [awarded in the Minneapolis Area Council] were earned by 289 boys. At least one examination was given during 1926 in each of the 65 merit badge subjects, except Botany, Insect Life and Stalking. The highest number of examinations given in one merit badge subject was 113 in First Aid to Animals. Craftsmanship came next with 112 examinations.

— **Minneapolis Council 1926 Annual Report**

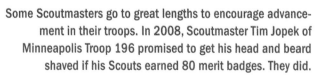

Some Scoutmasters go to great lengths to encourage advancement in their troops. In 2008, Scoutmaster Tim Jopek of Minneapolis Troop 196 promised to get his head and beard shaved if his Scouts earned 80 merit badges. They did.

Merit badge counseling at Square Lake Camp, early 1920s.

One of the most vivid things I can remember about my early Scouting days was the night I received my Tenderfoot badge. Dad pinned the badge on me and I recall his hands were shaking so badly I was afraid for my life.

— John Goodrich, Champlin Troop 276, to Scoutmaster Paul Wethern, September 17, 1960

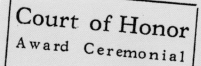

Court of Honor
Award Ceremonial

WEDNESDAY
JAN. 13
(Second Wed. each month)
7:30 to 9 o'clock

TEMPLE ISRAEL
5th Av. S. & 10th St.

Award of Promotions, Merit Badges and Honors.

Award of Efficiency Streamers.

For all Scouts, Parents, Friends and the Public

A Court of Honor at Temple Israel, Minneapolis, 1925.

Since the mid 1950s, Scouts belonging to Protestant denominations have been eligible to earn the God and Country Award.

APPLICATION FOR
GOD and COUNTRY AWARD

No. 4023
60M1162

C7385

Send to
Protestant Committee on Scouting
National Council — Boy Scouts of America
New Brunswick, New Jersey
(See reverse side for instructions.)

Certification by Leader and Minister

Candidate .... Bruce Otto .... Age ... 15
Must be under 21

Candidate's denomination .... Baptist

Scout rank .... Star .... If an Explorer, how long has he served as an Explorer? ....

Street address .... 3301 33rd Avenue South

City ... Minneapolis ... Zone ... 6 ... State ... Minn.

Type of unit ... Troop .... No. ... 150
Troop, post, ship, or squadron

Unit sponsored by .... First Baptist Church
Chartered institution

Unit leader .... Joseph Gasior

This candidate for the God and Country Award has fulfilled all of the requirements as outlined in the *Service Record Book,* and his work in this program has been reviewed and approved by an official board or committee in our church (session, vestry, consistory, Christian education committee, etc.).

Clergyman .... Rev. David Herwaldt

Church .... First Baptist Church

Address .... 1020 Harmon Place

City ... Minneapolis ... Zone ... 3 ... State ... Minn.

Denomination .... Baptist

Date of application .... May 29, 1963

NOTE: The minister sends this application to the local council

Certification of Scout Record

This certifies that the candidate has attained First Class rank or has served at least one year as an Explorer. He is under twenty-one years of age and is in good standing as a member of the Boy Scouts of America. We support the recommendation of his church.

Scout Executive .... Roy L. Williams

Council ... Viking .... No. ... 289 ... Date ... 6/14/63

NOTE: The Scout executive sends this application to the chairman of the local Protestant committee on Scouting or to a representative of the candidate's denomination on the committee.

Approval of Local Committee

The local Protestant committee on Scouting arranges an interview with the candidate and his minister. A pastor of the candidate's denomination should be on the reviewing committee. The chairman or a member of the committee approves this form.

Chairman or Member of Committee (See Item 2 on reverse side.)

Address .... 6421 Upton Ave So.
Mpls. 23, Minn.

Date of approval .... June 3, 1963

In areas where a Protestant committee on Scouting is not functioning, this approval may be signed by an officer of a local denominational or interdenominational ministerial association or Protestant church federation.

NOTE: The committee receives the necessary fees from the local

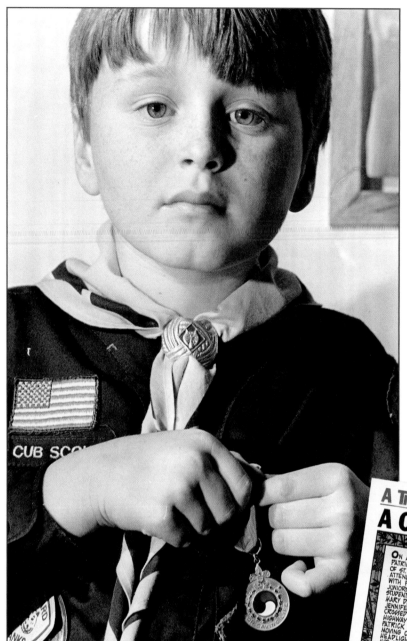

Nine-year-old Cub Scout Brian Christensen of Lindstrom became one of Minnesota's youngest Honor Medal recipients in 1981. He received the award after rescuing his baby sister from a water-filled drainage ditch.

Boys' Life has featured several illustrated stories of heroism by Minnesota and Wisconsin Scouts over the years. This one, about St. Paul Scout Patrick Tretter, appeared in the March 1993 issue.

Tomorrow is Howard Sallows' big day.

It is the day he receives the National Council gold medal for saving life as part of the Boy Scout celebration of the fifteenth anniversary of the birth of the organization.

It is a big day for Minneapolis Scout-dom as well for this is the first medal of the kind any Minneapolis Scout has ever received.

The medal is given only in recognition of the most unusual heroism in saving of life at imminent risk of one's own. [Howard jumped into the ice cold waters of Glenwood Lake to save a drowning man.]

— *Minneapolis Star,* February 10, 1925

The highest and most sought honor of Camp Tonkawa is election to the Order of the Arrow. This is recognition, by vote of fellow campers, of the best all-around Scouthood and campership of each period.

The Indian mysteries of the order are revealed at the close of the period to those awarded this high privilege. All members of the order will assemble at Camp Tonkawa some time during the fall for exemplification of the second degree.

— *Be Prepared*, October 1925

Two rare views of mid-century Order of the Arrow ceremonies: a 1956 Tonkawampus Lodge conclave, probably at Many Point Scout Camp; and similar Agaming Lodge conclave, date unknown, at Tomahawk Scout Reservation.

1930s >

AS THE NEW DECADE DAWNED, Scouting in the Twin Cities and the surrounding areas looked stronger than ever. The number of Scouts in the two councils had nearly doubled during the 1920s, thanks in large part to the addition of many counties beyond the metropolitan region. There was little reason to doubt that the coming years would be any less successful. In St. Paul, Scouting officials set high goals for 1930. Among other things, they expected at least 75 percent of the council's Scouts to spend one week or more at summer camp and decreed that every troop should schedule at least four overnight hikes. Council leaders admitted they were aiming high, but they insisted their goals were attainable if everyone—Scouts, Scoutmasters, and Scouting officials—worked together. The council's annual report ended appropriately with a quotation from a poem by J. Mason Knox.

> It ain't the individual,
>   Nor the Army as a whole,
> But the everlasting teamwork
>   Of every bloomin' soul.[1]

Few Scouts realized just how important teamwork would soon turn out to be.

In October 1929 the New York stock market crashed, smothering the economic boom of the previous decade. Within months, the United States and much of the rest of the world was sliding into what became known as the Great Depression. Businesses shut down. Farms failed. Millions of Americans lost their jobs. By early 1931, one out of every six workers in Minneapolis was unemployed and the numbers were only slightly better in St. Paul.[2] During the first few years of the Depression—before President Franklin D. Roosevelt launched his "New Deal" to provide relief to the poor

< Chow time at the 1932 State Fair Boy Scout Exposition.

Twin Cities Eagle Scouts build a trail through Itasca State Park, 1935.

EAGLE SCOUTS Trail Building in Itasca Park

and out-of-work—local governments and private organizations had to cope on their own with the effects of the economic crisis. In the Twin Cities and elsewhere, Boy Scouts were among the first to offer help.

Minneapolis-area Scouts set an example worth following in the autumn of 1929 and the winter of 1930, when they rallied to help a local charitable organization called the Sunshine Society. As a reporter for the *Minneapolis Journal* explained, the effort was a direct response to the plight of an unlucky boy, just a few years short of Scout age. "A 9-year-old boy came into the offices of the Sunshine Society," the reporter wrote. "It was cold yesterday, and the snow was blowing after school. He wore a light cotton shirt, no coat and no underwear. His mother, ill in bed, had sent him for clothing for himself, but the society supply was so low, all Miss Eva Blanchard, secretary, was able to give him was a ragged light cotton sweater."[3]

The story of the boy with no coat and no underwear aroused the sympathies of hundreds of Scouts in and around Minneapolis. Within days, troops mobilized to collect mounds of used clothing for the needy. Within a week

they gathered nearly 600 pounds of jackets, sweaters, trousers, socks, and shoes. By the end of the year, their collection topped two tons. "This is the most helpful thing Minneapolis Scouts have ever done," the council's chief executive, George Wyckoff, exclaimed.[4]

Scouting itself was not immune to the ravages of the Depression. The Minneapolis Area Council, which was heavily subsidizing the expansion of Scouting into rural areas, discovered that many struggling farm communities were reluctant to contribute money to the cause. Council leaders called the situation "a serious embarrassment," and strained to keep budgets balanced.[5] In an effort to reduce costs, the council stopped providing merit badges free of charge to Scouts, and advancement rates suffered as a result.[6] Public schools, which had financial troubles of their own, began charging troops rent for the use of school facilities.[7] Financial problems were further compounded when the social agencies that provided the bulk of the councils' funds—the Community Fund in Minneapolis and the Community Chest

Left: Scouts on parade at the Minnesota State Fairgrounds, 1930.

Right: Minnesota's activist Depression-era governor, Floyd B. Olson, was at the height of his popularity when he posed with these Boy Scouts in 1932.

Hadley Miller of St. Paul Troop 17 was among the lucky Depression-era Scouts who could afford a new uniform.

in St. Paul—began reducing their Scouting allocations. With economic conditions deteriorating, the two community funding organizations began shifting resources to charitable groups providing direct aid to the poor, homeless, and unemployed. In Minneapolis, the Community Fund reduced the council's requested allowance 17 percent in 1932 and 5 percent the following year.[8]

Scouts and their families often fared only marginally better than the people they were trying to help. For many families, the cost of a uniform became prohibitive. The Minneapolis Council addressed the problem by setting up a "uniform exchange" for Scouts who couldn't afford to outfit themselves.[9] Several troops, including Troop 118 in Farmington, held fundraisers to help their Scouts pay for new uniforms.[10] In some cases, troops resorted to even more radical solutions. Hubert H. Humphrey, who would become one of Minnesota's most popular elected officials and serve four years as vice president of the United States, was among the Scoutmasters who banned new uniforms altogether. "In those days our people were pretty down on their luck from dust storms and the Depression," he recalled. "We had a rule that no one could have a new uniform because we didn't want any boy to feel inadequate or inferior. So we passed around second-hand uniforms and tried to outfit each boy from the hand-me-downs of older brothers."[11] Although Humphrey was living in Huron, South Dakota, at the time, conditions there were nearly identical to those in some of the Minneapolis Council's far western districts.

Streaming into Good Medicine Lodge at the St. Croix River Camp, 1937.

The Minneapolis Area Council introduced its covered wagon recruiting tours in 1930 and continued the expeditions through most of the decade.

With hard times gnawing at almost every Minnesotan's pocketbook, local Scouting officials looked for creative ways to bring new Scouts into the fold—especially in hard-hit areas outside the Twin Cities. In 1930, the Minneapolis Area Council introduced a new recruiting tool that proved effective and popular throughout much of the decade— the annual covered wagon expedition. Each summer, a group of selected Scouts piled into a truck gussied up to look like a covered wagon, and headed out on a two-week tour of the council's western counties. In 1932, the expedition traveled 1,030 miles and visited 58 towns. Most Scouts reported that they thoroughly enjoyed the experience, although some suffered from occasional motion sickness. Mindful of queasy stomachs, Scoutmaster Magnus Johnson urged covered wagon planners to think carefully about food. "It should be of the kind that is easily digested," he wrote, "and chosen with the thought of the Wagoners who . . . sit for longer or shorter periods in a crowded wagon, being shaken and [bumped] considerable."[12]

Through it all, local Scouting leaders tried to maintain and, when possible, improve the programs that attracted boys in the first place. At a meeting of Scouters in Excelsior, David Jones, the senior deputy commissioner of the Minneapolis Council, urged his colleagues to remain "boy-conscious." He reminded them that the boys of the Great Depression were growing up in "an atmosphere of despair and unrest," and that "the bulwark of the future depended upon the continuance of such influence as the Boy Scout program."[13]

For years, Scouting officials on the national and local levels had struggled with what was often referred to as the "older boy problem." Boys tended to drift away from Scouting once they turned 15 since there were few programs to hold their interest. (Organized sports, for example, had long been frowned upon by the BSA, which decreed as early as 1914 that "competitive athletics have no place in Scout work.")[14] Sea Scouting, a program designed specifically for older boys, had begun in coastal areas of the United States shortly after the formation of the BSA, but had failed take root in Minnesota. A Minneapolis unit known as Sea Scout Ship 1 had launched with considerable fanfare in 1924—"Ahoy! All hands to quarters! House the topmast, break out the ensign, and launch the dinghy!"[15]—but it disbanded within a couple of years. It wasn't until the 1930s that the Minneapolis and St. Paul councils began making a concerted effort to keep older boys in the Scouting ranks.

In the summer of 1930, the Minneapolis Council established a new Sea Scout base at Camp Robinson Crusoe, the council's camp on Lake Minnetonka's Wawatasso Island. The base had its own cutter, the *Marchioness IV*,

The christening of the Minneapolis Sea Scout Ship Santa Maria, 1939.

and several canoes on which Sea Scouts could train. It also had a "dryland ship," an imaginary vessel, constructed on shore, consisting of two telephone poles (the masts), concrete footings, and webs of rope rigged with block and tackle. Despite high hopes, the first two summers of the Sea Scout program fell far short of expectations. "Worn and frayed" oars disintegrated "when subjected to hard pulling against a strong wind." Efforts to beat back poison ivy on the dryland ship proved fruitless. Attendance at the new base verged on paltry. Only two Minneapolis "ships"—the designation given to Sea Scout units—were active during the summers of 1930 and 1931. The efforts to attract and hold the attention of older Scouts were getting off to a slow start.[16]

Over the next few years, however, Sea Scouting finally took off in the Twin Cities. The Minneapolis area, with its wealth of lakes, was especially active. At one point the Minneapolis Council boasted 11 Sea Scout ships including S.S.S. "Admiral Byrd" (Westminster Presbyterian Church), and S.S.S. "Minnehaha" (Minnehaha Lutheran Church). In 1938, nearly 250 Twin Cities Sea Scouts gathered for a two-day rendezvous on Lake Minnetonka—an event significant enough to warrant mention in the *New York Times*:

The rendezvous combines camping and sailing. The Sea Scouts determine a place for their camp, sail to it in their boats and at nightfall pitch their tents. Here boys from various communities live together and swap experiences and techniques. Here is friendly competition in the tug-of-war, life-saving

Exploring Carver's Cave, St. Paul, 1930s. Boating adventures were not limited to Sea Scouts.

demonstrations, rescue drills, abandon-ship drills, first aid, signaling, rope-ladder climbing, model and sail-boat racing. In the evenings there are campfire programs in which yarns are spun, sea chanties sung and various "stunts" staged.[17]

By the end of the decade two other BSA programs were vying with the Sea Scouts for the attention and loyalty of older boys. About 300 Twin Cities

A pair of older Scouts at the 1932 State Fair Exposition.

Scouts joined Explorer posts and patrols in which they could pursue their interests in outdoor adventure. Much less successful was the new Rover Scouting program for young men between the ages of 18 to 25, which attracted only a few dozen members. Beginning in 1935, the BSA and the local councils bunched Sea Scouts, Explorers, and Rovers under a new heading, "Senior Scouting."

Although Senior Scouting established itself as a viable program during the 1930s, its success paled in comparison to the decade's other major Scouting expansion initiative: Cubbing. Boys younger than 12 had been clamoring for years to become Boy Scouts, but the BSA had resisted their entreaties. Chief Scout Executive James West, for one, felt the BSA could not afford to

This sign hung at the entrance of the original Pine Bend Scout Club cabin.

In March 1932, after a late-winter thaw, a group of St. Paul Boy Scouts floated three rafts of discarded telephone poles 18 miles down the Mississippi River to a spot called Pine Bend. With the help of a team of horses, the Scouts then hauled the poles up a ravine to a clearing where they planned to build a log cabin.[22] Over the next six months, the Scouts hiked down to Pine Bend every chance they got, and slowly the cabin took shape. On October 30, 1932, the 36 charter members of the Pine Bend Scout Club formally dedicated their new "home."[23]

The club continued to thrive through the 1940s, but then industrial development along the river began encroaching on what had been a secluded refuge. In the late 1950s, a group of the club's alumni—the Pine Bend Association—sold the Pine Bend site for $45,000 and used the proceeds to purchase a 320-acre property on Round Lake, near Onamia. That property, Birch Bend, now serves as home to the Pine Bend Association's outdoor training program, the College of Wilderness Knowledge.[24]

024   6877 (7284) 8427

... 69.5 6889 7381 7869 7945 8298 8701 8572 9557 10764

MEMBERSHIP-12/31/37   (7284)
NEW BOYS AND LEADERS
ADDED DURING THE
YEAR 1938   3480
             TOTAL SERVED 10,764

WE SERVED IN 1938

10,764

In its 1938 annual report, the Minneapolis Area Council boasted that it counted 1,737 Cub Scouts among the 10,764 boys and men it served that year.

shift resources away from boys in the 12-to-16 range, who he believed were most likely to benefit from Scouting. But in 1929, after a five-year study, the BSA introduced Cubbing, a new experimental program designed for 9-, 10-, and 11-year-olds. Cubbing became an official BSA program the following year, and in 1931 it arrived in the Twin Cities.[18]

Bethlehem Lutheran Church in St. Paul sponsored the Twin Cities' first Cub pack. It was an experimental unit—no official uniforms or badges—with 22 young members and three adult leaders.[19] The St. Paul Council proceeded slowly with the expansion of Cubbing, adding only two new experimental packs during the next two years. Meanwhile the Minneapolis Council, hampered by Depression-induced funding cuts, delayed introduction of the program until money became available. Finally, in 1934, Cubbing took on official status in both St. Paul and Minneapolis. That first year, the two councils registered seven packs and 171 Cubs. By the end of the decade, the tally showed 81 packs and more than 1,800 Cubs.

Scouting officials went out of their way to draw clear lines between Cubbing and Scouting. "[Cubbing] is not Junior or Cub *Scouting,*" a memo from the Minneapolis Council explained. "There is to be 'no trespass' on the Scouting Program. Cubs are not handled as part of a Scout Troop. Cubs are not Troop 'Mascots.' They are not 'tag-alongs,' 'under aged' or 'waiting list' Scouts. 'Cubbing' is a separate, distinct program in itself." Where Scouting focused primarily on the outdoors, Cubbing revolved around home and the family. Although the mothers of Cubs were encouraged to supply "steadying influence, near at hand," they were expected to remain largely in the background. Cub leaders, like Scout leaders, were to be men—not women.[20] For the moment, the position of den mother remained an unofficial one.

As the 1930s came to a close, the economic crisis that defined the decade was finally abating. But all was not well. War was raging in Europe, Japan was terrorizing its neighbors, and the United States was preparing for the possibility that it might have to join the fight. Apprehension about the future was widespread, but Scouting, strengthened by an infusion of older and younger boys, approached the new decade with confidence. A poem written by an unidentified Minneapolis Eagle Scout during the first year of the Depression helped explain Scouting's enduring appeal:

Scouting was made for boys like me,
Boys with souls that have no key.
Boys whose hearts are filled with fear,
A mind of evil to the second [tier].

For as we near that precious age,
When life starts on the second page,
Some kindly looking, stalwart man,
Comes and takes us by the hand.

He can handle boys like me,
For in his words is found that key
That opens up a life anew,
And locks that box of things untrue.

Yes, 'tis this man that puts us to
These Scout laws to follow through.
But there are two men I wish to thank,
That is God and—
My Scoutmaster, second in rank.[21]

The message on this 1930 postcard, depicting a camping scene along the St. Croix River, read: "Scouts like to camp? O boy!"

OUTING >

CORWIN DIAMOND HAS BEEN IN THIS POSITION BEFORE. He and his fellow guide, Matt Swallow, have led a small band of snowshoers to the middle of a frozen-over lake, the size of a glorified pond. The group consists of two adults and eight boys— two sixth graders, four seventh graders, and two eighth graders. Few of the boys have snowshoed before, and it shows. Several have already tripped over their elongated feet and landed face first in powder. They embarked on their excursion about five minutes ago, and already they're getting antsy. Diamond tries to grab their attention with a rhetorical question. "Is it a good idea for us to stand out here on the ice all clumped together?" he asks.

No answers, just mumbling interspersed with laughter.

"No, it is not," he barks. The boys, suddenly aware of the drawbacks of clustering too close together on ice of unknown thickness, disperse into groups of two and three.

The eight boys are all members of Boy Scout Troop 89 in southwest Minneapolis. They've come to Stearns Scout Camp, near Annandale, to spend the last weekend of February camping outdoors in temperatures no higher than the teens. The North Wind Winter Adventure program at Stearns is one of a relatively small number of places in the United States where Scouts can learn winter camping skills in a natural outdoor setting. A few of the Troop 89 boys sampled winter camping a year before at the Northern Star Council's companion program, Spearhead, at Tomahawk Scout Reservation, but most are new to the experience. By the time they arrive back at the main lodge tomorrow morning they will have spent 24 consecutive hours outside in temperatures near or below zero.

After absorbing a few minutes of instruction on the properties and formation of lake ice, the boys tramp off toward their destination, a small rise on the far end of the lake known as Spider Island. As they soon discover, the island gets its name from a man-made obstacle at the top of a hill. A web of black, elastic cord has been stretched between two tree trunks. Diamond tells the boys that they have to figure out how to get everybody through the web without disturbing the big, fuzzy, black spider that stands guard over the obstacle. "And, oh, by the way," he adds. "Everybody has to go through a different hole in the web."

Mayhem results. The Scouts start yelling at each other. A wrestling match

Previous pages: St. Paul Scouts, probably from Troop 9, on an overnight campout, 1920s.

The Scouts of Minneapolis Troop 89 at Stearns Scout Camp's "Spider island."

breaks out. One Scout crawls beneath the web, taking the path of least re-sistance. Another tries to dive through one of the holes.

"You just got eaten," the second guide, Matt Swallow, informs the diving Scout.

"Do you think all this pushing and shoving is helping the cause?" Diamond asks.

For about twenty minutes, the Scouts of Troop 89 attack the problem with little success. They seem incapable of banding together to come up with a solution. But finally they begin working as a team.

"Parker and Sam, lift Kesecki!"

"Get on your hands and knees, Parker!"

"Why, so you can hurt me?"

After getting everybody from one side of the web to the other—to the good-natured satisfaction of Diamond and Swallow—the boys head back to base camp, a clearing in the woods that the North Wind staff calls the North Pole. (The troop has temporarily renamed itself the "Peary Crew" in honor of polar explorer Robert Peary.) The sun is slipping below the horizon. It's time to start work on the weekend's most imposing task—turning a large mound of snow into an overnight sleeping shelter known as a quinzee.

Digging out a quinzee.

The boys had created the mound earlier in the day by shoveling snow onto a pile of sacks containing, among other things, their sleeping bags. Now they have to hollow out the mound and retrieve their supplies, so they have a place to sleep tonight. The six oldest boys get to work on the quinzee. The two sixth graders join Swal-low and Diamond at the "kitchen counter," a length of plywood topped with three tiny propane burners used to boil water and heat dinner.

As dusk fades to darkness, an almost grim sense of purpose takes over the camp. The quinzee crew digs deeper into the snow mound. ("Remember guys, you want to go in and up!") The two youngest Scouts try to get the hang of the propane burners, but eventually abandon their posts out of frustration and a deepening realization that the night is only going to get colder. One of the troop's assistant Scoutmasters, Marc Krumholz, circles the camp offering candy as an incentive to keep working. "Want a Rollo?" he asks. The candies' centers have frozen into caramel flavored rocks.

Swallow and Diamond cook dinner by dropping Ziploc bags filled with rigatoni and garlic breadsticks into pots of boiling water. The Scouts huddle around the kitchen counter and shovel the food into their mouths. Most use plastic forks and spoons, but one of the sixth graders—ignoring warnings about exposed skin—uses his fingers instead. The main topic of conversation is the cold, and how sitting in one place only seems to make matters worse.

The older boys get back to work on the quinzee. Swallow, his full beard now frozen into what he calls a "beardsicle," admits he's concerned about their progress. "I've never had a crew that was still working on its shelter past sundown," he says. Still, he's pretty sure they'll get the job done.

Preparing dinner at the "kitchen counter."

By 8:30, the quinzee is finished. All the packs have been retrieved and seven sleeping bags have been tightly arranged on the floor in a parquet-like pattern. (The remaining members of the crew will sleep in three other shelters—a tent, a tarp-covered tree trunk, and an army surplus parachute suspended from a branch.) Diamond and Swallow lead the crew on a 45-minute night hike meant to push the boys to the brink of exhaustion. The boys return to camp and collapse into sleeping bags warmed by Nalgene bottles filled with hot water.

Overnight the temperature drops to 7 degrees below zero. In the morning, back at the lodge, each member of Troop 89 receives a "Zero Hero" patch to recognize his accomplishment.

IN ONE OF THE EARLIEST KNOWN LOCAL ACCOUNTS of the infant Scouting movement, the *St. Paul Pioneer Press* reported on August 28, 1910, that nothing was more important to a Scout than spending time outdoors. "The wild woods are the best place to camp," it explained, "but Boy Scouts learn how they can get pleasure and benefit from living in a tent on a town lot, or on a porch."[1]

In the years and decades that followed, countless boys in Minnesota and Wisconsin learned what it meant to be a Scout by venturing outdoors and experiencing nature up close. In the beginning, before the establishment of permanent camps such as Tonkawa and Square Lake, hiking was the most popular form of outdoor adventure, and most destinations were close to home. Scouts often rode streetcars to the end of the line and set out on their excursions from there. Usually Scoutmasters led the way, but some Scouts, seeing little need for adult supervision, hiked off on their own. Overnights were relatively rare.

As Scouting developed, outings became more and more adventurous. Scouts came to expect that they would go on overnight camping excursions to distant places. Winter camping no longer seemed so intimidating. Arduous canoe trips became the norm. With the establishment of new "high adventure" Scouting destinations such as the Charles L. Sommers Wilderness Canoe Base on northern Minnesota's Moose Lake (established in 1923) and Philmont Ranch in New Mexico (established in 1938), more Scouts than ever before had the chance to develop and test their outdoor skills.

Scouts from Minnesota and Wisconsin have been making annual high adventure trips to Philmont Ranch for decades now. During the 1980s, the Indianhead Council even acquired a bus to carry Scouts to New Mexico and back. These days, local troops, posts, and crews (including Hutchinson Troop 246, shown here in 2007) arrange their own transportation.

Champlin Troop 176 on an autumn hike, 1930.

Now is the season of all seasons for Scouting out of doors. The hike is the thing. Open air and campfire meetings spell romance and adventure. The overnight hike is joy complete. There is just enough tang and zest in the air to fill the days with vigor and the nights with most perfect slumber.

— *Be Prepared* (Minneapolis Council newsletter), October 1923

St. Paul Troop 17 embarks on a hike to Boiling Springs, near Savage, 1917.

Five members of the St. Paul Scouts' 1915 hiking expedition to San Francisco. L–R: Fred Marcellus, Leon Blehert, Harry Marcellus, H. S. Sorrels, and Max Bernstein. At least two of them—Blehert and Bernstein—completed the trek.

While hundreds of persons of all ages looked on and waved farewells, the party of six Boy Scouts under H. S. Sorrels, former Scout executive of St. Paul, started out from the Old Capitol yesterday at 10:30 a.m. on their 2,800-mile hike across the continent to San Francisco. As the boys took hold of the "prairie schooner" containing their provisions and camp equipment and started down the street, a cheer went up from the crowd. A large number followed the hikers beyond the city limits.

— *St. Paul Pioneer Press*, April 12, 1915

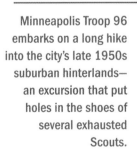

Minneapolis Troop 96 embarks on a long hike into the city's late 1950s suburban hinterlands— an excursion that put holes in the shoes of several exhausted Scouts.

As evidence of what can be done by trained Scouts who know how, a party from Excelsior Troop 40, among them Jamboree Scout Edgar Pierson, camped in a pup tent erected in a ravine near Shakopee during the entire holiday vacation. Although the temperature went as low as 25 below zero, and hovered between 15 and 20 below most of the time, the Scout campers were not indoors once during six days and five nights.

— *Be Prepared* (Minneapolis Council newsletter), January 1925

Minneapolis Troop 342 on a winter camping adventure during the late 1960s.

A snowstorm greets an outbound crew of Scouts at Camp Stearns' North Wind Winter Adventure program.

Pausing during a hike to St. Paul's Battle Creek, 1921.

Blankets come in two sizes: Those not long enough and those six inches too short. When you sleep double, blankets are what keep the other fellow warm all night. If you sleep single, you should roll up in your blankets. You should always roll up in the same direction, and you should make a note in your book of which direction you must roll in the morning to untangle yourself. Many a man, otherwise healthy, has rolled himself desperate because he could not remember which way he should turn over to get the blankets off.

— *Be Prepared* (Minneapolis Council newsletter), January 1923

North Branch Troop 411 goes cave camping at Eagle Cave, south of La Crosse, WI, 2008.

A Minneapolis Scout and his trusty bed roll, late 1910s.

Swimming has always been favorite activity among Minnesota and Wisconsin Scouts—at least during the summer. This 1920s watercolor, by the father-and-son artistic duo known as Hy Hintermeister, captures the joy of a warm-weather dip. It's one of a series of original Hy Hintermeister paintings on display at Many Point Scout Camp.

While it is a minor matter, sunburn is mighty painful. My Scouts learned that by experience a few days ago when I went on a fishing trip with them. They insisted on running around in the sun all afternoon in their bathing trunks, although I told them repeatedly they would blister their backs. They did, too, before night, and they know better now.

— Prof. D. Lange, Ramsey Council #1
Instruction Committee Chairman, 1911[2]

St. Anthony Park
Troop 17 cooks out,
1951.

A skeptical taste tester,
1957.

Eating Scout food is a truly remarkable experience, particularly when 28 of those Scouts are novices at cooking and washing dishes outdoors for the first time. . . .

For the first few days, the eager young Scouts bombarded my taste buds with powdered eggs mixed with pine needles and lichens, pancake batter topped with generous portions of sand and fire ashes, all served on plates that looked suspiciously as though they had last been washed at the 1972 campout.

All this is washed down with gallons of a concoction I soon dubbed bellywash, better known to the Boy Scouts as grape Kool-Aid. . . .

After two days of this kind of cuisine, I stumbled wearily to my tent where I lay wheezing and moaning for the next two days while my stomach struggled wearily to adjust itself to the rigors of outdoors life.

— Parent Jim Shoop describing a Scout outing in the *Minneapolis Star*, August 13, 1975

What challenge now to the campfire cook when preparation of the morning oatmeal means only adding hot water to the instant product in the cereal bowl? What valiance necessary to produce flapjacks when they're cooked from prepared pancake flour? What bravery must come to the fore to empty a container of instant soup into hot water? What contrast to camp cookery of half a century ago—before instants, ready-mixes, plastic and aluminum foil!

— *St. Paul Dispatch*, February 14, 1964

Scouts of St. Paul Troop 195 prepare dinner outdoors during an urban camping excursion, about 1950.

Assistant Scoutmaster Gerald Walsh and Scoutmaster Fred Nelson of Farmington Troop 118 pass out bottles of pop during a campout at Crystal Lake, 1947.

I wanted to share a Pack 120 tradition, the chocolada. It evolved from the smaco (s'more fixings in a hard corn taco shell) that we learned about at Webelos Camp at Stearns when we were at a friend's cabin and they had only soft flour tortillas. The chocolada solves the eternal problem of the s'more—no one can wait for the marshmallow to melt the chocolate!

You'll need: chocolate bars, marshmallows, soft tortillas, aluminum foil, very hot campfire coals, and long fire tongs.

Instructions: Cut each tortilla in half (unless you're using very small ones); Wrap a square of chocolate and marshmallow in the tortilla: Wrap the tortilla in aluminum foil: Cook for several minutes (this will depend on the heat of your fire).

Warning: The interior is very hot and runny—it's best to let them cool for a bit and to have plenty of napkins!

— Louis Hoffman, Pack 120, in *Navigator*
(Northern Star Council newsletter), August 2007

1940s >

BY LATE 1940, MANY AMERICANS—and many Minnesotans and Wisconsinites—were coming to the uneasy conclusion that the United States would soon be drawn into the wars raging in Europe and the Pacific. Isolation no longer seemed a viable option. In Minneapolis, Scouting officials strongly considered—but ultimately rejected—a request from an interventionist group called the Committee to Defend America by Aiding the Allies to participate in a mass anti-isolationism rally.[1] About a month later, in February 1941, the *Minneapolis Star Journal* praised the Boy Scouts for setting an example worth following.

> *Here is a democratic movement that begins where such movements should begin—among youth; which cuts through all classes and social strata; which unites every American boy, rich or poor, in a brotherhood which is patriotic without jingoism, idealistic without sentimentalism, obedient without regimentation.*
>
> *Contrast the qualities and individual gifts which Scouting develops with the traits which Hitler, Mussolini and Stalin are trying to inculcate into their youth and you can measure at a glance the difference between freedom and goose-stepping, between the development of individual human personality and its submergence in the will of the State.*[2]

As the nation prepared for what seemed to be inevitable war, a sense of dread began to set in. "Today no man dares to predict the things which are to come," Scout Executive L. D. Cornell declared at a December 4, 1941, meeting of the Minneapolis Council's board of directors. "Suddenly we find ourselves face to face with the stern reality of a suffering humanity . . . nation against nation . . . a world full of distrust and hatred into which our youngsters are being born."

< Minneapolis Scouts practice first aid in the dark
as they prepare for possible duty during wartime blackouts.

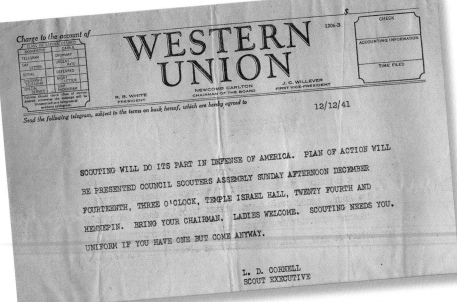

Charge to the account of

WESTERN UNION

1206-B

R. B. WHITE
PRESIDENT

NEWCOMB CARLTON
CHAIRMAN OF THE BOARD

J. C. WILLEVER
FIRST VICE-PRESIDENT

12/12/41

Send the following telegram, subject to the terms on back hereof, which are hereby agreed to

SCOUTING WILL DO ITS PART IN DEFENSE OF AMERICA. PLAN OF ACTION WILL
BE PRESENTED COUNCIL SCOUTERS ASSEMBLY SUNDAY AFTERNOON DECEMBER
FOURTEENTH, THREE O'CLOCK, TEMPLE ISRAEL HALL, TWENTY FOURTH AND
HENNEPIN. BRING YOUR CHAIRMAN. LADIES WELCOME. SCOUTING NEEDS YOU.
UNIFORM IF YOU HAVE ONE BUT COME ANYWAY.

L. D. CORNELL
SCOUT EXECUTIVE

Minneapolis Area Council Scout Executive L. D. Cornell rallies Scouting's troops following the attack on Pearl Harbor.

Three days after Cornell delivered that anxious assessment, Japan attacked Pearl Harbor and the United States was officially at war. Men of all ages (and even some boys trying to pass themselves off as 18-year-olds) flocked to Army, Navy, and Marine recruitment centers to volunteer for military service. Others took new jobs at defense plants, manufacturing everything from bullets to bombers.

Locally and nationally, the Boy Scouts faced a sudden shortage of adult leaders. By the summer of 1941, the St. Paul Area Council was struggling to cope with a 75 percent turnover in its leadership ranks.[4] Nearly every other council in the United States—including the Minneapolis Area Council—faced similar leadership shortages and continued to do so for the duration of the war. For the

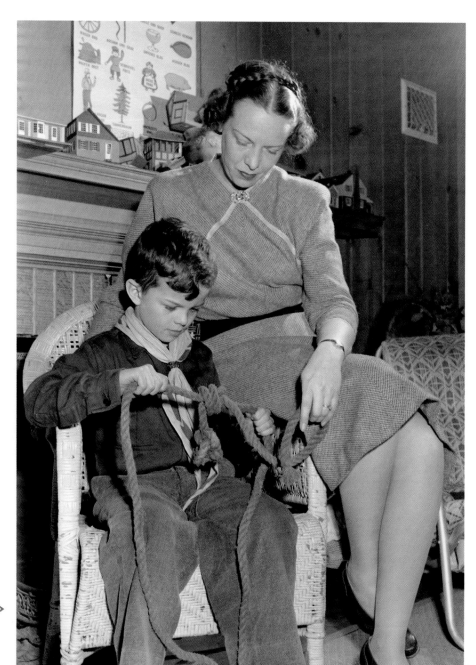

A sudden shortage of available men thrust more women into Scouting leadership roles—especially in Cub Scout dens.

first time, den mothers began taking over the leadership of Cub dens. (The number of den mothers in the St. Paul Area Council grew tenfold during the war, from 20 in 1941 to 208 in 1945.) Some Scout units, like Troop 33, sponsored by Minneapolis's Westminster Presbyterian Church, were forced to rely on 14- and 15-year-old Scouts for leadership. Newspapers such as the *St. Paul Pioneer Press* issued urgent pleas for new Scoutmasters.

> *The number of Scoutmasters under arms has raised a serious problem for the organization here at home.... So long as there are still adults who can qualify for leadership, no Boy Scout troop should be permitted to go undermanned, nor any needed new troop unorganized. Adolf Hitler, remember, abolished the Scout organization in Germany and all occupied countries. That alone is evidence enough of its contribution to freedom.[5]*

Compounding the problems created by the Scoutmaster shortage was a simultaneous spike in interest among Scouting-age boys. "Boys have more than the normal desire to belong to an organization where they feel they can render their country a service," a report issued by the St. Paul Area Council concluded. "The Scout Program, with its uniform, is particularly appealing and popular at the present time."[6] The combination of more Scouts and fewer Scoutmasters threatened to weaken Scouting programs that had steadily improved over the previous three decades.

Still, despite wartime constraints, thousands of Scouts from the Twin Cities councils managed to make real and measurable contributions to the nation's war effort. In the first few months of confusion after the Pearl Harbor attack, local Scout leaders struggled to fashion a coordinated response. Early planning focused primarily on salvage collection, but the programs were slow to develop. In the fall of 1942, Scouts in Minneapolis and St. Paul finally got their first big chance to shine as the two cities engaged in a good-natured competition to see which one could collect the most scrap metal during the course of a weekend.

Sea Scouts pull an old 11-ton dredge from the bottom of Lake Minnetonka as part of Mound's 1942 scrap drive.

Minneapolis Scout Willis Lund helps Mildred Matta dispose of two World War I artillery shells during the 1942 scrap drive. The article accompanying the photograph did not explain where the shells came from.

Minneapolis was first up in the competition, and local Scouts fanned out across the city, helping residents toss unwanted junk onto the backs of flatbed trucks and into huge scrap piles. The following weekend, St. Paul Scouts performed a more specialized duty, planting small American flags in the front yard of each household that contributed to the effort. "The Boy Scouts [of St. Paul] did a magnificent job," the *Pioneer Press* reported. "Smartly dressed in their khaki uniforms, they carried, placed and saluted the American flags. When the day was done they reported back to their leaders and without exception all asked: 'Isn't there something else we can do?'" In the end, St. Paul and its flag-planting Scouts emerged victorious, with about 6,700 tons of scrap collected compared to Minneapolis's 6,000.[7]

Minneapolis Scouts volunteering as air raid emergency messengers were required to have their fingerprints on file.

Twin Cities Scouts assumed even greater responsibilities the following year when a small army of them—more than 500 in Minneapolis alone—trained to become emergency messengers.[8] Fears of possible air raids remained high during the first two years of the war, and the Scout messenger corps was an integral part of both cities' civil defense apparatus. The Scouts trained to deliver messages by hand if normal communications channels were disrupted by air raids or sabotage. Neither city was ever attacked during the war, but the Scout messengers got plenty of practice during blackout drills. Minneapolis Scout John Calvin described the experience to the *Minneapolis Tribune:*

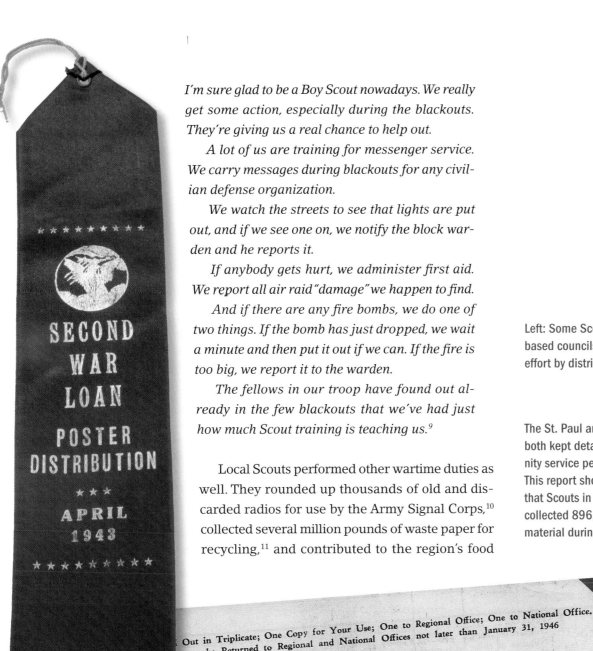

I'm sure glad to be a Boy Scout nowadays. We really get some action, especially during the blackouts. They're giving us a real chance to help out.

A lot of us are training for messenger service. We carry messages during blackouts for any civilian defense organization.

We watch the streets to see that lights are put out, and if we see one on, we notify the block warden and he reports it.

If anybody gets hurt, we administer first aid. We report all air raid "damage" we happen to find.

And if there are any fire bombs, we do one of two things. If the bomb has just dropped, we wait a minute and then put it out if we can. If the fire is too big, we report it to the warden.

The fellows in our troop have found out already in the few blackouts that we've had just how much Scout training is teaching us.[9]

Local Scouts performed other wartime duties as well. They rounded up thousands of old and discarded radios for use by the Army Signal Corps,[10] collected several million pounds of waste paper for recycling,[11] and contributed to the region's food

Left: Some Scouts in the Twin Cities-based councils contributed to the war effort by distributing war loan posters.

The St. Paul and Minneapolis councils both kept detailed records of community service performed during the war. This report shows, among other things, that Scouts in the St. Paul Area Council collected 896,968 pounds of scrap material during 1945.

Fill Out in Triplicate; One Copy for Your Use; One to Regional Office; One to National Office.
Copies to be Returned to Regional and National Offices not later than January 31, 1946

BOY SCOUTS OF AMERICA
1945 WAR TIME SERVICE REPORT

Includes GREEN THUMB CAMPAIGN

REGION No.

COUNCIL No.

NAME OF COUNCIL _____ (STATE)

LOCATION OF COUNCIL OFFICE

INCLUDE IN THIS REPORT ONLY 1945 ACTIVITIES

NATURE OF WAR SERVICE RENDERED	No. Communities Covered	Total No. Different Cubs and Scouts Participating	Total No. Different Troops and Packs	Total Volume of Material Handled By Boys	SPACE FOR YOUR COMMENT (If Completed — Include Date of Completion)
				896968 Lbs.	Unit Citations Awarded 13 / Eisenhower Medals Awarded 707
WASTE PAPER COLLECTION General Eisenhower - Boy Scout Campaign March - April 1945	22	707	80	Lbs.	
WASTE PAPER COLLECTION (Total of entire year)	33	1007	119	Lbs.	
SALVAGE OF SCRAP RUBBER	8	37	11	10510 Lbs.	
SALVAGE OF SCRAP METAL (Scrap Banks)	3	94	7	27152 Lbs.	
	6	247	13	49505 Lbs.	

SECOND WAR LOAN POSTER DISTRIBUTION

★ ★ ★

APRIL 1943

supply by planting thousands of "Victory Gardens."[12] In western Wisconsin, Scouts collected milkweed pods. (Floss from the pods was used in Navy life jackets.) At camp, even the most routine daily duties took on a sense of urgency. In a move that set a nationwide example, the Minneapolis Area Council converted its primary summer camp, Camp Tonkawa on Lake Minnetonka, into a far-reaching experiment in boy-powered food production.

The experiment began in the summer of 1942, with a small, one-sixth-acre garden maintained by Tonkawa campers. The following summer, Tonkawa's entire program was expanded and retooled to focus almost exclusively on the production of food. Scouts at the new "Victory Camp" tended vegetable gardens planted on 35 acres of farmland adjacent to the camp and contributed more than 100,000 hours of labor.[13] Much of the food they produced went straight to the camp kitchen. The rest went to market. "We have felt that camping merely for the sake of camping should be out for the duration [of the war]," Scout Executive L. D. Cornell explained. "We could justify the operation only in terms of its direct contribution to the war's end!"[14]

At the 1947 National Scout Executives Conference in Bloomington, Indiana, a men's chorus from Region Ten—the Scouting area that included Minnesota and parts of Wisconsin—debuted a new song based on the Scout Oath. The song's composer, longtime Twin Cities Scouter Harry Bartelt (he had gone on to serve as Scout executive of the North Star Council in Duluth), had no idea that his creation, "On My Honor," would soon become one of Scouting's most familiar and popular tunes. "Although I possessed great interest and enthusiasm for music, I lacked experience and good training in composition," he later admitted. "The reason for the effort in the first place was the hope that the Scout Oath might be sung instead of verbally repeated. It seemed to me that on certain occasions a musical Scout Oath might be especially effective."[22]

Above: An early copy of "On My Honor," with guitar chords added.

Left: St. Paul Area Council Assistant Scout Executive Harry Bartelt during a 1919 camping trip to the Canadian border.

The "Minneapolis Area Council Plan," as the Tonkawa food production program became known, quickly caught the attention of national Scouting officials. "We have been greatly interested in seeing [your] plans," Chief Scout Executive Elbert Fretwell wrote in a letter to Arthur Larkin, president of the Minneapolis Area Council. "We hope of promoting Scout Camps along the line that you are pioneering."[15] During the summer of 1943, Scout councils around the country operated 41 food production camps based on the Minneapolis plan.

The Tonkawa experiment was, if anything, too successful. The number of Scouts attending Tonkawa more than tripled in 1943, due in large part to the camp's new, heightened emphasis on food production and on the desire of boys to contribute to the war effort. Tonkawa was ill prepared to accommodate such a large influx of new campers, and the program suffered as a result. Chief among the problems were the camp's "filthy and malodorous" latrines.[16] "Our present facilities at Camp Tonkawa are inadequate to a degree which jeopardizes the health and welfare of groups of campers," the council's camping chairman, Charles Velie, reported.[17] The problems encountered during the summer of 1943 forced the council to significantly scale back its food production goals in 1944, and to begin thinking seriously about replacing Tonkawa with a new camp. (The resulting search process culminated in the establishment of Many Point Scout Camp in 1946.)

The end of the war in August of 1945 triggered outpourings of relief and joy, but it also marked the beginning of a short but challenging period for the Boy Scouts, both locally and nationally. "Those good men who took over at the beginning of the war, to carry the Scouting program on through the war years, became anxious for relief as soon as the war ended," St. Paul Scout Executive Paul Hesser said. Many wartime Scouters were counting on returning servicemen to "take over the reins" after they came home, but military veterans were often reluctant to assume Scouting leadership roles—at least right away. The resulting upheaval in the leadership ranks led to an unusually high rate of lapsed units and a general "letdown of Scouting morale."[18]

It did not take long, however, for morale to rebound. Scouting officials recognized the threat of a post-war malaise, and they moved quickly to

These Minneapolis Scouts were among the hundreds who tended crops at Camp Tonkawa's "Victory Camp" during the summer of 1943.

Farmington Troop 118 gets back to full strength after four years of wartime disruption, 1947. Sitting: Assistant Scoutmaster Gerald Walsh. Standing L–R: Patrol Leaders Ronald Ersfield, James Gerster, Paul Gerster, Robert Peterson, and James Freer.

Older Scouts, like these from Farmington Sea Scout Ship "Monitor" (left) and the Minneapolis Sea Scout Ship "Santa Maria" (right), were folded into the BSA's new Explorer program during the late 1940s.

counteract it. In the fall of 1946, councils around the country—including the St. Paul and Minneapolis councils—participated in the inaugural National Round-Up, an organized recruitment campaign that quickly established itself as an annual event on the Scouting calendar.[19]

The following year, the BSA chose the Minneapolis Area Council (and eleven others around the country) to test a new program aimed at addressing one of Scouting's most persistent challenges—the "older boy problem."

Like most other councils around the country, the Minneapolis Council had long struggled to keep boys 15 and older in the Scouting fold. Local leaders had hoped that Sea Scouting, Explorer Scouting, and a new program introduced during the war—Air Scouting—would hold the interest of older Scouts, but success was fleeting. By the end of 1946, "Senior Scouting" (the term under which the three programs were often lumped) was limping along in Minneapolis. The council listed 16 registered Explorer units, but most of them were inactive. Its Sea Scouting program, which had enjoyed a spike in interest during the war, was just "striving to carry on" now that the fighting was over. Air Scouting, despite its supposed appeal to aeronautically inclined teenagers, had so far attracted only a few Scouts. Minneapolis Council leaders called Senior Scouting a programmatic "step child," and they spoke of an urgent need to develop "a different kind of program" to meet the needs of older Scouts.[20]

The primary goal of the BSA's Senior Scouting experiment was to merge all existing Sea Scout ships, Explorer posts, and Air Scout squadrons into new units called Senior Outfits. Under the test program, older Scouts received new badges and uniforms, and operated under a reconfigured advancement sys-

tem. The experiment began in early 1948 and was scheduled to last three years, but the early results in Minneapolis and elsewhere were so encouraging that the BSA decided after one year to adopt the program nationwide—albeit under a slightly different name. From now on, Scouts 14 and older would be registered as Explorers—not Senior Scouts or Explorer Scouts. They could wear either the standard Boy Scout uniform or a new green Explorer uniform. They also were given the choice of remaining in their current troop (as part of a new Explorer crew) or joining a separate unit known as an Explorer post.

By the end of the decade, local Scouting officials were looking forward—with mounting apprehension—to the years to come. The combined membership of the Minneapolis and St. Paul councils had nearly doubled during the 1940s, and every demographic trend suggested that growth rates over the next few years would only accelerate. Scouting programs were about to be put to a severe test.

Thankfully, local boys could continue to count on the efforts of hundreds of dedicated Scouters—people like Ray Winkel. The story of Ray Winkel had begun spreading around the country when the war was over. Winkel had joined St. Paul's Troop 30 at the age of 12, and was one merit badge away from earning Eagle rank when he left to join the Navy. He went off to war, saw battle on Guadalcanal, and figured his days with the Boy Scouts were done. But as a national reporter later explained it, Winkel's friends back home weren't about to forget him:

With the decade coming to a close, Scouts Edwin Burton of Anoka Troop 204 and Donald Talbot of Anoka Troop 276 present the 1950 Boy Scout calendar, illustrated by Norman Rockwell, to Anoka businessman J. W. Freeburg (in suspenders). Flanking them are the troops' Scoutmasters: C. Rudolph Johnson (Troop 204); Paul Wethern (Troop 276); and Kenneth Burton (Troop 204).

Now one thing about Scouting is that it makes sense. During the Spring Jamboree the Scoutmaster of Ray Winkel's troop—Troop 30, St. Paul, Minn.—suggested that such formal requirements as making a fire by rubbing sticks together, or putting a model raft together with tree-bark and vines, had really been met in Winkel's case by what he had done in the Navy's Construction Battalion in the field. And at St. Paul's annual Boy Scout banquet in 1943, the Eagle Scout badge was presented to Ray's mother.[21]

Winkel received his Eagle Scout badge while he was still stationed in the Pacific. When he finally returned home, he signed on as an assistant Scoutmaster with his old troop.

CAMP PART 1 >

NOW ✦ THEN

NOW ✦ THEN

THE BLACKFOOT CAMPSITE sits in a small clearing overlooking Lake Nielsen on the southwest side of the Tomahawk Scout Reservation. It's part of the Chippewa sub-camp. The Scouts of Mahtomedi Troop 89 consider Blackfoot the best camping spot at Tomahawk, and their Scoutmaster, Jim Schuster, tells the story of how his troop ended up here. Back in 1984, a troop that previously had enjoyed sole claim to the Blackfoot site during the last week of July forgot to send in its deposit. Troop 89's Scoutmaster at the time heard about the opening and immediately wrote a check to secure Blackfoot for his Scouts. The troop's been coming here ever since.

Previous pages:
"Tent #6," at Square Lake Camp, 1924.

The Blackfoot campsite at Tomahawk's
Chippewa sub-camp.

It's 7:25 a.m. Reveille sounded about a half hour ago, and in the time since then the campsite has come reluctantly to life. Thirty-six Scouts ranging in age from 11 to 17 have stumbled out of their canvas tents and lined up, groggily, by patrol. Those who care to notice see that the rising sun has illuminated the lake's far western shore.

"Color guard, advance!"

The next few minutes follow a familiar script: the posting of the colors; the Pledge of Allegiance; and finally, announcements. Senior Patrol Leader Alex Westad tells the Scouts that the day's activities will culminate in an evening water polo match against Troop 13 and the election of new troop and patrol leaders. Oh, and the Flaming Arrow patrol has K.P. duty.

At 7:55, the Scouts of Troop 89 join all the other troops at Tomahawk for morning assembly, including the all-camp flag raising. Five minutes later they're streaming through the doors of the dining hall to take their places for breakfast.

This morning's meal consists of Apple Jacks cereal, dry, tasteless hash browns (made palatable by liberal slatherings of ketchup), bean burritos that look suspiciously like yesterday's dinner, and a few bags of sliced white bread. As always, jars of peanut butter and jelly are available to anyone in search of extra protein. Each table accommodates 12 or so Scouts, with an adult leader sitting at the end. Conversation is kept to a minimum.

"Pass the cereal."

"Wyatt, can you get some more milk?"

Only on the way out of the dining hall do the boys return to their normally talkative selves. "That was probably one of the worst meals I've had here," confides one of the older Scouts. "And that's saying something."

Some of the Scouts head back to Blackfoot. Others drift off toward the beach and the Scoutcraft area to kill some time before the day's programs get underway. By 9 a.m., almost everyone has reported to one of Chippewa's eight merit badge locations or the campfire ring, where aspiring Tenderfoot Scouts participate in the camp's Brownsea program. At the handicraft area, boys intent on earning their woodcarving badges crowd around six workbenches, scraping grooves into six-by-six squares of wood. Across the way, Scouts in crash helmets inch their way up the climbing tower as their friends on the ground offer yelps of encouragement. And at the base of a tree near the dining hall, 15 boys including Troop 89's Alex Voytovich are working on their first aid badges with the camp's health officer, Jake Piekarski.

"Compound fractures," Piekarski says, introducing the day's subject. "There's only one bone in your leg that, if it breaks, you better call 911. What is it?"

"Tibia?"

"No."

"Femur?"

"Right."

For the next ten minutes, Piekarski and his Scouts discuss various types of bone fractures and how to treat them. Then it's time for some hands-on training. Alex Voytovich is among the Scouts who volunteer to be "victims." In this exercise, Alex is to lie on the ground and act as if he has a broken radius or ulna. His partner begins sliding a wooden splint under his arm.

"Does this hurt?" his partner asks.

"No."

"Does this hurt?"

"Argh!" Alex proves to be an excellent actor.

Breakfast at the Chippewa dining hall.

All around camp, Scouts are developing skills that they might never have had a chance to learn anywhere else. There's basketry and leatherwork at the handicraft area; horsemanship at the horse corral; lifesaving and sailing at the aquatics area; orienteering at the Lake Nielsen Marina; and astronomy, nature, and fish and wildlife management at the ecology area. And that's just the morning session. The afternoon program features everything from canoeing to fly-fishing to shotgun shooting to wilderness survival.

Camp is more than merit badge instruction, of course. The Scouts at Tomahawk have plenty of time during the day to rest or goof off. Back at Blackfoot, there almost always seem to be at least a few Scouts doing something to pass the time—paging through the Scout Handbook, playing cards, rummaging for some kind of personal item in the metal "bear box," or simply staring into space. When the afternoon merit badge session is over, the campfire becomes Scout central. A half-dozen boys settle into nylon chairs arranged around the fire pit. A crew-cut 12-year-old entrepreneur named Marcell Primeau is trying to sell marshmallows.

"I've got a new sale going on," he announces. "Fifteen cents apiece. I'll accept IOUs."

Afternoon rest and relaxation around the campfire.

He gets no immediate takers, so he switches to a complementary product line.

"Westin," he says, directing his pitch to one of his fellow Second Class Scouts, "I've got another job for you. Every new sharpened stick you bring me, I'll give you ten cents." Westin remains in his chair, apparently disinclined to act on Marcell's offer.

As everyone around the fire pit knows, this is steak night, the one time during the week when troops are expected to prepare and eat dinner at their campsites. Most troops have the boys do the cooking, but in Troop 89, the adult leaders prefer to treat their Scouts to a night off. By 5 o'clock, afternoon is blending into evening and preparations for dinner are well underway. The Tomahawk staff has supplied steaks and potatoes. The troop has brought along its own corn on the cob and garlic bread. The adults have spread a small carpet of charcoal briquettes next to the fire pit and thrown foil-wrapped potatoes into the coals.

One more scheduled activity remains before dinner is served. The older members of the troop have challenged camp staffers to a beach volleyball match. A small contingent of younger Scouts heads over to the aquatics area to watch the match-up and cheer on their team. The Troop 89 volleyballers make a game of it, but the staff team prevails. Nobody seems particularly surprised or disappointed. "Oh well," says one of the young spectators. "At least now I get to go back to camp for steak dinner."

IT TOOK A FEW YEARS for long-term camping to catch on among Twin Cities area Scouts. The region's first permanent Scouting camp, established in 1911 at a property called Crocker's Point on Lake Minnetonka's Harrison Bay, had few amenities. Scouts were expected to provide their own food, tents, and other supplies. The Hennepin Council arranged to dig a well and have the camp's drinking water tested by a city bacteriologist (waterborne diseases such as typhoid fever were a major public health concern at the time), but that was about the extent of its involvement.[1] The second generation of camps—the Hennepin Council's camp on Lake Minnetonka's Maxwell's Bay (later known as Camp Rotary) and the St. Paul Council's camps on Silver Lake, Lake Charlotte, and Lake Emily—were only slightly more sophisticated.

The camping experience for local Scouts improved dramatically with the establishment of the St. Paul Council's Square Lake Camp, north of Stillwater, in 1918 and the Hennepin Council's Camp Tonkawa, on Lake Minnetonka, in 1921. These council-owned camps were capable of accommodating hundreds of Scouts each summer and continued to operate for about two decades. As the years passed, both councils added new properties—including, most notably, the St. Paul Council's St. Croix River Camp (later renamed the Fred C. Andersen Scout Camp) and Camp Neibel—that further enhanced camping opportunities for local Scouts.

Most Scouts in the region went to council-owned camps, but many others attended smaller camps operated by districts within the councils and, in some cases, by troops and their chartered organizations. One of the troop camps—Camp Ajawah, on Linwood Lake in Anoka County—has served as Minneapolis Troop 33's summer camping home since 1934.

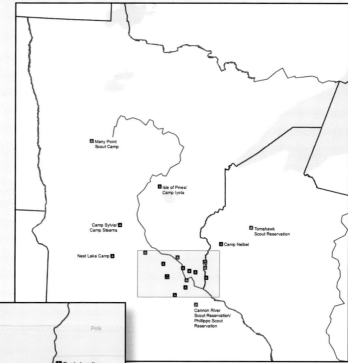

Current Council camps are in red. For a listing of the camps with locations and dates of operation, see page 222.

The Scouts of St. Anthony Park Troop 17 on their way to Square Lake Camp, 1918.

Dear Mom and Dad,

They told us to write home so here goes.

It sure seemed funny riding on a street car through the country all the way from St. Paul to Stillwater. They met us with a big truck with high sideboards, threw in our suitcases and blanket rolls and told us to get in. We stood up all the way to camp which is nine miles and it was rough riding. Nobody got hurt.

— Arvid H. Edwards, describing his trip to Square Lake Camp, August 1927[2]

The most popular pastime that Scouts do, besides eating and sleeping, is reading comic books. During rest periods a person can find ¾ of the camp lying on their beds, chewing candy bars, saturated with mosquito lotion, delving into such superhuman tales as "Captain Zingo" and "Oscar the Wonder Boy." Or maybe reading how "Watta Man" captures 5 million gangsters. Perhaps a Scout's fancy turns to the fair sex. (Mine does.) These boys will enjoy half an hour with "Madam Gangrene" and the "Legions of Death."

— *The Dope* (Camp Neibel newsletter), July 2, 1942

St. Paul Troop 38 enjoys a cookout at the St. Croix River Camp, 1940.

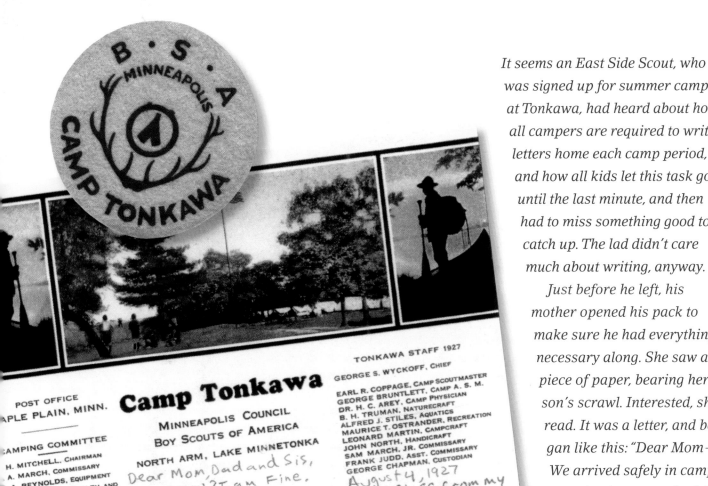

It seems an East Side Scout, who was signed up for summer camp at Tonkawa, had heard about how all campers are required to write letters home each camp period, and how all kids let this task go until the last minute, and then had to miss something good to catch up. The lad didn't care much about writing, anyway.

Just before he left, his mother opened his pack to make sure he had everything necessary along. She saw a piece of paper, bearing her son's scrawl. Interested, she read. It was a letter, and began like this: "Dear Mom— We arrived safely in camp. I am having a wonderful time and—." That was enough of that. But the mother was a real sport. She put back the letter, smiled to herself a bit, and fastened the pack-sack. Some boy still thinks he pulled a "fast one."

— *Minneapolis Journal,* September 4, 1935

POST OFFICE
MAPLE PLAIN, MINN.

CAMPING COMMITTEE
H. MITCHELL, CHAIRMAN
A. MARCH, COMMISSARY
W. A. REYNOLDS, EQUIPMENT
DR. HUGH AREY, HEALTH AND SANITATION.
J. H. COLLINS, PROGRAM

Camp Tonkawa
MINNEAPOLIS COUNCIL
BOY SCOUTS OF AMERICA
NORTH ARM, LAKE MINNETONKA

TONKAWA STAFF 1927
GEORGE S. WYCKOFF, CHIEF
EARL R. COPPAGE, CAMP SCOUTMASTER
GEORGE BRUNTLETT, CAMP A. S. M.
DR. H. C. AREY, CAMP PHYSICIAN
B. H. TRUMAN, NATURECRAFT
ALFRED J. STILES, AQUATICS
MAURICE T. OSTRANDER, RECREATION
LEONARD MARTIN, CAMPCRAFT
JOHN NORTH, HANDICRAFT
SAM MARCH, JR. COMMISSARY
FRANK JUDD, ASST. COMMISSARY
GEORGE CHAPMAN, CUSTODIAN

Dear Mom, Dad and Sis,
How are you? I am Fine.

August 4, 1927

I got to camp okay. When we arrived, Len and Cliff, from my troop and I were assigned to the Hodag Patrol. We make up a Patrol of boys from all over Minneapolis Area Council. The rest of the Hodags are swell. I think our Patrol is best. I was chosen the Patrol Leader.

We are staying in a tent city, rows of tents. The camp staff inspects our tent each day, then we go to the Dining Hall. The eats are great! On Sunday we will get ice cream.

The swimming beach is sure a peach. Yesterday I learned to swim on my back. I can't wait to show you when we go for a picnic at Lake Calhoun.

We had the Council fire last night. The older campers sat in the inner circle, while the outer circle was us new campers. Chief Wyckoff told us the story of Tonkawampus. Tonkawampus was a great man and a great leader.

Today we had the High Council meeting. I went as the Hodags Patrol Leader. We talked about how to make camp better and what our patrols should do. We decided to have boxing instead of wrestling tommorrow. I'll keep my left up like you showed me Dad.

Last night we went on a hike by patrols in the moonlight. After a while we stopped to rest by an old cemetery. The moon went behind a cloud. It was the creepiest situation I have ever been in.

I have learned a lot about being a leader that I will bring back to our troop. I also have many stories to tell you about Tonkawa.

Oh yes, Mom I am keeping my ears clean. Say Hello to Rose and give Spot a scratch for me.
Love, Buzz

P.S. Dear Sis, I have enclosed my pet wood tick for you. His name is Calvin Cootie.

The waterfront at Camp Neibel as it appeared in the 1940s.

A race of war canoes at Camp Tonkawa, 1921.

The war canoe race that was supposed to take place on Sunday evening was held Tuesday evening immediately after retreat. The Horse Patrol was appointed to conduct the race and proved very efficient. . . .

The race started about a mile down the North Arm and the canoes raced toward camp. Due to the inexperienced crews, the canoes lost a great deal by taking a zig zag course. It seems that the Gooses took a few more jumps sideward than the War Horses because the Horses arrived at the finish fully a length and a half ahead of the Gooses.

A grand water fight between the two crews finished the program for the evening.

— *Tonkawampus Tales* (Camp Tonkawa newsletter), July 30, 1927

You have no doubt noticed a thin green substance on the surface of the water. This is known as "Dog Day's Dilemma" or "Bath Tub Scum." Several Scouts have complained that this substance hampers swimming. This point will not be discussed here as only 10% of the camp have been sucked into slimy death.

At times "Bath Tub Scum" gets so thick that slight concussions and brain tumors occur when a dive is attempted. Of course this fact is blamed on the diver alone because he should use a crash helmet in a predicament such as this.

— *The Dope* (Camp Neibel newsletter), August 13, 1942

The diving platform at Camp Tonkawa was a Scout favorite for many years.

A moment of reverence at the Minneapolis Council's Camp Iyota, near Deerwood, 1938.

The Scouts of Osseo Troop 219 and Champlin Troop 276 horse around at Camp Manomin, near Fridley, 1935.

Chow time at Square Lake Camp, probably 1930s.

Rules for Scouts at the Table

1. *Never let a dish pass you without grabbing something off it.*
2. *Don't say "Please," always yell gruffly, "Slip the beans along, etc."*
3. *In eating, hump over your plate like a question mark, shovel 'er in with both hands, and watch your neighbor out of the corner of your eye like a dog.*
4. *If there is anything left on the adjoining plates grab it.*
5. *Be sure to get the largest cup and pass it twice for helpings.*
6. *Stand up, you can reach farther.*

— **Be Prepared** (Minneapolis Council newsletter), October 1923

That Camp Tonkawa grub "sticks to the ribs" is abundantly proven by the report of the commissary chief, Samuel March, Jr., for the second camping period ending July 16. Six hundred and 10 pounds net gain is made by 112 boys in 12 days, or 36 meals. This is an average gain per boy-meal of almost two and one half ounces, and is the visible result of 575 pounds of bread, 712 pounds of meat, 150 pounds of butter, 1,655 pounds of potatoes, 193 gallons of fresh milk, 210 dozen eggs and 20 gallons of ice cream, besides unweighed quantities of fresh fruit, fresh vegetables and a whole truckload of staples. The food is served on a balanced ration, prepared by Mrs. Schultz.

— *Minneapolis Tribune*, July 24, 1927

St. Paul Troop 38 lines up for breakfast at the St. Croix River Camp, 1942.

Tent inspection at Camp Rotary, late 1910s.

This Camp Rotary patch may be the oldest surviving camp emblem from the territory now included in the Northern Star Council.

Fellows who are late for formation get it. They have to run the gauntlet and everybody whales them with a belt. The other form of punishment is worse. That is bunk fatigue, which you get for bad offenses, like disobedience. A fellow who gets it has to stay in his bed undressed all day, but every time the bugle blows he has to get up, dress and report to the bugler. Then he goes back to bed again. The only thing worse than that is to get sent home, which doesn't happen very often.

— Scout Charles Morris, describing the first summer at Camp Tonkawa, *Minneapolis Journal*, August 7, 1921

In 1923, Camp Tonkawa introduced its "scalp program," a system designed to encourage advancement. Campers were eligible to earn up to three "scalps" (beanies) each summer. Scalps came in different colors and represented specific levels of achievement. The scalp program lasted for nearly 40 years, first at Tonkawa and later at Many Point Scout Camp.[3]

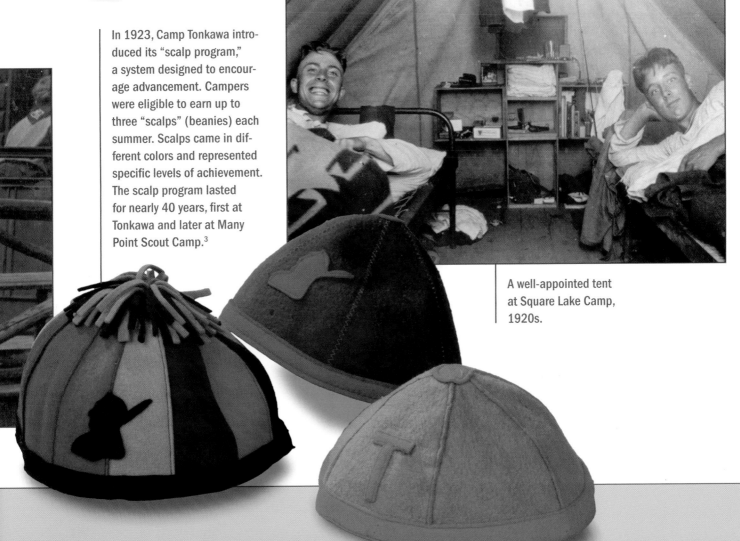

A well-appointed tent at Square Lake Camp, 1920s.

1950s >

THE UNITED STATES was in the midst of a baby boom. The national birth rate had made its first big jump in 1941 and had continued to rise during the war years. But it truly accelerated when the troops began coming home, getting married, and starting their own families. Now, as the new decade got underway, the nation was awash in babies, and few states were proving more fertile than Minnesota. For whatever reason, Minnesota's baby boom was outpacing—and was destined to outlast—that of the nation as a whole.[1]

The post-war demographic explosion had obvious implications for the Boy Scouts. By 1950, the first youngsters of the baby boom generation were reaching Cub Scout age. (The BSA had recently lowered the age requirement for first-year Cubs from nine to eight.) The combined membership of the St. Paul and Minneapolis councils jumped a whopping 10 percent during the first 12 months of the decade, prompting St. Paul Area Scout Executive Paul Hesser to declare that "we are literally 'bursting out at all seams.'"[2] The growth rate tailed off a bit in the years that followed, but by the end of the decade the number of boys served by the two councils (about 45,000) was nearly double the 1949 total.

At first, the jump in membership was most noticeable at the Cub Scout level. In the St. Paul Area Council, for example, Cub membership jumped more than 15 percent in 1951 while the number of Scouts and Explorers barely budged. But as time passed and the new crop of Cubs approached Scouting age, a new problem arose: there weren't enough Scout troops to accommodate the large numbers of graduating Cubs. As a result, only about a third of the Cubs in the St. Paul Area Council continued on with Scouting. Scout Executive Hesser warned that "this appalling loss of Cubs" would only get worse if the council did not act quickly.[3] The trick was to make Scouting

< A successful early 1950s paper drive by Minneapolis Troop 195.

Harbingers of Scouts to come: Cubs of St. Paul Pack 67 get down to work during the 1949–1950 school year.

Many Point owed much of its early success to this group of older Scouts who, under the guidance of Scoutmaster "Boots" Hanson (Many Point's first camp ranger), spent much of the summer of 1946 building the camp's roads and buildings, and clearing camp sites.

more appealing and relevant to a new generation of youngsters growing up during the second half of the 20th century.

Scouting officials with both of the Twin Cities-based councils had been considering ways to update their programs since the final months of World War II. By the early 1950s, their efforts were bearing fruit, most noticeably in their camping programs. The St. Paul Area Council was making final preparations to replace Camp Neibel with a new property on Wisconsin's Long Lake. (It would eventually become known as Tomahawk Scout Reservation.)

The Minneapolis Area Council was already basking in the glow of its newest acquisition, Many Point Scout Camp, near Itasca State Park in northwestern Minnesota.

Many Point was, in some ways, a groundbreaking experiment. During Scouting's first four decades, going to camp usually meant spending a week away from home with a bunch of other Scouts, most of whom were not members of your troop. Camp Tonkawa had tried to introduce the "troop camp" concept back in the 1930s in hopes of convincing more units "to camp together under leadership of their own Scoutmaster," but most Scouts and Scoutmasters preferred the old method.

Many Point, which opened in 1946, broke the old camp mold. Its developer, longtime Minneapolis Scouting professional Wint Hartman, believed camps should strengthen troops, and he designed Many Point so that boys camping with their own troops could graduate from one area to the next, developing camping and leadership skills as they went. "It is important that the troop sees their leaders as the heroes, not our staff," he was fond of saying. "It is the staff member's job to make sure the troop leader has the right tools to run the troop."[4] As the 1950s progressed, more and more camps around the country began to emulate the Many Point example.

Wint Hartman

Still, Scouting officials in Minneapolis and St. Paul knew they had to do more than open new camps if they were to effectively respond to the needs and concerns of the baby boom generation. The United States was entering a new era of unprecedented prosperity and unsettling global tension. After years of privation brought on by depression and war, Americans were embracing consumerism—buying everything from cars to refrigerators to new homes in the suburbs. But they also were confronting a new world order in which America and the Soviet Union were threatening each other with atomic weapons. The country was once again at war—this time, in Korea—seeking to protect an ally from communist aggressors. At home, many Americans worried that the liberties they cherished were under attack by shadowy communist sympathizers. Scouting began tailoring its programs to respond to the realities of what became known as the Cold War.

As the decade progressed, Scouts from the Minneapolis and St. Paul councils participated in a series of nationwide efforts designed to instill in them the ideals of patriotism, citizenship, and service to country. The first campaign, launched to coincide with Scouting's 40th anniversary in 1950, was dubbed the "Crusade to Strengthen the Arm of Liberty." Literature distributed by the BSA warned of "tyranny abroad and malice within our borders," and urged local councils to take the lead in preparing young men and boys for the many challenges facing the nation.

Liberty is not only a heritage, it is a fresh conquest for each generation. In a few years the youth of today will take part in that conquest. Our country will be given into their hands. They will run our farms, conduct our business, manage and work in our factories, lead us spiritually, make our laws and deal with world affairs.

Upon their shoulders we are laying a burden heavier than any ever imposed on any generation of American youth. Their problems, foreign

This replica of the Statue of Liberty remains on display to this day in the lobby of the Scott County Government Center in Shakopee.

Liberty Bell door hanger from the 1952 "Forward on Liberty's Team" campaign. Scouts in the Twin Cities-based councils hung thousands of these election reminders on their neighbors' doorknobs.

and domestic, will far surpass those with which we struggle today. Will they deal wisely and fairly with their responsibilities? Will they live by the faith of our forefathers in the fatherhood of God and the brotherhood of man?[5]

Although many of the initiatives of the 40th anniversary crusade were soon forgotten, one in particular left an indelible mark. In 1949 and 1950, about 200 troops around the country raised money to donate eight-and-a-half-foot-tall copper replicas of the Statue of Liberty to the communities in which they lived. The miniature Lady Libertys cost $350 apiece and were manufactured by a veteran Scouter from Kansas City. The BSA promoted them as reminders "that freedom, like life itself, is preserved only through vigilance and care."[6] At least three of statues—one each in Shakopee, South St. Paul, and Northfield—found homes within the boundaries of the Twin Cities councils.[7] The effort inspired a similar project, more than a half century later, to place bronze replicas of the famous Tait McKenzie Boy Scout statue in public spaces around the Northern Star Council.

Over the next few years, Twin Cities area Scouts took part in a series of national campaigns designed to build on the themes established during the 40th anniversary crusade. In 1952, the year the BSA launched a new program called "Forward on Liberty's Team," local Scouts hung thousands of Liberty Bell-shaped get-out-the-vote reminders on doorknobs throughout the cities. Two years later they joined in a national "Conservation Good Turn," planting thousands of trees and participating in a host of soil, water, fish, and wildlife conservation projects.

In the mid-1950s, during the height of what became known as the "Red Scare," Scouting's message assumed overtly patriotic and religious tones. A four-year nationwide campaign called "Onward for God and My Country" presented Scouting, at least in part, as a bulwark against what many Americans referred to as "Godless Communism." "This program is being launched at a time when it is evident that increasing emphasis on our free way of life is important," the BSA proclaimed. "For the safety and welfare of the United States, patriotism of the highest type is essential—a patriotism built on a firm spiritual foundation."[8] Once again, national Good Turns were a major component of the campaign. In 1956, for example, St. Paul area Cubs, Scouts, and Explorers distributed 30,000 posters promoting the American Red Cross, Christmas Seals, voting, and civil defense efforts.[9]

Local troops often attached Cold War-era streamers like these to their troop flags.

With Cold War tensions building between the United States and the Soviet Union, civil defense was becoming a national obsession. Schoolchildren hid under their desks in "duck and cover" air raid drills. Families built bomb shelters to protect themselves from a possible atomic attack. Local Scouting officials, reflecting the national mood, acclaimed the "universal value" of civil defense training during "the present troubled times."[10] At least one Cub Scout pack furnished bomb shelters as a service project. In Minneapolis, the fixation on civil defense even left a mark on one of the local council's most popular programs.

In the fall of 1952, the council—working in cooperation with the Minneapolis Fire Department—introduced a new emergency training program for Explorers, complete with an especially effective recruiting tool: a fully equipped emergency response van. Trainees learned advanced first aid techniques as well as other skills that might prove valuable in an emergency—skills such as crowd control, lighting, and electronic communications. Each year the council's emergency service unit responded to a variety of fires, floods, drownings, plane crashes, and missing-person searches. It quickly earned a vaunted reputation among first responders around the Twin Cities. During the summer of 1953 it won the praises of the Mahtomedi Fire Department after responding to a drowning at White Bear Lake:

The Explorer Emergency Service Unit was one of the most visible programs of the newly named Viking Council.

The truck and equipment which you sent to Mahtomedi this past week to aid our Department in trying to locate the body of one of our respected citizens, lost in a boating accident in White Bear Lake, has inspired our Rescue Squad to greater aims.

Your activities at the scene of the accident were not only informative, but also instructive. The manner in which the boys conducted themselves and the "know-how" in which they went about their duties has been an inspiration to our Department and we will always remember your crew for their very fine performance. By your activities, Americanism has been demonstrated 100 percent and we of the Department are deeply appreciative.[11]

Although the emergency service unit began as a cooperative effort with the Minneapolis Fire Department, its role soon expanded in response to the community's growing Cold War apprehensions. Civil defense became an integral part of the unit's mission. Crew members were encouraged to take ad-

Many established city troops, including St. Anthony Park Troop 17, continued to thrive during the 1950s despite the demographic shift to the suburbs.

ditional civil defense training courses. Those who completed the training were issued special civil defense identification cards. Scouting officials made it clear that the unit would continue to respond to routine calls, just as it always had, but would now be made available to city, county, and state authorities in the event of a "general catastrophe."[12] To everyone's relief, no such general catastrophe ever occurred.

Even as the Twin Cities councils jockeyed to offer programs that reflected Cold War anxieties, other trends were forcing them to redefine themselves in different ways. By the early 1950s, Scouting officials were noticing a significant population shift—from the cities to the fast-growing suburbs. Many believed that if Scouting were to succeed during the second half of the century, it would have to concentrate more of its efforts in those places where families were moving. The Minneapolis Council responded by redrawing its map to include, among other changes, a new district (Dan Patch) encompassing the booming communities of Richfield, Bloomington, and Savage. The St. Paul Council also kept its eye on the area's shifting residential map, but it was more deliberate in its approach, limiting its boundary changes to the merger of two districts in western Wisconsin.

Other changes were more cosmetic. In 1951, the Minneapolis Area Council decided the time had come to choose a new name for itself—one that reflected its true geographical reach. It put out a call for suggestions, and Scouts from around the region responded by the hundreds. Most of the submissions were worthy of consideration, but a few—"Bacon Strip," "Massacre," "Missile," "Tutokanula," "Goodeedoers," and "Prowling Snakehead"—produced only chuckles. In June of 1952, the council's executive board unanimously chose a new name: Viking Council.[13]

The suburbanization of the Twin Cities-based councils was reflected on the shoulders of local Scouts.

Distributing home emergency handbooks in Minneapolis during a 1958 Good Turn.

The St. Paul Area Council held onto its name for a while longer than its counterpart across the river, but by 1954 it too was ready for a change. More than 500 Scouts took part in the council-wide naming contest, and by early 1955 the judges had whittled down the list of possibilities to six contenders: "Wissota," "Indianhead," "Many Waters," "Seven Rivers," "Evergreen," and "Wakon-Teebe." In the end, the council chose Indianhead, explaining "the course of the St. Croix River running through the Council territory between Wisconsin and Minnesota forms a natural Indian head looking in either direction."[14]

As the decade progressed and the first wave of Twin Cities area baby boomers advanced through the ranks—from Cubs to Scouts to Explorers—Scouting programs evolved to keep up with them. In 1954, the BSA established a new advancement level for Cubs called Webelos (an acronym for "We'll be loyal Scouts") in an attempt to address the persistently high dropout rate among 11-year-olds. The increased focus on younger boys seemed to pay off. The decade of the 1950s soon established itself as the first in which Cubs accounted for a majority of boys registered with the Viking and Indianhead councils.

On October 4, 1957, the Soviet Union launched Sputnik, the world's first Earth-orbiting artificial satellite, into space, forcing the United States to reconsider its long-held assumptions about American technological superiority. Although the U.S. government did not create NASA, the National Aeronautics and Space Administration, until the following summer, Scouts in St. Paul were already looking far into the future when they held their annual

"circus" in May 1958. The Indianhead Council's "Centen-O-Rama" coincided with the 100th anniversary of Minnesota's statehood. This cartoon, created by an unidentified Cub Scout, depicted the theme of the show's highlight act, "Cubs Invading the Moon." In the years that followed, space exploration continued to be a common theme at local Scouting events.

Scouts sometimes expressed their fascination with the space race on their neckerchiefs and slides.

While Cub Scouting steadily grew throughout the 1950s, Exploring continued to struggle. Despite changes made to the Explorer program after World War II, the Twin Cities councils—like their counterparts around the country—still had trouble holding onto Scouts once they reached their 14th birthday. The number of Explorers fluctuated wildly from year to year. In 1959, after years of study, the BSA once again revamped its program for older boys. The new program's main innovation was the introduction of "specialty" Explorer posts in which young men could gain experience in fields as diverse as auto mechanics, astronomy, and broadcasting. In the Twin Cities, aeronautics was especially popular, with Northwest Airlines and the local Air Force Association sponsoring two of the first new Explorer units. Local officials expressed confidence that Explorer membership would double in the new program's first year, setting the stage for even greater growth during the 1960s.[15]

All three levels of Scouting—Explorers, Scouts, and Cubs—were represented in this local publicity photograph, taken to commemorate the BSA's 47th anniversary. The oversaturated colors in this image were common in early tinted newspaper photos. Left to right: Gary Fehring of St. Paul Explorer Post 9; William Whalen of St. Paul Troop 9; and Professor McKinney of St. Paul Pack 9.

Working to solve the "older boy problem" during the 1950s: St. Paul Air Explorer Squadron 424, chartered by the Ray S. Miller Squadron of the Air Force Association (left); Members of the Pine Bend Scout Club aboard the St. Paul Sea Scout Ship "Savage" (right).

NOW ☆ THEN

CAMP PART 2 >

NOW ☆ THEN

DINNER IS ABOUT A HALF-HOUR AWAY, and every member of Troop 89 has now returned to the Blackfoot campsite. After the flag-lowering ceremony and announcements, the boys busy themselves as the adults make the final preparations for the meal. In the mess tent, Senior Patrol Leader Alex Westad helps freckle-faced 11-year-old Blake Nicholson prepare for his Tenderfoot examination.

"Let's go over the Scout Oath and Law," Alex says. "What's it mean to be clean?"

"Don't talk trash and wear clean underwear."

"Okay. Helpful."

"Help other people with different things."

"Obedient."

"Do what you are told and do it well."

"Morally straight."

Previous pages: An annual rite of passage: the sorting of campers according to swimming ability.

Blake stumbles on this one. After a few seconds of hemming and hawing, he gives up. "Maybe you need to think more about this," Alex says. "Come back to me after dinner."

About a dozen of the boys are lounging in the nylon chairs surrounding the campfire. Most of the adults hover over the cooking grates, monitoring the progress of 40-some steaks. "Check that one," Assistant Scoutmaster Eric Linner says. "It's pretty burnt on the bottom and raw on top."

By 6:15 dinner is ready. All the boys are seated at tables with their mess kits. Alex begins calling them forward by patrol. One by one they take their places in the chow line, where a phalanx of adults fills their plates with steaks, corn, bread, and baked potatoes. Back at the mess tents, Chaplain Aide Jordan Erickson holds up three fingers and says grace. The Scouts dig into their suppers with relish. Everyone seems to agree that this meal is far superior to their dining hall breakfast.

As the boys devour their dinner in the mess tents, the adults squeeze together at a picnic table off to the side. Most of them seem to enjoy the food just as much as the boys do. Scoutmaster Jim Schuster, in particular, appears to be in his element. Schuster did

Down time at the checkerboard.

not grow up in Scouting, but he has two sons who were Scouts, and he's been Troop 89's Scoutmaster for seven years. He looks forward to his weeks at Tomahawk if for no other reason that it gives him the opportunity to spend time with what he calls "quality kids." "That's why I continue to do this," he says, "even now that my sons have grown out of Scouting."

A little before 8:30 the Scouts of Troop 89 start heading toward the aquatics area on Long Lake for what promises to be the highlight of the evening—the water polo match with Troop 13. There's not much sun left now. The western sky is mottled with blue and purple clouds set against an orange background. A loon yodels from somewhere on Lake Nielsen.

The boys of Troop 89's water polo team strip down to their bathing trunks. With the light fading, they are now silhouettes of varying shapes and sizes. As the match gets underway, the troop's cheering section—made up mostly of younger Scouts—finds it increasingly difficult to make out who's who. By the time the match is over (Troop 89 wins in sudden death) even the players are having a hard time distinguishing their teammates from their opponents.

Back at Blackfoot, the campsite has assumed an end-of-the-day look. Stray, soggy socks, T-shirts, and underwear are scattered about. A few Scouts shuffle in and out of the shadows, like toy robots running on low batteries.

Troop 89's adult leaders serve up a steak dinner as a treat to the Scouts.

At the far end of camp, near the adults' tents, 11-year-old Robert Kancans is undergoing his examination by a three-member board of review. He wants to advance in rank to Tenderfoot.

"What's your favorite part of camp, Robert?"

"Archery."

"What's your least favorite part?"

"Some of the tents, like ours."

Robert is seated on a bench in front of his three questioners. He is compulsively scratching his knees, elbows, and face.

"What does it mean to be trustworthy, Robert?"

"You need to trust people," Robert says. "Like today, this guy was giving out IOUs for marshmallows. A Scout has to be trustworthy, so stuff like that works."

At 9:30 the troop gathers near the Scoutmaster's tent for the last big event of the day—the election of a new Scout leadership team. Doug Larson and Tom Westad are running against Zach Winkler and Sam Schroeder for the positions of senior patrol leader and assistant senior patrol leader. All four candidates are dressed in khaki shirts and merit badge sashes. Each is given the opportunity to present his platform to the troop.

"I know a lot of you had nothing to do during the summer," Doug says. "So we want to have more campouts."

Leadership candidates address the troop.

"I'm going to have a new system," Zach explains. "Every time your patrol comes with shirts tucked in, you'll get points. And at the end of the year, whoever has the most gets a pizza party personally paid for by me."

When the ballots are counted, Zach wins. Pizza pays.

It's 10 o'clock. Some of the boys have retired to their tents. Others have gathered around the fire. Marcell Primeau is still trying to sell marshmallows for 15 cents. He finds few takers. Alex Westad appears in the fire's glow and announces mail call.

"Jordan. Bradyn. Aaron."

"I got a letter from my dog," one Scout observes. "How sad is that?"

"Jonathan. Marcell. Jesse."

It's been about 15 hours since the Scouts of Troop 89 roused to the sound of reveille. If they were back home, many of them would probably stay awake for at least a couple more hours watching television, playing video games, and hanging out with friends. But not here, not now. When mail call is complete, the Scouts begin moving toward their tents. Someone calls out, "Time to go to bed!" And as if on cue, a bugler plays taps.

THE ESTABLISHMENT IN 1946 of Many Point Scout Camp, with its trailblazing commitment to troop-led outdoor experiences, ushered in a new era of camping for Scouts in the Twin Cities and the surrounding region. Seven years after Many Point opened, the St. Paul Area Council established Tomahawk Scout Reservation near Rice Lake, Wisconsin. The two Twin Cities-based councils now operated two of the nation's newest, largest, and best-equipped Scout camps, along with several other popular properties including the St. Croix River Camp, Camp Manomin in Fridley, and the original Camp Stearns near Annandale.

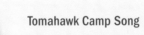

In the decades that followed, the newly named Viking and Indianhead councils continued to expand their camping programs with the additions of Rum River Camp in 1957, Cannon River Scout Reservation (later renamed Phillippo Scout Reservation) in 1965, Camp Heritage (later renamed Camp Stearns) in 1966, and Kiwanis Scout Camp in 1989. New programs such as winter camping and overnight camping for Cub Scouts increased the camps' use and allure.

In the century since the opening of the Twin Cities area's first overnight Boy Scout camp on Lake Minnetonka, the Northern Star Council and its predecessors have assembled an impressive collection of camp properties totaling close to ten thousand acres. Few, if any, councils in the United States can offer their Scouts so many different camping opportunities. And yet, despite the growth of the council's camping program over the decades, some things have changed hardly at all. As Scout Charles Morris put it after attending Camp Tonkawa in 1921, "Scouting is a great life, and in camp, even for two weeks, it becomes real bliss."

The Many Point Ballad (*First Verse*)

Hear the loon's mournful call
By the shores of Many Point.
Calling Scouters one and all
To the shores of Many Point
Always there's a fire bright,
Burning through the deep, black night,
Carrying Scouts' eternal light
From the Shores of Many Point.

Tomahawk Camp Song

All Hail Camp Tomahawk campers,
All Hail who've gathered here!
With hearts for outdoors' grandeur,
And adventure through the year.

To you a joyful greeting,
To you a loud Hurrah!
As camp staff we salute you,
All Hail! Camp Tomahawk!

Lunch at the Buckskin dining hall, Many Point, 1990.

Two plans that never came to fruition at Many Point: separate base camps for Air Scouts and Sea Scouts.

To the Editor:
I have just returned from my first visit to the Boy Scout camp on Many Point Lake near Ponsford, Minn., where I spent several exceptionally interesting and extremely pleasant days. I want to take this means of assuring those parents, who may have any qualms or fears about sending their boys up there, to dismiss such worries from their minds. Inasmuch as two of my sons are there I, too, was somewhat apprehensive, but after my observations I have no further worries. . . .

— Donald A. Hillstrom, writing to the *Minneapolis Tribune*, early 1950s

During its early years, the Many Point trading post was a mini-grocery store carrying everything from laundry detergent to fresh fruit to stew beef at 78 cents a pound.

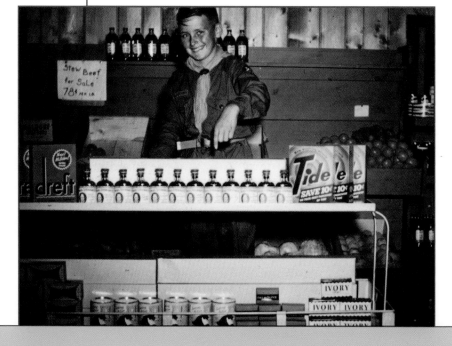

Scenes from Tomahawk:
Pitching tents . . .

mail call . . .

physical exams.

*Lists in
hand, [we] go
from site to site dropping off
or picking up gear. Attempts are
made to leave, at each site, the
required gear for the incoming
troop. If wet, the tents are allowed to stand and dry. If dry,
they are picked up, but only
after the departing occupants
have been suitably advised of
their total lack of folding apti-
tude. Cots are sorted, broken
and unbroken. The departing
campers are ruthlessly interro-
gated to give up the hiding places
of the missing cot cross-bars.*

— Former staff member Tom Wilson on
"changeover" Saturdays at Tomahawk[1]

Cub Scout day camp at Kiwanis Scout Camp, 1990s. The first day camps, established during the 1980s, operated on the district level with volunteer leaders.

Canoeing at Rum River Camp, 1970s.

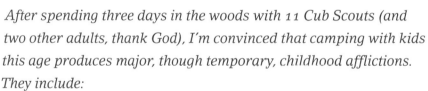

After spending three days in the woods with 11 Cub Scouts (and two other adults, thank God), I'm convinced that camping with kids this age produces major, though temporary, childhood afflictions. They include:

- *Loss of hearing: This condition is a group phenomenon, surfacing when phrases like "put down those sharp sticks" or "wash your plates and silverware" are uttered. At first, you think they are ignoring you. Then, after noticing a glazed quality in their eyes, you realize that they're listening to the call of the wild.*

- *Loss of sight: A tiny toad or a hapless daddy longlegs is instantly spotted, but ask them to pick up trash or the dropped food that rings picnic tables and they are struck with sudden blindness. Trash? What trash?*

- *Loss of motor skills: Food seems to flee from their plates to the ground. Milk erupts from their drinking cups. This phenomenon strikes at mealtime—followed by sudden blindness during cleanup.*

— Reporter David Hawley on camping with Cub Scouts, *St. Paul Pioneer Press,* July 4, 1994

Experiencing the thrill of achievement on the Camp Stearns climbing tower, 2008.

My son Alex (Webelos 1) went up the climbing wall about eight feet and froze. [Two staff members] . . . did everything they could to get him down without bruising his ego. They did an incredible job. After supper Saturday we had free time. My son was determined to try the wall again. [Staffers] "Q" and "Rabbit" were working the wall; my son scaled up to about 22 feet and after some hesitation mixed with the proper encouragement from "Q" and "Rabbit," he made it to the top. Thus, bringing to life one of my son's greatest achievements in Cub Scouting. Not to mention a father's pride.

— **Excerpt from an email describing a Cub camping weekend at Camp Stearns, July 2007**

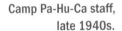

Camp Pa-Hu-Ca staff, late 1940s.

Dressing up in goofy get-ups became a time-honored camp tradition during the post-war years. Scouts at Many Point Camp looked forward to Lumberjack Days (center) while those at Camp Stearns donned appropriate costumes on Pajama Night (right) and Lone Ranger Day (bottom).

Tuesday supper was a somewhat informal affair for which everyone wore pajamas or better still, some other original costume.

Roger Vegdahl won second place with a brassiere, a bathing suit, and a piece of mosquito netting for a skirt.

Wednesday was Lone Ranger or Wild West Day with everyone in appropriate costume.

There were no ratings for costumes but our gang did very well with one cowboy, two Indian suits, and a pair of Texas Longhorns robbed from the wood pile.

— O. A. Nelson, Minneapolis Troop 228, reporting on his troop's experience at Camp Stearns, 1949

Monday we found out that a thief had been raiding our supply tent. We thought it to be a raccoon so we set live animals traps. We caught a very strange raccoon [that] had a bushy tail and a white stripe down its back. It kind of reminded me of a skunk. My theory was put to fact when Steve was sprayed by it and had to soak his uniform in hot water for 12 hours to get the smell out.

— Harold Rochat, Troop 334, describing his troop's experience during a two-week stay at Many Point in July 1968

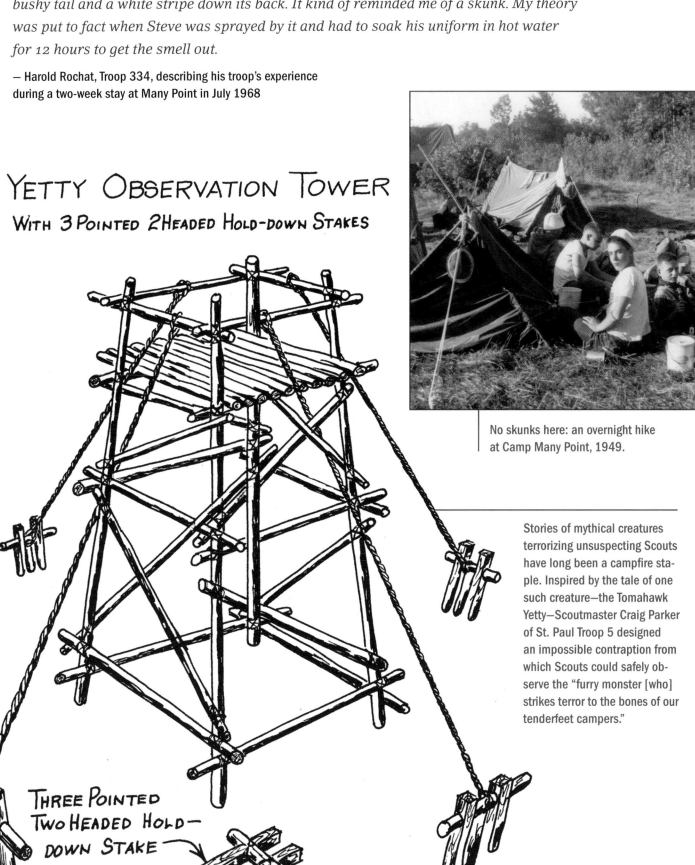

YETTY OBSERVATION TOWER
WITH 3 POINTED 2 HEADED HOLD-DOWN STAKES

THREE POINTED TWO HEADED HOLD-DOWN STAKE

No skunks here: an overnight hike at Camp Many Point, 1949.

Stories of mythical creatures terrorizing unsuspecting Scouts have long been a campfire staple. Inspired by the tale of one such creature—the Tomahawk Yetty—Scoutmaster Craig Parker of St. Paul Troop 5 designed an impossible contraption from which Scouts could safely observe the "furry monster [who] strikes terror to the bones of our tenderfeet campers."

1960s >

1960 WAS THE 50TH ANNIVERSARY of the Boy Scouts of America and its two largest Minnesota-based affiliates, the Indianhead Council and the Viking Council. Scouts from throughout the councils' combined territory marked the occasion with big springtime celebrations in Minneapolis and St. Paul. The Viking Council's Boy Scout Circus at the Minneapolis Auditorium featured everything from Cub Scouts on parent-pulled "Magic Carpets" ("If the excitement overcomes you, there is a doctor in attendance," the program notes proclaimed) to a "pint-sized hotrod" race pitting power hungry Explorers against each other ("The more noise, the better").[1] The Indianhead Council's Golden Anniversary Show at the State Fairgrounds Hippodrome entertained more than 30,000 people with history-themed skits, Order of the Arrow Indian dances, and music by a group called the Den Mothers Kitchen Band. As Indianhead Council Scout Executive Paul Hesser pointed out, the number of Boy Scouts in the St. Paul area had grown from 60 (it was unclear how he came up with that figure) to nearly 20,000 in 50 years. If that wasn't reason enough to celebrate, what was?[2]

The signs of Scouting's robust health seemed to be everywhere. Local Scouts looked on with pride as Robert Hoel of Hutchinson traveled to the White House to participate in Scouting's Report to the Nation—the first time a Viking Council Scout had taken part in the annual presidential tradition since its establishment in 1948.[3] In St. Paul, the printing presses at Brown & Bigelow churned out more than a million golden anniversary Scout calendars, which, as usual, sported a reproduction of an original painting by Norman Rockwell.[4]

When it came to spreading the good word about Scouting in Minnesota and western Wisconsin, nothing could match the public relations punch of the Indianhead Council's Drum and Bugle Corps. Formed in 1958 under the

< Thomas Samways and Terry Hansken of St. Louis Park Explorer Post 369 take a breather during a two-week excursion down the Minnesota River, 1964.

50th Anniversary
VIKING COUNCIL
BOY SCOUT CIRCUS
MINNEAPOLIS AUDITORIUM APRIL 28-29-30

"FABULOUS FACTS FOR OUR FIFTIETH YEAR"

There are 5,043,195 boys and leaders enrolled in the Boy Scouts of America today.

300,872 women serve in the Boy Scouts of America as Den Mothers in Cub Scouting.

Each President since Taft, in 1910, has been Honorary President of the Boy Scouts.

Scouts distributed 37,500,000 home emergency handbooks to America's homes in one day.

Latest world Scout membership in 69 associations show 7,589,183 boys and leaders.

Local Council Scout camps have a total value of $85 million.

The Boy Scout International Bureau is located in Ottawa, Canada.

Scouting's top Eagle Award was conferred on 19,548 Scouts and Explorers in 1959.

The new Johnston Historical Museum in New Brunswick, N.J., will be Scouting's showcase.

The 2,000-acre Reverse J. Diamond Ranch at Colorado Springs, Colorado, will be the scene of the 5th National Scout Jamboree, July 22-28, 1960.

Three of every four boys want to become Scouts and one of every two actually join.

More than half the men at West Point and Annapolis each year report they were Scouts.

Boys' Life, published by the Boy Scouts of America, has over 2,000,000 subscribers.

Scouts will put on their third non-partisan Get Out The Vote Campaign in 1960.

An unknown British Boy Scout's "Good Turn" to an American led to Scouting in the U.S.

sponsorship of the First National Bank of St. Paul, the corps already ranked among the top groups in the nation. In 1960 alone it made 46 public appearances around the country, garnering a slew of top prizes.[5] In the years that followed it continued its trophy-winning ways, reaching its pinnacle with a first-place showing at the 1962 World's Fair in Seattle. The St. Paul drum and bugle corps consisted of two contingents—the elite, competition-ready "A corps" and a "B corps" made up mostly of musical novices. The corps owed much of its success to its executive director, Herb Johnson, a retired bank executive with a love for martial cadences. Johnson had formed the drum and bugle corps shortly after his wife died, and he credited the corps' 80 Scouts with helping him through the grieving process. "Those boys have substituted for my wife," he said.[6]

At the same time Herb Johnson and his drummers and buglers were winning widespread acclaim, another St. Paul Scouter was using the magic of music to turn a group of young urban dwellers into one of the sweetest sounding Boy Scout troops ever assembled. Bob Plante had been the Scoutmaster of Troop 274 since its formation in 1955. The Scouts of Troop 274 all lived in McDonough Homes, one of St. Paul's first public housing projects. Plante had agreed to form them into a troop after listening to the concerns of parents who feared their sons might fall prey to gangs sprouting within the project. On the night of the troop's first meeting, he received a

The "A corps" of the Indianhead Council's Drum and Bugle Corps made regular appearances at community events around the Twin Cities, including this early 1960s parade on St. Paul's Rice Street.

Three members of the Indianhead Council's Drum and Bugle Corps—identified only as "Corky," "Herb," and "Bloyer"—perform at the State Capitol, 1960.

sobering piece of advice. "Don't walk across the middle of the room," someone told him. "Stay along the edges or they'll jump you."[7]

A soft-spoken man with an aversion to drill-sergeant techniques, Plante quickly hit on a unique way to channel the abundant energy of his high-spirited Scouts: He taught them to sing. With their Scoutmaster accompanying them on a small electronic organ, the Scouts of Troop 274 sang just about anywhere they were asked to perform—nursing homes, hospitals, schools, houses of worship. "We have one rule here," Plante explained. "You don't have to sing good to belong to Troop 274, just good and loud."

But they were good. One evening, during a performance at the Indianhead Council's headquarters, the boys of Troop 274 outdid themselves with a moving rendition of Harry Bartelt's "On My Honor." When the song was over, one hardened Scouting veteran stood up and excused himself. "I've heard the Scout oath recited thousands of times before," he said later. "But when those boys sang it, it did something to me. I had to leave the room. Scout leaders aren't supposed to cry."[8]

Scoutmaster Bob Plante and the singing Scouts of St. Paul Troop 274.

Bob Plante's work with the young residents of McDonough Homes was an early example of Scouting's renewed urban focus. For years Scouting officials in St. Paul and Minneapolis had tried to address the needs of inner city youth but now demographic shifts and social upheavals were creating new challenges demanding new solutions. The postwar prosperity of the 1950s had fueled a phenomenon known as "white flight" in which middle-class families—most of them white—migrated from the cities to the suburbs. By the 1960s

Minneapolis and St. Paul, like most other urban areas, were shrinking in population and their remaining residents were increasingly likely to be African American, Hispanic, or American Indian. As downtown businesses joined the rush to the suburbs, jobs disappeared, property values plummeted, poverty increased, and crime rates jumped. The cities were in trouble.

Dedicated Scouters like Bob Plante had been working for years with inner city kids, but it wasn't until the mid-1960s that the Indianhead and Viking councils started making a concerted effort to address the needs of disadvantaged youth in the troubled urban core. Plans began to crystallize in the spring of 1964 when Larry Harris, the director of Minneapolis's Youth Development Planning Project, presented some sobering numbers to a gathering of Viking Council executives. Harris's statistics showed that childhood

During the mid-1960s, Brown & Bigelow commissioned Twin Cities artist Howard Sanden to create a series of paintings for its annual Cub Scout calendars. "Each year I had to think up some appropriate activity for my Cubs to do," Sanden recalled years later. "I honestly enjoyed this work, and blithely continued on, year after year, working in the styles of other artists [including Norman Rockwell]." After finishing his work with Brown & Bigelow, Sanden went on to establish himself as one of the country's premier portrait artists. He is shown here with two of his models for the 1968 calendar, Edina Cubs Kevin Ciresi and Joseph Peria.[19]

poverty, school dropout rates, and juvenile delinquency were rising to alarming levels in several Minneapolis neighborhoods. He told his Viking Council hosts that he believed the Boy Scouts could play an important role in addressing those problems, especially if local leaders were willing to abandon what he called the "normal Scouting approach."[9]

Evidence suggested that Scouting was indeed failing to keep pace with changing demographic trends in the Twin Cities. A study conducted in 1962 found that while a quarter of all Scouting-aged boys within the Viking Council's geographical borders participated in the Scouting program, only 8 percent of the boys on Minneapolis's near North side and 12 percent of the boys on the city's south side were Scouts.[10] The Indianhead Council saw similar numbers in some of St. Paul's most disadvantaged neighborhoods.

In 1965, the two councils began seeking funds to launch new programs aimed at reaching more urban-dwelling boys. In St. Paul, the Indianhead Council focused the bulk of its efforts on what it called the Capitol District, an area encompassing several economically depressed neighborhoods near the State Capitol. With a special allocation from the Greater St. Paul United Fund, the council hired a coordinator to establish new packs and troops throughout the Capitol District and in several low-income neighborhoods outside the district's borders. Over the next two years the council boosted the number of Scouting units within the Capitol District from three to 11 and reached more than 30 percent of the area's Scouting-aged boys.[11]

The Viking Council launched a similar recruitment program in several of Minneapolis's most disadvantaged neighborhoods, and the early results

Troop 405, chartered to St. James AME Church in St. Paul, was among the Twin Cities' most active African American Scouting units during the 1960s. Among those pictured, kneeling fourth from left, is William Finney, future St. Paul police chief.

were encouraging. *Minneapolis Tribune* columnist George Grim, who for years had chronicled the achievements of a generation of Minneapolis Scouts, attended a meeting of Troop 199—led by Scoutmaster Joe Steen—in the basement of South Minneapolis's Abbott Hospital to see for himself the changing face of Scouting:

> *I looked at the troop's four patrols. Happy faces of Indian, Hawaiian-Chinese, Japanese, Negro, Hindu-Indian parentage, Irish, Scandinavian and more all went into the mix. More than half of these Scouts come from mother-only homes. The sense of belonging they find in Troop 199 is as powerful as it is personal.*
>
> *"Good evening and tuck your shirt in," Joe greeted a latecomer. (In went the shirt.) Three new prospects were there—watching, listening, eager to become a part of the group. Maybe they'd be able to go on that adventurous overnighter. . . .*
>
> *From the flag salute at 7 until the Scoutmaster's "quiet moment" at 9, Wednesday nights in Abbott Hospital's basement are filled with fun and comradeship for these neighborhood boys. To watch them is to gain a measure of Scouting's worth.*[12]

Although the councils' initial efforts to recruit more Scouts within the cities produced promising results, lasting change proved elusive. By the late 1960s it was becoming obvious to local and national officials that Scouting still had plenty of work to do in urban neighborhoods where it was sorely needed. A new national recruiting campaign dubbed "Boypower '76" encouraged local councils to increase membership—especially in urban settings—over the next eight years, but it was not clear how successful the campaign would be. "We do not claim total success in our outreach, as many challenges still need to be met," Indianhead Scout Executive Carl Martindale admitted. "However, we are doing an effective job within the resources available to us."[13]

The changing urban landscape was just one of several challenges confronting Twin Cities Scouting programs during the 1960s. The decade was a time of social upheaval with African Americans, Native Americans, women,

Many Scouts, such as these Explorers from Cokato (left) and these Eagles from Hutchinson (right), presented a neat and disciplined appearance at odds with the decade's increasingly indulgent culture.

St. Paul Post 17 Explorers John Sheldon, Newton Johnson, and Gerry McKay, Jr., 1960. As the decade wore on, the Indianhead and Viking councils found it more and more difficult to keep older teenagers in the Scouting fold.

and many others rising up in protest against racism, sexism, and all forms of injustice. At the same time anti-war activists were staging increasingly vocal demonstrations against America's escalating military involvement in Vietnam. Many Scouts and Scouters—even those who supported the protesters' aims—rejected the demonstrators' methods. They believed the tumult of the 1960s reflected a general decay of traditional American values, and they hoped that Scouting would provide a much-needed corrective. During a speech to a group of Scout executives in St. Paul, U.S. Army Chief of Staff General William Westmoreland—himself an Eagle Scout and former Scoutmaster—spoke for many in the audience when he proclaimed that "in an age of apparent ethical obsolescence, the Scouting oath of 'on my honor, I will do my best' still provides a suitable moral guide." Outside, a minor dust-up occurred when a Scouter confronted a longhaired anti-war protester in an Explorer uniform.

"You're no Scout!" he shouted. "Where's your registration card?"

The protester ignored the man's demand for identification.[14]

As more and more young, impatient Americans rebelled against authority and tradition, membership in the Viking and Indianhead councils began to suffer—at least among the ranks of older boys. While the Cub Scout program grew at a 23 percent clip over the course of the decade (roughly matching general population growth in the

Cubs from Farmington Pack 118 head off to day camp at the St. Croix River Camp, 1960.

Twin Cities metro area), the number of Scouts increased by just 18 percent and the number of Explorers *declined* by 12 percent.[15] Scouting officials had struggled for years to find ways to keep older boys from dropping out of the program once they reached high school, but the problem had rarely seemed so intractable. The decline in the number of Explorers happened despite some highly publicized local efforts to make Scouting more relevant to high schoolers.

The BSA had revamped its older-boy program in 1959 in hopes of holding onto the waves of baby boomers who were just then heading into their teen years. The new program's main innovation was the introduction of "specialty" Explorer posts in which young men could gain experience in a wide variety of career fields. As the 1960s progressed, older Scouts throughout the Twin Cities metro region and beyond began teaming up with a wide mix of sponsors to form posts catering to their own specific interests.

Among the most notable of the Twin Cities' early Explorer units was Viking Council Explorer Post 467, based in Bloomington. Its sponsor was, appropriately enough, the Minnesota Vikings of the National Football League. The post was the brainchild of brothers Frank and Charlie Kniebel, juniors at Bloomington's Kennedy High School. The Kniebel boys served as managers of the Kennedy football team, and their interest in sports led them to approach the Vikings with a proposal to sponsor an Explorer post focused

Minneapolis Cub Scouts appeared on WCCO Television's "Clancy and Company" morning kids' show to promote the 1965 Scouting Exposition at Metropolitan Stadium.

on sports management. To their surprise, the team agreed. For several years during the mid-1960s, Post 467 could confidently claim that it was the country's only Explorer unit sponsored by a professional sports team. The Scouts of the post met regularly with members of the Vikings' staff including equipment manager Jim Eason and trainer Fred Zamberletti. A group of Vikings personnel including offensive lineman Grady Alderman served on the post's advisory committee.[16]

Although most Explorer post sponsors did not boast the boy-attracting appeal of the Minnesota Vikings, they did offer the kind of expertise that many Explorers were seeking. The Archer Daniels Midland Company sponsored a post focusing on chemistry. Lutheran Brotherhood worked with boys interested in ministry and social work. A post supported by the Izaak Walton League concentrated on environmental issues. And the Minneapolis office of the Federal Aviation Administration sponsored a flight-fancying unit known as Post 707 (named after the ubiquitous 1960s-era Boeing passenger jet). "These boys had an interest in aviation, but didn't know much about the industry or how to get into it," explained Edward Blazejack, an assistant control tower chief at Minneapolis-St. Paul International Airport. "We're trying to further the aviation education of 24 outstanding young men."[17]

As most Scouting officials were fully aware, Explorers were interested in more than football, planes, and whatever else they might be able to learn from their adult mentors. Boys were interested in girls, and the revamped Explorer program in the Twin Cities area created plenty of opportunities for older Scouts to meet and spend time with members of the opposite sex. As *Minneapolis Tribune* photographer Duane Braley noted, many posts held regular "chaperoned activities calculated to help the young men learn how to get along with other people and to sharpen their social savvy." The get-togethers included pool parties, river cruises, and movie nights. "Girls finally have found their way into the Boy Scouts of America," Braley wrote. "They're not registered members, but they've become important factors in the activities of Explorer Scouts."[18] Girls would have to wait until the next decade to officially break into the Explorer ranks.

Top: Explorers Charlie and Frank Kniebel get a locker room view of sports management from Minnesota Vikings equipment manager Jim Eason.

Bottom: Explorers with the aptly named Post 707 visit the Minneapolis maintenance hangar of North Central Airlines, 1967.

B·S·A·

WINNER
ALL CITY CONTEST
1920

NOW · THEN
GATHERING ›
THEN · NOW

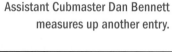

THE GYMNASIUM AT MALONE ELEMENTARY SCHOOL in Prescott, Wisconsin, has undergone a temporary transformation. On the far end, opposite the cafeteria tables and the hot dog stand, young boys and their parents gather in front of an impressive collection of high tech gizmos. An aluminum track stretching across much of the gym's width dominates the scene, but it's the other odds and ends that give the place a 21st-century feel. There are video cameras placed at strategic locations, two digital projectors, a matching pair of large video screens, and—less obvious—an array of tiny lasers situated at the end of the track. Malone Elementary is ready for Cub Scout Pack 133's annual Pinewood Derby.

Registration begins at 9:30 a.m., a full 90 minutes before the races are scheduled to start. Each car needs to pass inspection, and many of them initially fail. Experienced Cubs and their parents know it's important to arrive early, in case they have to make adjustments to their entries.

Assistant Cubmaster Dan Bennett is the pack's derby coordinator. He also mans the inspection table. After several years of practice, he's fine-tuned the inspection process into an efficient series of easy-to-follow steps. First he places the car on a scale to confirm it weighs no more than five ounces. Then he inserts it in his "go-no-go" box to see if it adheres to BSA width requirements (no more than two and three-quarters inches) and to make sure it's raised high enough on its wheels to clear the track. Finally he pulls out a flashlight to check that the insides of the wheels have not been lathed to give the car an illegal advantage. Cubs and their dads line up and wait for Bennett to pass judgment on their work.

A fourth-grade Webelos places his orange car on the scale.

"Five-oh-one," Bennett winces. "Just a little over."

The Cub's father has come prepared. He produces a pair of pliers and removes a small weight from the car's underbelly. The entry goes back on the scale.

"Four-ninety-nine," Bennett announces. "You got it, Dad."

The car is assigned a number, entered into a computer program, and taken away to await its fate. Father and son step away from the inspection table with smiles on their faces.

Thirty-one cars will race today. Each entry will run four times—once on each of the track's four lanes. Heats are assigned by age groups: Tigers race against Tigers, Wolves race against Wolves, and so on. Dan Bennett's intricate set-up, with its laser eyes and computerized ranking system, will make it easy for Cubs and their parents to keep track of the re-

Previous pages: Minneapolis Troop 17 dominated many all-city competitions during the 1920s.

Assistant Cubmaster Dan Bennett measures up another entry.

sults. It also will reduce the chances of potentially ugly disputes regarding the results.

Most of the boys say they think their cars will perform well, but one Cub, fourth-grade Webelos Sam DuBois, seems particularly confident. Last year Sam went all the way to the Northern Star Council's championship derby at the Mall of America, where he placed 13th out of 222 competitors. His entry this year—a sleek blue wedge with red wheels and flaming-eyeball decals—may be an upgrade. "We tested it against last year's car," he says. "This one's faster."

Other boys with less derby experience seem less sure of themselves. Another fourth-grader, Dakota Lefevre, has produced a wrench-shaped car with flames on it. It lacks the polished finish of the car belonging to his fellow Webelos, Sam DuBois. "I painted it," he says. "I sanded the wheels and the axles. I think I'll do pretty good."

Questions about the proper level of parental involvement have been a part of the Pinewood Derby since it became an official activity of the Cub Scout program in 1955. Cubs are supposed to build their own cars, but parents are expected to help when needed—especially if power tools are involved. Some adults, though, do more work than others, and the difference in approach sometimes creates tension. No one at the Pack 133 derby is threatening to make a scene, but everyone understands that some families take the competition very seriously while others do not. "I watch how much some of the dads do," one father chuckles. "It's ridiculous."

Even if some adults are aware of the difference in quality among the cars, the boys don't seem to care. As the clock ticks down to 11 a.m., the Cubs take their seats on the floor, behind a yellow rope. Cubmaster Gary Zielinski tries to rev up the excitement with a few Cub Scout cheers. The boys chime in only half-heartedly.

Making last-minute adjustments.

They want the races to begin. Finally Dan Bennett calls out the question everyone's been waiting to hear. "You ready to race?" he asks.

"Yes!" The screams linger for at least ten seconds.

The first heats feature the Tiger Cub cars. Then come the Wolves and the Bears. At one point the races are suspended while a father tries to repair a car whose back wheels refuse to turn. (He diagnoses the problem as an overly generous application of super glue.) At 11:30, it's time for the fourth grade Webelos.

Sam DuBois and Dakota Lefevre are now sitting next to each other behind the yellow rope. There will be six heats in this group, and the cars belonging to Sam and Dakota will race each other twice, in the first and the last runs.

Sam DuBois and Dakota Lefevre snag front-row seats for the big race.

The two boys engage in no trash talk. In fact, they say barely a word to each other. Their attention is focused on the track.

In the first heat Sam's car races to a first place finish. Dakota comes in third.

In the next two heats, Dakota's car again finishes third.

In heat four, Sam scores another first place finish, setting a new track record in the process. He continues his domination in the fifth heat.

When the time comes for the sixth and final heat, the outcome is hardly in doubt. Sam and Dakota are still sitting together. Both are smiling. When Sam's car crosses the finish line in a new track record time of two-point-eight seconds, the two boys react hardly at all. There's no celebration on Sam's part, no slumping shoulders from Dakota. Sam will be one of ten Cubs from Pack 133 who go on to the district finals. Dakota's Pinewood Derby dreams are done for the year. Both Cubs seem perfectly satisfied with the results.

BOY SCOUTS IN THE TWIN CITIES and surrounding areas have been finding reasons to get together in large numbers since their earliest days. The first mass gathering occurred in May 1911, when Scouts from the Ramsey Council held a rally dubbed "Camp Seton" near the Mississippi River bluffs between Fort Snelling and Minnehaha Falls. A few months later, Scouts from across Minnesota gathered for the first statewide Boy Scout encampment at the Minnesota State Fairgrounds. Since then, hardly a month has gone by when local Scouts have not come together in large numbers on a district, council, or inter-council basis.

The names and locations of these events have varied over the years. During the 1920s and 1930s, the Minneapolis Area Council held annual citywide competitions called Wali-Ga-Zhus at indoor venues such as the Minneapolis Armory and the Minneapolis Auditorium. (Wali-Ga-Zhus later became strictly district events.) Its public exhibits and pageants were known variously through the 1950s as Wali-Ga-Zips, Boy Scout Reviews, Scout-O-Ramas, and Boy Scout Circuses. For many years the St. Paul Area Council held most of its annual gatherings—Roundups, Scout-O-Ramas, and Scout Expositions—at the Hippodrome on the State Fairgrounds. In the 1960s and 1970s, both councils shifted their shows to shopping malls.

There have been many other types of events as well. District camporees have been popular for decades. Pinewood derbies, introduced during the 1950s, have given several generations of Cub Scouts an opportunity to compete at the pack, district, and council level. Scouts itching for a little winter competition have been participating in Klondike Derbies since the 1960s.

By the late 1920s, many districts within the local Scouting councils had grown large enough to hold their own get-togethers. This district Wali-Ga-Zhu was held at Minneapolis's Holy Trinity Church in 1928.

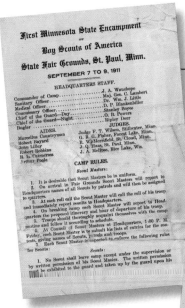

Plans for the first statewide Boy Scout encampment at the Minnesota State Fairgrounds, 1911.

Signal towers have been common sights at Scout gatherings through the years—especially those held at the Minnesota State fairgrounds. Shown here: the 1921 Scout Exposition and the 1998 Scout Fair.

Program from the earliest known indoor Scouting show in the Upper Midwest, 1912.

The Viking Council's annual Scout-O-Ramas at the Minneapolis Auditorium were huge events featuring 400 or more demonstration booths. Although the demonstrations put on by the Scouts were impressive, the most remarkable accomplishment may have been the speed with which the Scouts tore down the displays. In 1957 the whole show was broken down in a half hour—in the words of the *Minneapolis Tribune,* "a speed reminiscent of a circus big top being dismantled."

10:00 p.m.

10:10 p.m.

10:30 p.m.

The images projected by the posters for the Viking Council's largest gatherings evolved significantly between the mid-1960s and the early 1970s.

Local Boy Scouts at the 1952 State Fair. Council-wide get-togethers in the Twin Cities area often featured Scouts in garments inspired by American Indian customs and culture.

By the late 1960s, the Viking and Indianhead councils were beginning to shift many of their public exhibitions to suburban shopping malls

There was no chance to sell the story of Scouting to anyone [at the old Scouting expositions] because all of us there already knew it. Now things have changed for the better. The camaraderie is still present, but the story is being told to an interested and enthusiastic public.

— Viking Council President Pat Colbert, on the shift to mall-based expos, 1983[1]

Scouts of Waconia Troop 327 perform at Har Mar Mall in Roseville. In 1983, the Indianhead and Viking councils teamed up to present SCOUTEXPO '83, a series of public shows held at 10 malls—including Har Mar—across the metro area.

SCOUT CONTEST OCT. 28'16 TROOP 69 SECOND PLACE

Signaling competitions were extremely popular during Scouting's first few decades in the Twin Cities area.

For 15 years beginning in 1924, the Dan Beard Trophy (a framed and signed portrait of the famous illustrator, author, and outdoorsman) passed among the Minneapolis Council's fastest firestarters. The record, set in 1931 by Troop 28's Stan Eddy, was eight and three-fifths seconds.

After a while competition got too severe—it was getting out of hand; not so much with the boys but the men maybe got too excited when we won or we lost.

— Gale Frost, St. Paul Troop 17, recalling intertroop competitions during the 1920s[2]

Robert Likens and Jim Peterson of New Brighton Troop 132 win the fire-by-friction contest at their district's 1970 Camperall with a time of five and a half minutes.

The first Wali-Ga-Zhus were council-wide Scouting skills challenges, but they eventually evolved into district events.

4-30-28 B+D 7500 #16 85

MINNEAPOLIS AREA COUNCIL
Boy Scouts of America
Admit One to Annual
WALI-GA-ZHU
THE ARENA
S. Dupont & 29th St.
Hennepin Ave. Cars
May 10, 1928
7:30 O'CLOCK
COMPLIMENTARY--Present This Card at the Door. This
Ticket is for Admittance of Parents and Friends of Scouts.

To Whom it May Concern:
This is to notify the Scouts of Minneapolis and the rest of the world that I, Willard A. Tatam, do hereby challenge any Scout in the world to a trial of skill in that mystic art of producing a fire without the use of matches. I am ready at any time and at any place to compete against any bona-fide registered Boy Scout who is eligible for the Dan Beard trophy.
(Signed) Willard Tatam (19 ²/₅ seconds)

— *Be Prepared* (Minneapolis Council newsletter), December 1925

That's right, it's once again time for the Wild River District's Klondike Derby and Gold Rush Days. Make sure you have studied up on all Scouting trivia as the Claim Jumpers will be roaming around trying to stump even the experts in Scouting. With dog sleds, turkey bowling, canoe sledding, and snow, what else would you be doing February 12–14?

— *Navigator* (Northern Star Council newsletter, February 2009

An early Klondike Derby in Afton, Minnesota, 1972.

Wild River District's 2009 Klondike Derby.

Remember, [the Pinewood Derby] is a kid's project . . . It would be a great help for parents and Cubs if someone expanded the instructions to include what kind of sand paper to use, steps that a parent should be involved in, such as a power saw use, and the steps that should be left to the Cub, like sanding and painting.

— Guest commentary by University of Minnesota Associate Professor John Schultz in the February, 1980, edition of *Council Close-ups* (Indianhead Council newsletter)

The Pinewood Derby held at the Viking Council's 1964 Scoutcapades exhibition was a relatively small-scale affair.

By 2008, the Northern Star Council's Pinewood Derby finals was such a big event, it had to be held at the Mall of America.

In a rare case of inter-council cooperation, the Viking and Indianhead councils teamed up in 1976 for a Bicentennial Camporee at Fort Snelling State Park. The weekend included a variety of competitions including a bucket brigade event.

At the conclusion of the Bicentennial Camporee, some of the Scouts left the campsite by canoe.

During the mid-1990s, the Indianhead Council joined with the host council in St. Cloud for the Ripley Rendezvous, an expansion of the annual Scout gathering at the Minnesota National Guard's Camp Ripley, near Little Falls.

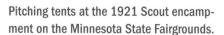

Fighting a fifth inning rain and the resultant hardships of pitching camp, 62 troops from six different areas attacked the [Minneapolis] parade grounds and dotted the countryside with multi-shaped tents to hail the second annual Boy Scout Camporee last Friday night. Regardless of a downpour . . . approximately 1,250 boys settled down to have themselves some fun, resolved that no rain could unseat them again.

— *Camporee Times* (Minneapolis 1941 Annual Camporee newsletter), June 8, 1941

Pitching tents at the 1921 Scout encampment on the Minnesota State Fairgrounds.

Flipping flapjacks at the 1933 State Fair Encampment. Food has always been an important part of any outdoor gathering of Scouts. In fact, some say that the 12-point Scout Law has an unofficial 13th point: "A Scout is hungry."

Mess tent at the 1942 encampment.

Bring a pot of your favorite chili recipe [to the Eagle Bluff District Chili Cookoff]. Please label it mild, medium, or hot. . . . Note: chili challenge winners are NOT determined by "heat" alone — please bring something to indicate the hotness level of your dish, that those with weaker tongues may stay away.

— *Navigator* (Northern Star Council newsletter), January 2009

Dutch oven cooking at the 1972 spring Camporee of the Viking Council's Mustang District.

Serving up barbecued steer at the Indianhead Council's 1964 Adventure Exposition.

1970s >

ON THE THIRD SATURDAY OF APRIL 1970, several hundred Boy Scouts from the Viking Council held their annual exhibition, Scout-O-Rama, at the Minneapolis Auditorium. It was billed as a special show celebrating 60 years of Scouting in the United States and the Minneapolis area. There were nearly 300 displays—everything from rope-tying demonstrations to canoes loaded with supplies for Canadian expeditions. Thousands of people attended. The following day, the *Minneapolis Tribune* ran a single photograph of the event, a picture of Scouts from Shakopee's Troop 218 putting on an exhibit of American Indian customs.[1] After reading the caption accompanying the photo, a *Tribune* reader identified as Mrs. Philip Bray shot off a letter to the editor bemoaning the newspaper's scant coverage of the Scouts and their show. "The men and boys worked hard to put on an excellent display and you saw fit to publish only one photo," she wrote.

"If hundreds of our young men were involved in rioting or demonstrating it would make headlines. Please make the public aware of the fine people in our city. Surely an entire page would not have been too much."[2]

Mrs. Bray's letter expressed the frustration that many Scouts, Scouters, and Scouting families were feeling as the 1960s gave way to the 1970s. To them, it seemed that many young people in the Twin Cities and around the country were doing what might charitably be called un-Scoutlike things. Kids were growing out their hair, experimenting with drugs, and challenging authority wherever they encountered it. Sit-ins, demonstrations, and marches were becoming regular occurrences at the University of Minnesota and elsewhere. African Americans, American Indians, women's rights proponents, and anti-Vietnam War activists all joined the growing chorus of protest.[3] To some, it seemed that the times had passed by the Boy Scouts.

< A Scout's burden: David Bartyzal of St. Paul Troop 99 enjoys (or perhaps endures) a weekend of hiking and camping at Cannon River Scout Reservation, 1973.

In St. Paul, Indianhead Council officials set out to rework Scouting's priorities amid this whirlwind of escalating social turmoil. They concluded that the "community's numerous problems" had a single root cause: a shortage of "character":

> Racism, discrimination, crime, delinquency, alcoholism and drug abuse, apathy toward high social values . . . the list is long . . . are all, we believe, products of and symptomatic of a deeper and more attackable "problem."
>
> Our social ills and problems are products of many individuals' attitudes, [personalities] and habits . . . in short, character. An individual's character is formed in youth. A community's character . . . is formed by its youth turned adult. When large numbers of individuals have negative character traits we reap [seemingly] insurmountable social problems.[4]

Not surprisingly, the council's leaders believed that Scouting could play an essential role in addressing society's perceived character deficiency. The question was, how best to reassert Scouting's relevance in a world suffering from "misplaced priorities"?[5]

Shakopee Troop 218 at the 1970 Scout-O-Rama. Some people believed Scouting deserved more publicity than it received during the early 1970s.

In the fall of 1971, BSA Chief Scout Executive Alden Barber told an audience at a volunteer recognition event in St. Paul that the Boy Scouts needed to change with the times. For one thing, he said, Scouting had to rethink its longtime devotion to camping and outdoor skills. "A boy in a small Minnesota town may find it valuable to draw a map of the wilderness area surrounding him," Barber explained, "but a boy in the Bedford-Stuyvesant area of New York City would have no use for such a map. So he draws a map of the subway system of New York."[6]

Barber's comments in St. Paul previewed what turned out to be one of the most audacious and controversial experiments in Scouting history. A study commissioned by the BSA in 1968 had found that many boys—especially older ones—believed Scouting was "too organized" and "kind of out of date." Now the BSA was initiating a new program aimed at changing those perceptions.[7]

With the establishment of the BSA's new "Improved Scouting Program"

Bloomington Scouts Jamey Zahn and James Kissell model the old uniform and the 1970s version.

in September 1972, Boy Scouts and Scouters throughout the country—including those in the Twin Cities and surrounding counties—operated under a new set of rules and expectations. "They don't require lots of the outdoor skills anymore, like chopping and sawing and taking care of your knife and axe," Eagle Scout Dennis Haney of St. Paul Troop 477 observed. "And you don't have to know knots."[8]

The new eighth edition of the *Scout Handbook* contained sections on issues that Baden-Powell, Seton, and Beard never would have thought to address: drug abuse, human sexuality, community problems, family finances, current events.[9] Merit badges were now available for a host of modern-day accomplishments including computer programming and "citizenship in the world." Many of the changes were designed to appeal directly to city boys. "In our day, we learned what to do for a snake bite," Indianhead Council Scout Executive Norman Swails said. "Today we also learn what to do with a rat bite."[10]

Many of the changes incorporated in the new program were inspired by Scouting's continuing ef-

Assistant Scoutmaster David Schmidtke, donning the new Scouting uniform's red beret, pulls Troop and Pack 118's float in Farmington's Centennial Parade, 1972.

For some troops, Scouting's renewed urban focus meant camping in the city. In 1971, the Scouts of Minneapolis Troop 91 pitched their tent in the shadows of the old Pillsbury "A" mill.

A portrait of Minneapolis's urban Boy Scout ranks, 1974. Front row, L–R: Frank Godwin, Troop 27; John Hinton, Troop 789; and Bernie Melcher, Troop 789. Back row, L–R: Larry Svien, Troop 700; and Richard Brown, Troop 789.

forts to reestablish a presence in the nation's troubled cities. The Viking and Indianhead councils had both tried to increase membership in Minneapolis and St. Paul's most disadvantaged neighborhoods during the 1960s, with only mixed results. Officials in the two councils now hoped the Improved Scouting Program's recognition of the realities of urban life would help convince more urban youth to give Scouting a chance.

In the early 1970s, the Viking Council took advantage of another new program—this one funded by the U.S. Department of Labor—to hire six community college students as full-time inner city re-

cruiters. The recruiters' main job was, in the words of the *Minneapolis Star*, to "convince black and Indian youngsters that Scouting isn't just for a bunch of sissified white middle-class kids with short hair." By the summer of 1974, records showed that the program had added about 800 minority-group Scouts to the council's rolls.[11]

On Minneapolis's South side, 26-year-old recruiter Roger Keller formed Troop 789 from a group of American Indian boys, most of whom came from single-parent families. Keller performed many of the traditional roles of Scoutmaster as well as several nontraditional ones—including making court appearances on behalf of youngsters who got in trouble with the law. "If any kids need Scouting programs," he said, "it's the kids with problems and on drugs."[12]

Another recruiter, 23-year-old Luther Holt, focused his attention on the South side's African American community. "I first went to Horace Greeley [Elementary School] and told them about Scouting and how it wasn't sissified," he recalled. "I invited anyone who was interested to see me after school. Five [black kids] showed up and we got them all." But as Holt soon discovered, most of the kids he tried to recruit remained deeply skeptical about Scouting. Typical of his experiences was the time he approached a street-savvy 10-year-old named Joey.

"How'd you like to be a Boy Scout?" Holt asked.

"How'd you like to take a swan dive in a pile of manure?" Joey responded. (Joey's exact words were less refined.) "I've got better things to do than hustle little old ladies across the street."

Holt refused to give up. Joey eventually agreed to attend a Scout meeting, "Just for laughs." It wasn't long before he joined Holt's troop.[13]

Holt, Keller, and the Viking Council's other urban recruiters found that the Scout uniform—even the new design with its red beret and optional neckerchief—was a major turn-off for many would-be city Scouts. Some boys objected to what they considered the uniform's vaguely military look. Others thought the pants, with their unstylishly narrow legs, were particularly obnoxious. ("They hurt my ankles," one Minneapolis Scout complained.) Those who found the uniform unacceptably burdensome were usually allowed to wear what they wanted.[14]

Minneapolis's inner city recruiters also faced another challenge common to Scouters in other communities—a reluctance on the part of adults to get involved with Scouting. Keller, for one, had only limited success in attracting parents of his American Indian Scouts, but he insisted those who did get involved benefited greatly from the experience. "I've seen parents that had a lot of home problems with their kids," he said, "and when they become involved in Scouting it straightens out."[15]

Although the Indianhead Council did not participate in the Labor Department-funded urban recruitment program, it continued to emphasize the need to serve disadvantaged city youth—especially those living in St. Paul's public housing projects. Bob Plante's Troop 274 and its slightly younger McDonough Homes sibling, Pack 274, remained the council's most notable urban success stories. Several of Troop 274's assistant Scoutmasters were former troop members who had returned to help out. "[You] were the pioneers in

Viking Council North Star District camporee near Anoka, 1974. Many troops significantly relaxed their uniform requirements during the 1970s.

Explorers Debbie Antonini and MaryJo Kvidera assist physical therapy patient Toni Boehm at St. Luke's Hospital in St. Paul, 1971. "Pretty funny looking Boy Scouts," Boehm laughed.

public housing's frustrations and trials and tribulations," Plante reminded his former Scouts at the troop's 15-year reunion. "You were the guinea pigs. The Dead End Kids with zero futures."[16] In 1974, Scout and Cub membership in McDonough Homes totaled 74, up nearly 9 percent from the year before.[17]

The Indianhead and Viking councils' emphasis on underserved urban youth was just part of a larger attempt to broaden Scouting's appeal in the Twin Cities and the surrounding region. The Explorer program, for example, continued to expand during the 1970s. The addition of special interest posts during the previous decade was one of the main factors in attracting high school-aged boys, but just as important was the decision in 1970 to begin welcoming teenaged girls into the program. Within a few months of the switch, "co-ed" Explorer posts—many of them focused on health care and law enforcement—were operating throughout the Twin Cities area.[18] In 1974 the Indianhead Council reported its Explorer program doubled in size over the previous year.[19]

In just one of many SOAR projects conducted by local Scouts during the early 1970s, St. Paul Troop 30 loaded boxes of glass onto trucks for shipment to a recycling plant. It would be several years before community recycling programs caught on in the Twin Cities area.

Concerns about pollution and the depletion of natural resources reached new heights during the early 1970s, and a nationwide conservation initiative called Project SOAR ("Save Our American Resources") inspired many Scouts throughout the Twin Cities and surrounding counties to get involved and focus on the environment. They collected newspapers, glass, and tin cans for recycling. They planted trees and lobbied local governments to protect wetlands. "We all need to start investing in the future of our earth," explained chairwoman Carroll Nelson of St. Paul Pack 25 during a Cub Scout recycling drive in the spring of 1971. "This is a program that everyone can participate in—the Cubs, their families, the community. It is a start, and we have to start someplace."[20]

The Twin Cities-based councils had a long history of making Scouting available to disabled youth (Minnesota organizer L. S. Dale established the nation's first troop of deaf Scouts in Faribault in 1911), but the 1970s was a decade of breakthroughs. In 1972, for example, a Minneapolis case helped convince the BSA to rethink its policies regarding Scouts with physical disabilities. Warren Rixmann, a deaf Scout from Minneapolis, had been led to believe that he could work on his Eagle requirements after his eighteenth birthday to compensate for his disability. But when he fulfilled those requirements at the age of 20, the BSA informed him that he was too old to qualify for Eagle. Rixmann wrote to the *Minneapolis Star* for help.

The Boy Scouts of America and St. Paul's Brown & Bigelow Company honored Norman Rockwell during an exhibit of his paintings at the BSA's 1973 annual meeting in Minneapolis. The event's program notes included a letter that Rockwell wrote specifically for the occasion. "For me, Scouting has always encouraged the best from each boy who is a member," he explained. "This is the feeling that I've really enjoyed conveying in my paintings over the years. In 1913 the movement was only three years old—I was 19 at the time—when I became art director for *Boys' Life.* My love for boys in the outdoors quickly merged with my admiration for the Boy Scout program. It has remained with me ever since. I'm particularly proud that my paintings have been so accepted as portraying its principles and practices."

Norman Rockwell at the Boy Scouts of America annual convention in Minneapolis, 1973.

Norman Rockwell Gallery Exhibit
of Original Paintings
Co-sponsored by BROWN & BIGELOW
and the Boy Scouts of America
MUNICIPAL AUDITORIUM
(Plaza Room)
WEDNESDAY   THURSDAY   FRIDAY
1 to 6 p.m.   9 a.m. to 8 p.m.   9 a.m. to 8 p.m.
NATIONAL COUNCIL   •   BOY SCOUTS OF AMERICA
ANNUAL MEETING   •   MINNEAPOLIS, MINNESOTA
A-9

WARREN M RIXMANN

TROOP 404   BLOOMINGTON MINNESOT
HAVING SATISFACTORILY COMPLETED THE REQUIREMEN
IS HEREBY CERTIFIED AS AN

EAGLE SCOUT

BY THE

BOY SCOUTS OF AMERICA

DATE JULY 26 1973
289

Richard Nixon
HONORARY PRESIDENT

Robert W. Reneker
PRESIDENT

Alden Barber
CHIEF SCOUT EXECUTIVE

NO. 28-708

Warren Rixmann at his Order of the Arrow recognition ceremony, 1966— and his Eagle certificate, issued belatedly in 1973.

I am having a lot of problems getting the Eagle badge I have been working toward for 10 years. I had all the merit badges needed and they failed me because I was too old. Before, they said it was OK to work to get it until I was 21. I always loved Scouting and want to be a Scoutmaster for a deaf troop some day. Please help me.[21]

With the *Star's* help, Rixmann eventually made Eagle. The BSA soon began reconsidering its strict age rules on rank advancement. In 1978, after a series of high profile cases similar to Rixmann's, the BSA formally revised its advancement age restrictions for Scouts with physical disabilities.[22]

Scouting was now more open than ever to young people with special needs. By the end of the decade the Viking and Indianhead councils were serving more than 1,000 Scouts with cognitive, emotional, and physical disabilities.[23] Many of those Scouts belonged to packs, troops, and posts catering to their special needs, but a growing number of them joined units in which disabilities were a secondary concern.[24]

Pack 215 at Hastings State Hospital in Hastings was one of the nation's few Cub Scout units for adults with developmental disabilities. The BSA had loosened membership-age requirements for the mentally disabled during the 1960s. The pack's organizer, Bernie McCoy, is shown here third from left.

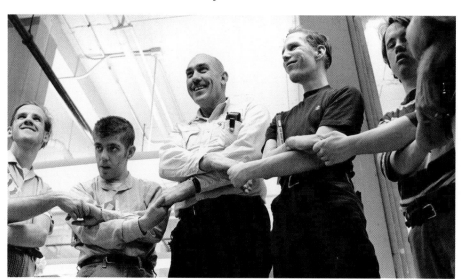

Although Scouting was working hard to become more relevant and more inclusive, its efforts were falling short. In the first six years of the decade the combined membership of the Viking and Indianhead councils actually dropped from just over 52,000 to just under 52,000.[25] Local Scouting officials attributed the stagnating numbers to a host of factors: a declining youth population; fewer neighborhood schools; smaller families; more single-parent homes; high unemployment; increased television viewing; the growing popularity of family camping; and the widening reach of organized sports and other extracurricular activities.[26] Making matters worse, wrote Indianhead Council Scout Executive Ron Phillippo in 1978, was the "lessening concern for patriotism, respect for others and their property, responsible citizenship, the family as the basic institution in our society, and the American free enterprise system."[27]

By the late 1970s, many local Scouters were heaping additional blame for the membership skid on the BSA's Improved Scouting Program, with its red berets and much-vaunted quest for relevance. Scouts and Scoutmasters had been grumbling for several years that the revamped program, while well intentioned, abandoned or downplayed many of the things that made Scouting great. ("You might end up with some boys out in the forest who don't know what they're doing," Eagle Scout Gregory Johnson of White Bear Lake Troop 431 observed.)[28] Now calls were growing for a back-to-basics approach.

Worries about stagnating membership could not dampen enthusiasm for the U.S. Bicentennial Camporee held by the Viking and Indianhead councils at Fort Snelling in the fall of 1976. About 5,400 Scouts took part in the event.

In early 1979, the BSA released its ninth edition of the *Boy Scout Handbook,* written by William "Green Bar Bill" Hillcourt, one of the nation's most respected teachers and proponents of traditional Scoutcraft. The new edition was thicker and denser than the one it replaced. Camping and nature study took up 284 pages instead of 116.[29] The BSA claimed the new handbook placed "greater emphasis on fun and adventure and [used] Scout skills to achieve the aims of Scouting."[30] The Indianhead Council's Ron Phillippo predicted it would be "a very popular book."[31]

By the time Bill Hillcourt arrived in the Twin Cities to promote his new handbook in the fall of 1979, it had sold more than a million copies. He told *Minneapolis Tribune* columnist Ron Schara that the book's success lay in its renewed emphasis on the out-of-doors. "I don't call that moving backward," he said. "It's going forward with fundamentals." Schara believed his readers—Scouts, Scouters, and outdoors enthusiasts of all stripes—would appreciate the change. The new handbook was "a veritable encyclopedia of outdoor know-how wrapped within the spirit of Scouting," he wrote. "The knowledge contained within the book, or the spirit, for that matter, wouldn't hurt anybody."

NOW & THEN
NOW & THEN

JAMBOREE >

THE MOTOR COACH PULLS INTO THE ROUNDABOUT arrival area and disgorges its occupants. Forty Scouts and Scouters from the Northern Star Council step off the bus into a scene of bustling humanity. As the Scouts unload their duffels and backpacks, the staging area takes on the characteristics of a large-scale revolving door, with one coach leaving and another arriving every two minutes or so. Amid the laughing and barking of instructions, snippets of unintelligible conversation filter through. The members of Boy Scouts of America Troop 301, as this unit is known, gather their gear and head down the road toward a clearing, about a half-mile away, that will serve as their campsite home for the next 12 days.

It's July 27, 2007, the first day of the 21st World Scout Jamboree at Hylands Park in Chelmsford, England, about 30 miles northeast of London. Hylands Park is an expanse of rolling greens and woodlands, large enough to accommodate 40,000 Scouts and leaders from nearly 160 countries. The landscape has been staked out to create a variety of themed villages, activity sites, and campgrounds. Troop 301 is one of 50 units from around the world assigned to Fjord Sub-Camp, a 10-acre triangle in the park's southeast corner.

After setting up their blue two-man tents in neat rows, the Minnesota and Wisconsin Scouts begin venturing out and exploring their surroundings. Before long they become familiar with a peculiar form of jamboree etiquette. It's possible that at any moment the general hubbub will be pierced by the voice of a friendly stranger.

"Jambo!"

With that cue, there is just one proper response.

"Hello!"

Although there are plenty of activities to keep Scouts busy—cultural exhibits, service projects, competitions of all sorts—few pastimes are more enjoyable than wandering the grounds and meeting new friends. Looking back on the experience, Ben Coder, an Eagle Scout from Coon Rapids Troop 406, is amazed by the easy camaraderie that can develop among strangers. "Even though we didn't speak the same language, we were able to communicate because we were all Scouts with the same values," he says. "I met Scouts from all over the world."

Nothing, it turns out, is better at breaking down cultural barriers than food. The Minnesota Scouts try a variety of delicacies from around the world—everything from Dutch pannekoeken to Saudi Arabian coffee to Scottish haggis ("Okay at first," reports Senior Patrol Leader Chad Heise. "Afterward, not so great. It kind of leaves that taste in your mouth.") In return, they introduce their non-American counterparts to several American culinary specialties. Popcorn is a big hit, but it can't match the drawing power of another familiar campfire staple—s'mores.

One evening, Ben Coder and a few other Scouts from Troop 301 pool their money to purchase all the necessary ingredients—graham crackers, marshmallows, and chocolate bars. They return to the campsite, assemble their concoctions around a fire, and begin handing them out to their Fjord Sub-Camp neighbors. "As time went on," Coder recalls, "our s'more-making operation

Previous pages:
Scouts from the Indianhead Council enjoy the fireworks at the 2005 National Jamboree.

became more and more popular until we completely ran out of ingredients." At the suggestion of a British Scout, the Americans and their neighbors close out the evening by sharing Scout songs from their respective countries. "I have to admit," Coder says, "that was one of the best memories I took away from the Jamboree."

Chad Heise thinks the theme of this year's jamboree, "One World, One Promise," fits well. Heise attended the 2005 National Jamboree at Fort A.P. Hill, Virginia, but while he enjoyed himself there, he realizes now that there is something especially uplifting about a world jamboree. "Typically when you go to another country, you kind of feel like a fish out of water," he says. "You don't really fit in with what's going on. But at a world jamboree, instead of having a bunch of people who feel that way, it's more of a feeling that we're all here together, we're all going to do this together." Chad is aware that the United States' international reputation has suffered in recent years, due in large part to the war in Iraq, but he's encouraged by the reception he's received from the Scouts he's met. "Everyone going into it was extremely open-minded," he says. "There were no grudges or competitions between countries that were rivals or politically didn't get along so well. It was basically—You know what? We're all Scouts. We're going to be here and have a good time and learn about each other and just enjoy it."

Troop 301's immediate neighbors in the Fjord Sub-Camp come from the Netherlands and South Africa. With proximity comes familiarity, and soon

BSA Troop 301 represented the Northern Star Council at the 2007 World Jamboree at Hylands Park in Chelmsford, England.

the American Scouts are developing friendships, some of which will last well beyond the jamboree. Heise becomes particularly close with a pair of Scouts from Dutch Troop 21, the "Spotvogels." Meanwhile Ben Coder is nurturing a friendship that began only a few hours after he stepped off the bus. "On the first day of the Jamboree, while waiting in line for the opening ceremony, I met an Italian Scout named Simone Menichini," he recalls. "Simone did not speak English and I definitely did not speak Italian, but we were still able to communicate. Throughout the Jamboree, I saw Simone in different places and we would catch up on each other's experiences. Toward the end of the Jamboree we exchanged e-mail addresses in the hope that we would stay in contact."

Ben will, in fact, remain in e-mail contact with Simone once he returns home.

Chad will continue to stay in touch with his Spotvogels friends.

In the months to come, both Scouts will reflect on the jamboree at Hylands Park, and both will conclude that it was, in Chad's words, "a unique and wonderful experience." Ben, in his final report to the council (he is, after all, the troop's scribe), will have little trouble summing up the experience. "Overall," he writes, "the 21st World Scout Jamboree was the most exciting and memorable time of my life to this point. I got to travel the world without really physically doing so, by meeting other Scouts and learning about other cultures. . . . I am overjoyed that I was able to represent myself, my family, and my country at such a life-changing event."

AS FAR AS ANYONE KNOWS, not a single Minnesota or western Wisconsin Scout was present at the first World Scout Jamboree in England in 1920. Four years later, though, two Scouts from the Twin Cities journeyed across the Atlantic to attend the second World Jamboree in Ermelunden, Denmark. Harvey Collins of St. Paul and Edgar Pierson of Minneapolis were among the 56 American Scouts who made the trip. The St. Paul- and Minneapolis-area councils held separate competitions to determine who would go, and the two winners did not meet until after they arrived in New York for their trans-Atlantic voyage.

In the years that followed, significantly larger contingents of Twin Cities-area Scouts traveled to a succession of jamborees, both at home and abroad. In 1929, BSA Region Ten, which included the Minneapolis and St. Paul councils, sent 24 Scouts and four adult leaders to the third World Jamboree in Birkenhead, England. At the first National Jamboree, held in 1937 in Washington, D.C., the Minneapolis Area Council boasted the largest contingent, with 178 boys.[1]

Many of the local Scouts who attended jamborees over the years forged friendships that endured for lifetimes. In 2007, 19 members of Paul Bunyan Troop 21—the Twin Cities-based unit that attended the sixth World Jamboree in Moison, France—held their 60th reunion. One of them, Bob McQueen, later described what it was like to see his old jamboree mates in a poem titled, "An Ode to Some Ageless Scouts." It read, in part:

The Scouts of Paul Bunyan Troop 21 at the 1947 World Jamboree and at their 60th reunion in 2007. Mike Galvin (front row, third from left) is a former council president.

We looked hard at each other for youthful traces
And for hints of recognition in our aging faces.
We greeted each other with a handshake and smile.
It's been 60 years for some and that's quite a while.

Harvey Collins's Jamboree medal

Edgar Pierson (standing right), shown here with three friends from other states, was the Minneapolis Council's sole representative at the 1924 World Jamboree in Denmark.

This photograph, with St. Paul Scout Harvey Collins in the center, was taken aboard the S.S. Leviathan en route to the 1924 World Jamboree.

A MIAMI ORANGE AND A MIAMI PEACH S.S. LEVIATHAN 1924

Scoutmaster Kyle Cudworth of Minneapolis Troop 33 (center) confers with Chief Scout Executive James West (right) at the 1937 World Jamboree in the Netherlands.

Harvey Collins's Jamboree certificate.

The boys are busy trading all kinds of articles, including stamps, and all will probably return with a large collection of interesting things to show the folks at home. Among Robert's collection is a pair of Dutch wooden shoes. The boys are keeping in condition by playing football frequently. They witnessed an interesting billiard tournament at the hotel where they stopped in Antwerp, and watched the three-time Swiss billiards champion play.

— Anoka Scout Robert Donaldson, describing the Fifth World Jamboree in the Netherlands, 1937[2]

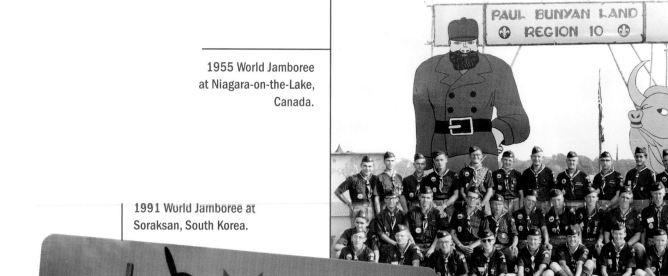

1955 World Jamboree at Niagara-on-the-Lake, Canada.

1991 World Jamboree at Soraksan, South Korea.

1953 National Jamboree at Irvine Ranch, California. Local Jamboree troops have long made a point of having their portraits taken in front of the elaborate gateways leading to their camps.

The drawling Texan who offered a live octopus would have gotten lots more action out of our patrol if he'd come around a few days earlier. By now we were veteran Jamboree swappers. So no one moved.

"'You all got anything to swap for an octopus,' repeated the drawl.

"'Please, not before breakfast,' someone mumbled.

The Texan, shrewd enough that he didn't want to hang around until he was maneuvered into asking instead of offering, ambled off to seek more spirited bidders.

— Minneapolis Explorer Dick Gardner, describing Jamboree swapping at the 1953 National Jamboree in California, *Boys' Life*, October 1953

A pair of swapped wooden shoes from the 1947 World Jamboree.

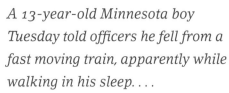
On the train trip back to Minnesota from the 1950 National Jamboree.

Catching a nap during a day trip away from the site of the 2005 National Jamboree at Fort A.P. Hill, Virginia.

A 13-year-old Minnesota boy Tuesday told officers he fell from a fast moving train, apparently while walking in his sleep. . . .

He was a passenger on a special train carrying a group of Boy Scouts to Glacier National Park prior to attending the national Boy Scout Jamboree in Colorado Springs, Colo.

[Jeffrey] Keating suffered only a gash on the head, but was hospitalized for observation.

— Associated Press, July 20, 1960

Swapping patches during the 1950 National Jamboree at Valley Forge, Pennsylvania.

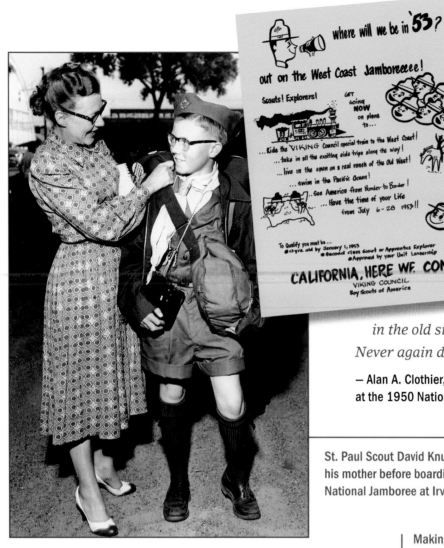

[I] was lucky enough to attend the 1950 National Jamboree at Valley Forge, Pennsylvania. . . . [I have] such memories as [the visit by] President Harry Truman, Texas long snapping whips, horned toads, Waterman's Monument, and, of course, the big outbreak of poison ivy all over the place. This was treated with calamine lotion dispensed in the old six-ounce pop bottles by the case. Never again did I drink Coke in a small bottle.

— Alan A. Clothier, Elk River Troop 90, recalling his experiences at the 1950 National Jamboree[3]

St. Paul Scout David Knutson gets a once-over from his mother before boarding the train to the 1953 National Jamboree at Irvine Ranch, California.

Making the best of an uncomfortable situation during the 1989 National Jamboree at Fort A.P. Hill, Virginia.

One 11-year-old Scout was taken by helicopter to Fairchild Air Force Base Hospital near Spokane, Wash., with possible appendicitis. It turned out he only had a bad stomach ache.

"He admitted to eating two eggs and milk at Missoula, Mont., a malt in Wallace, Idaho, and a banana split, a hot dog and a can of pop at another Idaho town a short time later."

— Account of St. Paul Troop 11's experiences at the 1973 National Jamboree in Idaho, *St. Paul Dispatch*, August 8, 1973

Most of the Scouts who attended the 1971 World Jamboree in Fuji-nomiya, Japan, had to evacuate camp when a typhoon hit. However, some members of the local contingent, including Scoutmaster Paul Johnson (far left), John Guthmann (second from right), and John Sproat (far right) stayed behind to guard the encampment.

In most cases a typhoon would have put a damper on the fun but with 23,000 Boy Scouts having too much fun already (games, trails, trading, meeting foreign friends, etc.), a typhoon merely changed the environment, from grassy plain to a mudhole.

— Scout Rick Kravik, describing the 13th World Jamboree in Japan, 1971[4]

Next was Tokyo. We stayed at the Tokyo Olympic Youth Centre. I still remember the words of the man in charge: "Gentlemen, I just want to make one thing clear: This is not a prison or army camp."

How wrong he was! However I suppose it was for our own protection considering that the centre is in the Red Light District of town.

— Scout Earl Rasmussen, describing the Thirteenth World Jamboree in Japan, 1971[5]

Viking Council Scouts Dave Tengdin and Andy Schuster show off some of the souvenirs they brought back from the Japan Jamboree.

A candlelight assembly during the 2005 National Jamboree at Fort A.P. Hill.

1980s >

THE 1980–1981 SCHOOL YEAR had just gotten underway at Minneapolis's Edison High School, and social studies teacher Dave Moore could tell something was different. Scattered among the hundreds of returning students who shuffled through the halls each hour were dozens of unfamiliar faces—young people who almost invariably looked lost and confused. "They nodded to me politely when I said hello to them in passing," Moore later recalled. "Sometimes they muttered a soft monosyllabic reply; in what language, I couldn't guess. But mostly they looked down at their feet, avoiding eye contact. They had their own teachers and their own programs. They were strangers."[1]

The strangers Moore encountered in the halls of Edison High School were part of a new wave of immigrants that had recently begun arriving in Minneapolis and St. Paul. The new arrivals were Hmong, a farming people from the highlands of Laos in Southeast Asia. The Hmong had allied themselves with the United States during the Vietnam War. When the war ended in 1975, and the communist Pathet Lao seized control of Laos, many Hmong fled the country, fearing for their lives. Some of them, sponsored by churches and local aid organizations, found their way to the Twin Cities. Soon others—often friends and relatives—followed them. By 1980 as many as six thousand Hmong were living in Minneapolis and St. Paul. Many of them were children.[2]

As the weeks went by in the fall of 1980, Dave Moore continued without much luck to engage the Hmong students he met in the hall. It wasn't until the following spring that he finally broke through. For the past 15 years, Moore had served as the Scoutmaster of one of the oldest Boy Scout units in Minneapolis—Troop 33, sponsored by Westminster Presbyterian Church. At the urging of a friend, he agreed to hold a Scouting information session in the high school gym and sent out an open invitation to any Hmong boy or girl who wished to attend.

< Having earned his Bobcat Badge, Cub Scout Nate Gagnor prepares to advance through the Wolf, Bear, Webelos, and Arrow of Light rank requirements.

159

Some of the early members of Minneapolis Troop 100.

About a hundred kids showed up.

"Now, at long last, I met the strangers who'd been hanging around the halls all winter," Moore recalled. "We had a regular Scout meeting, starting with a flag salute. It made no difference that we murdered the English language trying to say the pledge of allegiance and sing the national anthem. When we finished, we broke into spontaneous applause for our efforts."[3]

The meeting in the Edison gym led to a weekend camping excursion on the Rum River. (One of the campers, Xe Vang, impressed Moore by catching two heavy strings of fish with a reel rigged from a rock and a pop can.)[4] Not long after that, Moore formed Minneapolis Troop 100, a unit consisting exclusively of Southeast Asian boys—nearly all of them Hmong. As the decade progressed, Troop 100 established itself as one of the most active and accomplished Scout units in the Twin Cities. In 1986 it produced the nation's first Hmong Eagle Scout, Su Thao.[5] Moore believed that Hmong culture, with its emphasis on cohesion, discipline, leadership, and cooperation, made the boys of Troop 100 "natural Boy Scouts." "These are things the Boy Scouts try to teach," he said, "but Hmong kids know this already."[6]

Troop 274 of St. Paul's McDonough Homes neighborhood included some of the Twin Cities' first Hmong Scouts.

Troop 100 and its St. Paul counterpart, Troop 184, helped dozens of Hmong boys learn a new language, adjust to a new culture, and develop a true appreciation for the nation they now called home. In his application to become St. Paul's first Hmong Eagle Scout, Xia Yang of Troop 184 acknowledged his devotion both to the land in which he was born and the country he now called home. "I pray," he wrote, "that my small contribution to my people is also a contribution to my new home ... the United States of America."[7] Several years later, Xia joined the Indianhead Council's staff as an outreach specialist.

The success of the Twin Cities' first two Hmong troops contrasted sharply with the Viking and Indianhead councils' continuing struggles to establish additional viable Scouting units in the underserved urban neighborhoods of Minneapolis and St. Paul. Many of the urban troops formed during the 1970s lasted only a few years, and programs designed to increase membership among minority groups—including the U.S. Labor Department-funded initiative that employed Minneapolis recruiters Roger Keller and Luther Holt—vanished when funding dried up.

Despite their struggles to cultivate urban Scouting, the Viking and Indianhead councils refused to turn their backs on the cities. In 1983, eight Scouts spent a week camping atop St. Paul's tallest structure, the First National Bank Building. The project, called Sky Camp, was designed to promote the 1983 United Way fund drive.

Scoutmaster Bob Plante's Special Needs Troop 1984 at Tomahawk Scout Reservation, 1984. L–R: Mark Blaeser, Bill Erlandson, Curtis Nacy, Ben Hussman, John Beard, Chris Nacy, Duwayne Rogalla, and Steve Lape. Beard and Lape have continued with Scouting over the years and currently are working to earn Eagle rank.

The effort to build up urban Scouting in the Twin Cities hit its low point in 1980 when the *Minneapolis Tribune* reported that the Viking Council had listed as active 17 inner-city troops that did not exist. Viking officials pointed out that most of those troops had stopped meeting before their one-year charter expired, and that they remained on the books only because of a quirk in BSA reporting procedures. Nonetheless, the newspaper story led the Minneapolis United Way to temporarily reduce the council's funding until it demonstrated its inner-city recruiting program was producing results. Viking's funding was restored later that year.[8] The episode highlighted the difficulties that many councils with large urban populations were experiencing and prompted the BSA to issue a new directive urging all councils to improve and more closely monitor their urban programs.[9]

Partly in response to the negative publicity, Viking Council officials produced a 21-page plan to reinvigorate inner-city Scouting in Minneapolis. The plan included a five-week summer recruiting effort based in the city's parks, a proposal to send University of Minnesota students into housing projects as troop leaders, and a new campaign to sign up city-based corporations as troop sponsors. By 1982, the council was claiming success, with its primary urban subdivision, the Hiawatha District, listing 46 "active and growing units" (22 Cub packs, 22 Scout troops, and two Explorer posts).[10] In St. Paul, the Indianhead Council hired a new inner-city Scouting specialist to guide its urban efforts. By 1988 more than half of the Scouts in St. Paul were in troops operating under the inner-city program, although the problem of low participation rates among African American, Hispanic, and American Indian boys remained.[11]

As the Indianhead and Viking councils struggled to respond to the needs of inner-city kids, Scouting in the Twin Cities region continued to evolve with changing social customs and expectations. Efforts to reach more boys with physical and cognitive disabilities accelerated during the 1980s as the councils assigned staff and volunteers to new positions focused on Scouts with special needs. With grants from three local foundations, the Indianhead Council hired Suzette Heinze in 1983 to oversee its program for disabled Scouts. Heinze believed that Scouts with developmental disabilities were capable of achieving many regular merit badge requirements, and she regularly worked with them on projects such as first aid training, cooking, and camp preparation. "We use Scouting to expand the kids' whole life," she said. "Their independence skills, socialization and survival skills. It all ties into what Boy Scouts is."[12] In 1987, the council created a new Special Needs Division comprising units from all its districts. By the end of the decade, the division—which chair Sandy Klas called "the best kept secret in town"—was serving more than 2,000 young people.[13] One of those youngsters, Webelos Tim Hunt, appeared before a 1987 meeting of the Indianhead Council Executive Board to describe what he had learned about freedom during his time in St. Paul Pack 14:

In 1980 the Boy Scouts of America marked the 50th anniversary of Cub Scouting by recognizing 10-year-old Tony Blakey of St. Paul Pack 7 as the nation's 30 millionth Cub. The BSA acknowledged that it could never know who exactly was the Cub Scouts' 30 millionth registrant, but it figured Tony came close enough. After a random drawing determined that the lucky Cub should come from the Indianhead Council, local officials chose Pack 7's newest member for the honor. Tony is shown here with his sister, Brandi, and his mother, Sheila.[23]

The Tiger Patrol of Troop 330 at Faribault State School and Hospital, 1983.

Today, handicapped people are able to go to many places, but some places aren't set up for wheelchairs and this makes me feel less free. I hope this will change, so I can go anywhere I choose to go.

Sometimes, people don't know me well enough to understand what I am saying. So, I may have freedom of speech, but not always be understood. If people take the time to listen, they will find that handicapped people are just like them.

Sometimes freedom can mean things like being outside on a nice day with a full charge in my power wheelchair, or having gym and playing with my friends. Freedom can also mean being free to help others and to be able to ask for help if you need it.[14]

The Twin Cities area also became a center of innovation in the Cub Scout program during the 1980s. In 1981 the Viking and Indianhead councils participated in a one-year experimental project aimed at introducing seven-year-olds to Scouting. Developed at a national task force meeting in St. Paul, the Tiger Cub program was designed to encourage meaningful partnerships between adults and young boys, and to serve as a "bridge" to the Cub Scouts. In a typical Tiger Cub group, five to 10 boys met regularly with their adult partners—usually family members. There was no formal advancement system—just a series of activities built around "Big Ideas" such as "Getting to Know You," "Helping Others," and "Making Your Family Special." Each time a boy completed a Big Idea, he received a tiger paw iron-on to put on his Tiger Cub T-shirt. Among the findings of the test program: nearly 100 percent of Tiger Cubs joined regular Cub packs when they turned eight years old. In addition, many Tiger Cub leaders went on to become Cub Scout and Boy Scout leaders.[15]

The Tiger Cubs program was just one of several Cub Scout initiatives on which the Twin Cities-area councils provided national leadership. Their successful experiments with overnight Webelos camping during the early 1980s (at the Indianhead Council's Fred C. Andersen Scout Camp and the Viking Council's Camp Heritage) were instrumental in the BSA decision to approve extended camping for Webelos in 1984. When the BSA loosened its policies on camping for younger Cubs the following year, the Indianhead Council jumped at the chance to expand its camping opportunities. In 1986 it introduced an experimental overnight Cub Scout camping program called Akela, and set in motion plans to open a resident Cub camp called Camp Akela—

Seven-year-old Thomas Kane of Forest Lake held the distinction of being the nation's first Tiger Cub. In an inspired public relations coup, the Indianhead Council arranged for Thomas to pose for photographers holding a 2-week-old tiger cub at St. Paul's Como Zoo. The mother tiger was safely behind a glass wall.

first at Camp Kiwanis (1990–1992) and from then on at the Cannon River Scout Reservation. The Indianhead Council also helped convince the BSA to adopt Webelos Woods — a successful Webelos-to-Scouts transition program introduced in the 1980s by the council's North Lakes District—on a national scale.

Women had served for years as den mothers and, since 1976, as Cubmasters, but had long been barred from most other Scouting leadership positions, including Scoutmaster. Now the rules were changing. The BSA, facing frequent lawsuits stemming from its male-only leadership policy, decided in 1988 to let women become Scoutmasters and Webelos leaders. Many longtime Scouters believed the old policy helped provide boys with positive male role models, but as Indianhead Council Scout Executive Ron Phillippo explained, financial considerations had forced the BSA to capitulate.[16]

A month after the BSA changed the rule, Kim O'Donnell, a recreational therapist at Minnesota State Academy for the Blind in Faribault, became the first female Scoutmaster in Minnesota—and the second in the country. For seven years O'Donnell had served as the de facto Scoutmaster of Troop 335, a special needs unit based at the Faribault academy. (The previous troop leader was a woman too.) Now she had the official title. "I think a woman can be just as good a leader [for boys] as a man," she said. "I better have, since I've been doing it for seven years."[17]

Instructor Ed Buchwald teaches nature observation at Webelos Woods, Faribault, 1985.

O'Donnell's elevation to Scoutmaster did not immediately remove the misgivings that many Scouters felt, but most skeptics were willing to move on. Shortly after O'Donnell officially became a Scoutmaster, *St. Paul Pioneer Press* columnist Linda Kohl gently chided those who continued to predict a "catastrophe of some magnitude" would follow the dissolution of the male-only rule. "It has been two full weeks now," she wrote, "and to my knowledge the earth has not trembled and the sky has not fallen over southeastern Minnesota."[18]

As Scouting evolved to reflect changing social norms, the Viking and Indianhead councils simultaneously spent much of the decade confronting a perennial problem: money—or more accurately, a shortage of it. For decades, annual allocations from the United Way and its predecessor agencies, the Community Chest and the United Fund, had covered a large proportion of Scouting's expenses in the Twin Cities area. But in the economic recession years of the early 1980s, the United Way found it increasingly difficult to provide as much support as the Viking and Indianhead councils requested. Allocations to Scouting began shrinking. The Twin Cities-based councils responded by cutting costs where they could and by seeking new sources of revenue.[19] An increasing reliance on Sustaining Membership Enrollment (SME) campaigns (the solicitation of friends of Scouting such as parents and Scouting alumni) helped fill the funding gap, but more help was needed. For one of the first times in local Scouting history, the councils asked the boys themselves to become fundraisers.

The first experiment with Scout fundraising kicked off in 1981, when the Viking and Indianhead councils teamed up to present a series of local exhibitions called Scout Expo '81. The shows took place in six shopping centers throughout the Twin Cities and, as usual, allowed Cubs, Scouts, and Explorers to demonstrate a wide variety of outdoor skills. But unlike most previous Scouting exhibitions, Scout Expo '81 was designed to be a significant money maker. In the run-up to the show, Scouts went door-to-door selling $2 coupon books containing money-saving vouchers for goods and services throughout the Twin Cities. The results were gratifying. The Indianhead Council, which had raised just $2,000 at its 1980 show, netted more than $30,000 from the efforts of its coupon book-hawking Scouts in 1981. The numbers from the Viking Council were similar.[20]

Over the next few years, both councils—as well as their packs and troops—continued to rely heavily on the annual spring expo and its accompanying coupon book fundraiser. In an appeal to council board members, Indianhead Council Vice President of Program Betty Heath stressed that the coupon book's significance went beyond mere budget balancing. "This book is *terribly* important," she wrote, "because boys are using it to *earn their way to camp* and the council is using it to keep the cost of camping to boys and their families as low as possible."[21]

In 1984 the councils moved the fundraiser from the spring to the fall, and replaced the coupon books with plastic trash bags. After a successful initial fundraising campaign, sales of the bags dropped off considerably, and in 1986 the councils tried something different—candy. Through a partnership with St. Paul-based Pearson Candy Company, the Indianhead Council arranged for its Cubs, Scouts, and Explorers to sell more than 1,000 cases of Pearson's King Size Peanut Nut Rolls. Many Scouters, including Skyline District product sale chairman Dale Haag, were surprised at how successful the campaign was. "I know the units that participated were cautious at first," Haag said, "but when they found out how much the boys liked the sale and how easily everything went, we really sold a lot of product." When the final numbers were tallied, the council and its packs, troops, and posts had raised more than $120,000. Pearson's Nut Rolls remained a fundraising mainstay through the rest of the 1980s.[22] Scouting's most successful fundraising campaign, the annual popcorn sales drive, was still a few years off.

Responding to growing concerns about underage drinking and driving, the Indianhead Council in 1985 introduced SAFE RIDES, a program in which Explorers teamed with the St. Paul-Ramsey Medical Center to provide free and confidential rides home to teens who were in no condition to drive.

SERVICE >

"BRYCE, WHAT DO YOU WANT ME TO DO?"

"Bryce, should we just randomly fill the boxes with this stuff?"

Fifteen-year-old Eagle Scout candidate Bryce Palmer answers every question as best he can, even when he's not sure what the correct answer is. He's been preparing for this moment for the past few months, and now he's pinballing from questioner to questioner, trying to make sure everything goes smoothly.

A dozen Scouts from New Brighton Troop 106 and an equal number of adult volunteers have gathered in the banquet hall at VFW Post 6316 in Blaine, ready to do Bryce's bidding. They're shuffling among three long tables covered with assortments of nonperishable foods (ramen noodles, sunflower seeds, canned soup, SPAM), toiletries (toothbrushes, cotton swabs, shampoo, medicated foot powder), and sundries (tube socks, paperback books, DVDs, playing cards). As they squeeze past each other, they fill small cardboard boxes with whatever items strike their fancy.

The box-filling operation is the climax of Bryce's Eagle Scout service project—a plan to send at least 100 care packages to U.S. military troops in Iraq and Afghanistan. When asked how he feels, he pauses for a moment to come up with the right word.

"Overwhelmed," he says.

Right now Bryce has one main concern: that there may not be enough boxes to accommodate all the items he collected. The drop-off sites he set up at local grocery stores and churches proved to be much more successful than he anticipated. "Originally I had my goal set at 50 care packages," he explains. "I thought, 'Oh man, it's going to be so hard to get to 50 and get the donations to ship them all.' But after the first weekend I came home with two big boxes full of supplies and $100 worth of monetary donations. I couldn't believe it."

Previous pages:
The 1999 edition of Scouting for Food.

Bryce Palmer gives instructions to a few of his care package volunteers.

Bryce has been working with a statewide service organization, Operation Minnesota Nice, which specializes in this kind of work. Several Operation Minnesota Nice volunteers are here to help with the packing, but they're careful not to do too much. They know Bryce is in charge, and they defer to him, providing advice and encouragement only as needed. At one point, one of the volunteers steps in to assure the young Eagle candidate that he shouldn't worry about his apparent box shortage.

"You overplanned," she says. "But that's okay. It's going to be great."

As it turns out, Bryce need not have worried. Although he obtained only 100 mailing boxes from the post office—far fewer than he'll need to package all the donated items—there is no box shortage. The Operation Minnesota Nice volunteers brought along 100 boxes of their own. There are more than enough to get the job done.

Canned foods are among the most popular care package contents.

One hour into the packing operation, the tables that were piled high with donated odds and ends are beginning to look picked over. Some items, including the Girl Scout cookies, have completely vanished. Others, like the small plastic bags filled with ketchup, mustard, and barbeque sauce packets, have hardly been touched. Bryce, who until now has limited his instructions to one-on-one conversations, works up the courage to address the whole group of volunteers. "Great job so far," he announces. "Now the condiment baggies—if you could throw one of those into each box, that would be great. They don't take up too much room, and they're something the troops will definitely appreciate." His pep talk complete, he resumes his oversight of the boxing tables.

"Bryce, you got a marker?"

"Yep."

"Bryce, we're out of socks."

"That was quick."

Bryce's parents are among the adult volunteers participating in the packing operation. His mother, Flora Palmer, tears up when she thinks about what he's accomplished. "I think it's pretty special that a kid like that would do something that makes a difference," she says. "He knew he wanted to do something that would have a bigger impact than installing park benches or something like that. He just wanted to let the guys over there know that they're not forgotten—that they're appreciated and they're supported."

The sharp sound of unspooling packing tape cuts through the hubbub at regular intervals. The experienced volunteers from Operation Minnesota Nice are making sure each care package is stuffed with as many items as possible before it's sealed up for shipping overseas. A wall of taped-up boxes is taking shape on a table in the center of the banquet hall.

The stack of care packages grows as the evening progresses.

When the work is done, the final tally comes to 154 care packages. Bryce has enough donated cash to mail off most of them. He'll try to raise more money to ship the rest of them at a later date. Bryce knows he still has plenty of work to do—mostly administrative jobs like filling out customs forms and mailing labels—but he's relieved that this stage of his Eagle project is over. Not only did he oversee a successful packing operation, he proved to himself that he could accomplish a daunting task that would confound many adults. "Definitely a lot of stuff has happened tonight that I hadn't expected," he says. "But overall I'm definitely happy with how it went."

THE BOY SCOUT SLOGAN, "Do a good turn daily," has helped define Scouting in the public's mind—and in the minds of Scouts themselves—since the earliest days of the movement. In early 1911, the *St. Paul Pioneer Press'* new Scouting editor urged young Scouts to take the slogan seriously. "If you haven't been doing 'good turns,'" he wrote, "you'd better get busy, for you are not real Scouts, and you are missing one of the pleasantest parts of the work."

At first, good turns were seen primarily as altruistic acts to be performed by individual Scouts and troops. (One Minneapolis Scout even asked a local Scouting official "whether the licking of a neighborhood bully constituted a Good Turn.") But as the Scouting movement developed in the Twin Cities and elsewhere, the good turn tradition became more formalized. After successfully completing a series of community service campaigns during World War I, Scouts in St. Paul and Minneapolis began regularly participating in organized good turns coordinated by their local councils. They patrolled city parks, protecting wild birds from gun-toting "bad boys." They dug out fire hydrants from snowdrifts and directed downtown street traffic in an effort to reduce skyrocketing accident rates.

But of all the good turns performed by Scouts from the Twin Cities and surrounding regions, none could compare—in longevity, at least—to their ushering duties at the University of Minnesota. For nearly three-quarters of a century, beginning in 1923, Scouts from Minneapolis (and later St. Paul) volunteered as ushers at all Gophers home football games. By 1980, local Scouting officials were calling the U of M ushering program the "world's longest good turn."

The Scouting for Food campaigns of the 1990s and 2000s were good examples of the organized good turns that took precedence as Scouting developed over the decades.

In a real-life 1920s example of the iconic good turn, Scout Hy Krischner helps an elderly man cross a busy North Minneapolis street.

Cleaning up old campaign signs in Minneapolis, 1921.

Here is a good suggestion which will appeal to many of you. Your mothers are all fond of flowers, and especially violets. These dainty blossoms are now at their best. Take a hike into the country some afternoon and pick a good bunch for mother. Let her know that you got them especially for her. A little attention of this sort will bring to your mother untold happiness, for boys, as a rule, are thoughtless and apparently unappreciative of all the kind things their mothers do for them. Let mother know occasionally that you think of her and love her. It will do you both good.

— *St. Paul Pioneer Press*, May 11, 1913

Digging out fire hydrants after a heavy snow, 1920s.

Plenty of [fire]plugs were found needing "rescue" [from the snow], according to reports sent back by those who saw in this project that happy combination of fun for the boys, service to the community and, above all, that wise employment of spare time that leads to "participating citizenship."

Is it fair to anticipate that hereafter fireplugs will mean something more than a commonplace thing to the boys who played this game? Fireplugs are veritable sentinels of safety and as such should be of interest to Scouts in the same way they look upon first aid kits, don't you think?

— *Bulletin* (Minneapolis Area Council newsletter), March 14, 1939

Each winter, Scouts from the Northern Star Council's Kaposia District clear old holiday decorations from Fort Snelling National Cemetery. Staffers with the Department of Veteran Affairs say the Scouts finish in less than four hours what it would take the cemetery's staff three months to accomplish.

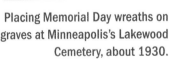

Placing Memorial Day wreaths on graves at Minneapolis's Lakewood Cemetery, about 1930.

You all know our good friend and pal, Mr. Elam L. Johnson, one of the most enthusiastic Scout leaders in town. Well, Mr. Johnson is in charge of "Ye Boye Scoute Toy Shoppe," which is now running at full blast. . . . If he calls on you for service, what are you going to do? Why, come a-running of course. That's always a Scout's response to a call for service.

After a few days of concentrated repair work . . . Santa Claus will have a whopping big load of good-as-new playthings to distribute through some of the friendly organizations of the city. And won't a few hundred of the less fortunate kids of the city be glad to get these rejuvenated toys? We'll say they will. And then won't you be happy that you are a Scout?

— *Be Prepared* (Minneapolis Council newsletter), December 1923

Toy repair in
Minneapolis,
about 1918.

Scouting for Food,
1992.

Scouts of St. Paul Troop 62
collecting donations for the
needy on the White Earth
Indian Reservation, 1921.

Usher Dave Williams of Minneapolis Troop 375 jokes with two fellow Scouts, Gopher football players Kenny Last and Bill Bevan, 1965.

Volunteer ushers gather outside the University of Minnesota's Memorial Stadium to participate in what would later be called Scouting's "longest good turn."

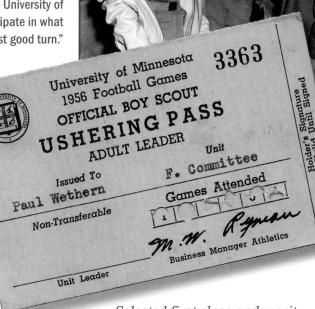

University of Minnesota
1956 Football Games   3363
OFFICIAL BOY SCOUT
USHERING PASS
ADULT LEADER

Issued To   Unit
                        F. Committee
Paul Wethern   Games Attended
Non-Transferable

                        M. W. Ryman
                        Business Manager Athletics

Unit Leader

Holder's Signature
Not Valid Until Signed

Minneapolis Scouts team up with Goodwill Industries, 1967.

Selected first class and merit badge Scouts will again be ushers at University of Minnesota football games in [Memorial] Stadium. . . .

It is required that each usher be completely and perfectly uniformed. This includes Scout hat, hat-badge, neckerchief in district color, troop numeral, insignia of rank, flannel shirt, official belt, breeches or shorts, and wool stockings. . . .

Chewing gum is at no time a part of the official uniform.

— *Be Prepared* (Minneapolis Council newsletter), October 1925

1923   1973
M
50 YEARS
OF SERVICE

The Scouts from Troop 319 in Hutchinson recently spent a day in Winona helping the American Red Cross and other emergency response teams by manning the victims assistance center [after the devastating floods in southeastern Minnesota]. . . .

The center was especially grateful to have the troop assisting them when they had several Hispanic families come in and 14-year-old Juan Carlos, who just joined the troop this spring, was able to be an interpreter.

— *Navigator* (Northern Star Council newsletter), October 2007

Hutchinson Troop 319, in Winona after the flood of 2007. L–R: Juan Carlos, Zane Keller, Humberto Delgado, Michael Reisewitz, C. J. Meyers, Robert Bustamante, Jonathon Bustamante, Tyson Steiner, and Zach Foede.

Before, after, and the Scouts of Minneapolis Troop 61 who did the work, 1921.

In 2008, Cub Scouts from Wayzata Pack 283 assembled fishing line recycling bins to reduce pollution caused by discarded monofilament.

Helping with the cleanup in Anoka after a devastating tornado in June 1939.

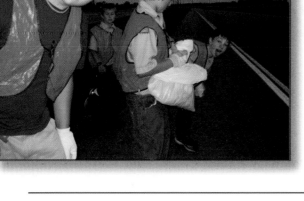

Scouts Evan Metzger, Josh Kamrath, Joel Emigh, Max Garaghty, and Parker Chase of Hutchinson Troop 246 pick up trash along a rural highway, 2007.

With community recycling still several years away, Matthew Isaak of Hopkins Troop 396 decided to act on his own. For his Eagle project in the winter of 1971, he collected boxes of glass and metal waste, and then arranged to have them hauled to recycling plants in Rosemount and North Minneapolis.

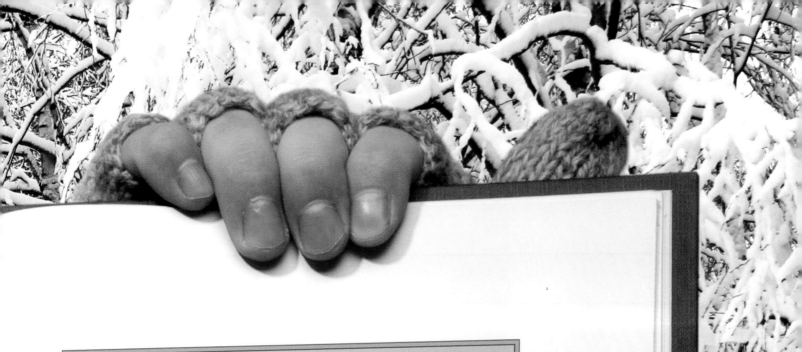

1990s >

ON A SUNNY SATURDAY in the fall of 1991, about 3,000 laughing, screaming, and roughhousing boys gathered at Camp Stearns for the Viking Council's annual Camperall. Although few of them realized it, they were all part of a grand experiment. For the better part of the day, they participated in a series of activities that soon would spread to councils throughout the country. They were, in effect, guinea pigs. And none of them seemed to mind.

At one end of a grassy field, two parallel lines of Scouts formed a horizontal "human ladder." Pairs of boys, standing face-to-face, held wood stave "rungs" between them. Then one by one, Scouts designated as "climbers" began creeping and crawling over the wobbly human contraption—about three feet above the ground—trusting that each pair of rung holders would hold on long enough to let him pass safely. Shouts of encouragement pierced the air.

"Come on, you've got it!"

"You're almost halfway there!"

Across the field 16 Scouts were lying shoulder-to-shoulder on the ground, passing a succession of boys above them in conveyor belt fashion. Each of the moveable boys declared his preference for a certain kind of cookie, and as he proceeded down the line, the "cookie machine" below him chanted the name of his favorite baked good. "Peanut butter!" "Chocolate chip!" "Snickerdoodle!" Usually the machine successfully performed its assigned function. Every once in a while, though, an unlucky cookie "crumbled."[1]

Everywhere you looked, Cubs and Scouts were playing what appeared to be simple games, but were actually much more than that. Six years earlier, in the summer of 1985, the Viking Council had asked the University of Minnesota's Center for Youth Development and Research (CYDR) to design a program to actively teach boys some of Scouting's longest held and most embedded principles—values such as trust, fairness, and caring. The result was

< Diversity takes center stage in this photo, which appeared on the cover of the Indianhead Council's 1990 annual report.

a series of activities and games in which kids encountered ethical issues by engaging in "concrete experiences" and then discussing the meaning of those experiences through a process called "reflection." The Cub program was known as DELV—Developmental Education for Lifetime Values. The Scout version was DELTA—Developing Ethical Leaders Through Action. The Viking Council and the CYDR tested and evaluated DELV and DELTA for several years, with help from several local packs and troops.[2] By 1990 the programs had merged into a single initiative called Ethics in Action. The games played at the Viking Council's 1991 Camperall constituted one of the first council-wide attempts to apply Ethics in Action concepts. The "human ladder" and "cookie machine" games, for example, both were designed to help Scouts learn and appreciate the value of cooperation and trust.

Shortly after the camporee, the Boy Scouts of America adopted Ethics in Action as an official Cub Scout program. It even published a special guidebook for Cub Scout leaders. (The Ethics in Action program for Boy Scouts

Climbing the human ladder at the 1991 Viking Council Camperall.

BOY SCOUTS OF AMERICA

DELV

CUB SCOUTS

VIKING COUNCIL
5300 Glenwood Avenue
Minneapolis, MN 55422

Cubs in action: right, 1999 Pinewood Derby winners from St. Paul Troop and Pack 356; next page, "Take a Tiger Fishing Day," 1997.

was never formalized.) The Viking Council had initiated the development of Ethics in Action to help boys make good decisions when confronted by "situations of real danger that their parents and grandparents may have only read about."[3] Now the BSA was introducing the programs developed in Minneapolis to Cub Scouts nationwide.

Ethics in Action had a short life span as a stand-alone nationwide program, but some of its most basic concepts and strategies lived on in regular Boy Scout activities. The program's "reflection" component, with its "What just happened?" discussion sessions was deemed particularly valuable. As committee chairman Charlie Levan of Anoka Troop 631 put it, "It's not the games so much as the process of sitting down after an experience and thinking and talking about it."[4] Years after Ethics in Action's disappearance as separate Cub Scout program, for example, new campers at Many Point Scout Camp were still being asked to reflect on their first-day experiences in Ethics in Action-style discussions.

Ethics in Action was not the only national Scouting program based on innovations developed by the Twin Cities area councils during the 1990s. In 1989, the Viking Council began field-testing Pine Tree, a redesigned version of

Youth staff member Corey Kline teaches conflict resolution skills at a mid-1990s Pine Tree camp. Kline later served as course director of Grey Wolf, the Northern Star Council's National Youth Leadership Training program.

the BSA's junior leadership program, at Stearns. At Pine Tree, 15-, 16-, and 17-year-old Scouts used Ethics in Action problem-solving techniques to teach leadership skills to Scouts only a few years younger than they were. Pine Tree participants typically summed up the weeklong experience in glowing terms.

"It was fun," one Scout said. "The best part was not having an adult with us."

"We learned we can be a lot more independent than we thought," another participant added. "We even had cherry cobbler for breakfast!"[5]

Pine Tree was, in the words of one of the program's early advisors, "a unique experience in living intensely the Scout Oath and Law."[6] In 1993, the BSA adapted the Pine Tree curriculum for use by councils throughout the country, and later renamed its program National Youth Leadership Training. The Indianhead Council's version of the program was known as Silver Pathfinder. When the Viking and Indianhead councils merged in 2005, the program took the name Grey Wolf. The objective: to make every troop in the council a boy-led troop, in which adults provided mainly guidance and encouragment.

The two councils also were among the leaders in a burgeoning national movement to connect American Scouts with youth from other countries. In the winter of 1989–90, 12 Scouts and three adult leaders from the Indianhead Council traveled to Costa Rica to help protect an endangered species — the leatherback sea turtle. The program grew out of a visit to St. Paul by the director of Costa Rica's National Parks Foundation. Costa Rica had established a leatherback protection plan that relied heavily on local Boy Scout and Girl Guide volunteers. On his visit to the Twin Cities, the parks foundation director inquired whether St. Paul Scouts would like to join in the effort. The answer he received was a resounding "Yes."

The Twin Cities area Scouts who traveled to Costa Rica during the first few years of the turtle program shared experiences they never dreamed they would have. Their main job was to help scientists protect and gather research data on the thousands of giant leatherbacks that came ashore each winter to lay their eggs on Costa Rica's Playa Grande (Big Beach). The Scouts discouraged poachers, chased away hungry birds, and trained tourists in turtle-watching etiquette. Sometimes they even counted eggs—as they were being laid.[7] Mike Hughes, a Scout with St. Paul Troop 1, was among a group of local Scouts assigned egg-counting duty during a mass nesting of 250-pound olive

Ridley turtles in early 1992. "You could not walk three feet in any direction without stepping on a turtle," he recalled. "It was by far the strangest and the coolest thing I've ever seen. . . . The turtles would literally lay the eggs into my hand and then I would set them in the nest."[8]

Although the program began as an effort to protect endangered turtles, it soon grew into something larger. Within a few years, Scouts from the Twin Cities were participating in a variety of conservation projects in Costa Rica, including tree planting and

The Scouts who participated in the Costa Rica turtle project performed a variety of jobs. Some measured the creatures while others, like Mike Hughes (above), counted eggs.

trail building. Costa Rican Scouts began making annual trips to Minnesota in what became a full-fledged exchange program. Soon Scouts from both countries were sharing a new, more sophisticated worldview. Mike Hughes, for one, made three trips to Costa Rica with the Scouts during the 1990s, and went back to stay with his host family more than a dozen times after that. His experience as a Scout ambassador inspired him to earn his college degree in Spanish. "It's had more of a profound impact on my life than anything else," he said, looking back on the experience. "We all knew we were doing something special."[9]

The positive experience in Costa Rica helped convince other Scouts in the Twin Cities region to broaden their outlook beyond the borders of the United States. The Indianhead Council expanded its exchange program to include Scouts from Bulgaria, Ireland, Argentina, and the Czech Republic.[10] Hmong Scouts from Minneapolis Troop 100 helped build an enclosed garden

A Scout welcoming party was waiting for Rahman Kasmi when he arrived at the airport in early 1998.

for a Twin Cities-based international human rights group, the Center for Victims of Torture.[11] And in 1998 the Indianhead Council, inspired by an article in a local newspaper, arranged to bring a destitute 15-year-old Albanian boy named Rahman Kasmi to St. Paul.

Rahman arrived in the Twin Cities with the clothes he was wearing, an empty knapsack, and a fifth-grade education. He spoke no English. Over the next three years, the Indianhead Council paid his tuition at a public school for international students (where he became fluent in English) and covered most of his expenses while he lived with local host families. When it was time for Rahman to leave, Indianhead Scout Executive Ron Phillippo, who led the campaign to bring him to St. Paul, marveled at his development. "The goal was to provide a young person of poverty an opportunity to experience a host family, school, and Scouting," he said. "He's made tremendous progress."[12]

Rahman had a name for Phillippo. He called him "Mr. Nice Guy."[13]

Even as local Scouts made new friends from overseas, they continued to expand their circle of friends closer to home. In 1994 the Indianhead Coun-

Next page, bottom: The fundraising trend that began during the 1980s with the sales of trash bags and nut rolls accelerated during the 1990s with the introduction of popcorn sales. In 1997, the Trail's End Company brought what it billed as the "World's Largest Popcorn Ball" to the Twin Cities to promote local popcorn fundraisers.

cil's Special Needs Division conducted a survey that found about 8 percent of the boys served by the Council had some form of disability—usually a behavioral problem, learning disability, or asthma. The findings helped spur the council to try to increase diversity by more actively recruiting new Scouts and staff members from the special needs community and other underrepresented groups.[14]

Efforts to increase diversity had their limits, though. In the early 1990s the Twin Cities-based councils were swept up in a brewing national controversy over the Boy Scouts of America's membership policies. Over the previous few years, courts in other parts of the country had issued conflicting rulings on whether the BSA had the right to exclude homosexuals, agnostics, and atheists from its ranks. Some of those cases were still on appeal. Now the courts in Minnesota were being asked to consider another membership question: whether girls could join the Boy Scouts.

The case involved a 13-year-old Bloomington girl identified in news reports as "Clare." Clare didn't fancy herself a trailblazer or troublemaker. She said she just liked to spend time outdoors, doing the kind of work Boy Scouts did to earn their merit badges. When asked why she wanted to be a Boy Scout, her answer was simple. "My older brother is in Boy Scouts," she said. "I thought it would be fun."[15]

Scout Mark Jamison of Troop 599.

Clare's case began attracting national attention in late 1991 when an agency of the state government—the Minnesota Human Rights Department—took her side. The department said there was probable cause that the BSA had discriminated against Clare when it refused to admit her. A few months later, a special assistant attorney general took the case to court.[16]

The case sparked indignation among many Scouting supporters who believed girls had no place in traditional Boy Scout programs. (The Explorer

program, which had welcomed girls since the 1970s, was another matter.) One of the most vocal Scouting advocates was State Sen. Bob Lessard, a former Scout. He introduced legislation—which later became law—that exempted the Boy Scouts, Girl Scouts and other private "single-gender youth organizations" from the state's human rights act. "I think there are cases where you can let boys be boys and girls be girls," he said.[17]

Clare's legal battle to join the Boy Scouts ended in the summer of 1992 when a Hennepin County district judge ruled that the BSA was an educational institution, which under state law was free to exclude girls. "If the court were to order the admission of Clare," the judge wrote in his ruling, "this could open the floodgate for similar requests of other young girls."[18] Although Clare and her family could have appealed the ruling, they decided to drop the case. Local and national Boy Scout officials were relieved.

"It has nothing to do with Clare personally," BSA attorney James Volling said. "It has to do with the right of the Boy Scouts to run itself as a private membership organization."[19]

The legal wrangling over the Boy Scouts' membership policies briefly overshadowed significant changes that were taking place in the local councils' leadership ranks. During the summer of 1990, the Tomahawk Scout Reservation hired its first female camp director—Mary Craig. Craig had been

In 1996, *Boys' Life* magazine celebrated its 85th birthday, and to commemorate the event, a special ceremony was held at the factory that churned out the magazine every month—the Quebecor printing plant in St. Paul. *Boys' Life* had not always been printed in Minnesota (Quebecor's St. Paul employees had been doing the job for only five years), but the old plant on Shepard Road seemed like the perfect place to mark the publishing milestone. The ceremony was rich with relics of Scouting's past, including enlarged copies of old *Boys' Life* covers and displays of some of the magazine's most memorable issues. The presence of two local Scouts dressed in historic BSA uniforms added a properly vintage touch. *Boys' Life* is no longer printed in St. Paul. The Quebecor plant closed in 2000.

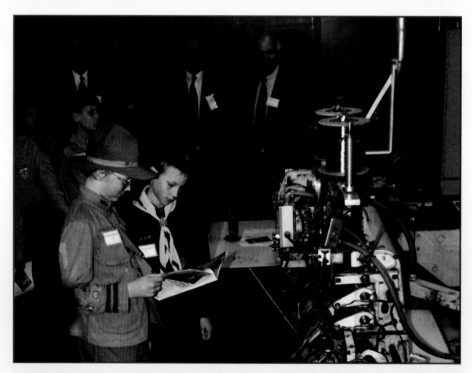

Scouts Warren Young and Adam Magnuson, dressed in vintage uniforms, get a close-up look at the printing presses that produce *Boys' Life.*

coming to Tomahawk since the early 1980s, when she joined Scouting's Explorer program. "I always wanted to be a Boy Scout," she explained. "I have brothers who went off to camp and I wanted to do that too." Now, at the age of 25, Craig was not only Tomahawk's first female camp director, she was one of the first women in the country to take charge of a Boy Scout camp. Her male charges seemed to take her groundbreaking status in stride.

"It just sounds different because the name says Boy Scouts," said 13-year-old Scout Scott Hedtke. "That's why people are surprised."

"I wish they were all [women]," added 12-year-old Shaun Bonacci.[20]

Five years after Craig broke the gender barrier at Tomahawk, another woman assumed an even higher leadership position in the local Scouting hierarchy. In 1995 Twin Cities businesswoman Kay Fredericks took over as president of the Indianhead Council, making her the first woman in the United States to head a metro council of the Boy Scouts of America. Indianhead Scout Executive Ron Phillippo had recruited Fredericks for the council's board of directors in 1984. In the years since then, Fredericks had established herself as an effective Scouting leader, both on the local and national level. She insisted she had always found the Boy Scouts to be "a very friendly, welcoming organization" in which women were encouraged to participate. "Women have always been active in Scouting and it's a natural thing," she said. "It's just as natural as men being involved in the activities of their daughters."[21]

At the same time, daughters were themselves becoming more and more involved in Scouting through a pair of programs aimed at older youth. Exploring had been open to girls since the 1970s, but in 1998 the BSA introduced a new program, Venturing, which further broadened Scouting's appeal. Among the many local participants was Kate Knuth, a young woman who said she couldn't remember a time when she didn't want to be a Boy Scout. (Her father and brother were Eagles.) After first joining a high adventure Explorer post, she became the charter president of Venturing Crew 367 in New Brighton. From there she went on to serve as the first female national Venturing president and later as one of the youngest members of the Minnesota legislature. "Scouting has been a huge part of my life and Venturing has given me many opportunities for adventure," she explained. "I've gained so many valuable lessons through those adventures that I want to give back to the program."[22]

Kay Fredericks was the first woman to serve as president of a metropolitan Boy Scout Council.

NOW ❖ THEN

SCOUTER >

Previous pages:
St. Paul Council Scout Executive
Frank Neibel demonstrates the
proper way to build a fire. Neibel
was the longest tenured Scout
executive among Northern Star
Council's predecessor councils. He
served from 1915 to 1937, when he
died in an automobile accident.

Bob Nelson in his element.

THE NONDESCRIPT RECTANGLE of a room that serves as Woodbury United Methodist Church's fellowship hall has emptied of most of the 30 or so Boy Scouts who were careening around just a few minutes ago. Troop 71 has scheduled its court of honor for next week, and tonight it's holding one last board of review session so each Scout can check his progress toward his advancement in rank. Most of the boys have retired to other rooms to huddle with adult leaders. The few who remain in the fellowship hall (including the gangly Scout who's managed to perch himself on top of two unopened pop cans) are either unconcerned with their progress or too young to fully comprehend the concept of advancement.

The seven Scouts gathered in a semi-circle at one end of the room fall in the second category. They have just crossed over into the troop from Cub Scout packs, and are now receiving an introduction to the Scout Handbook from senior patrol leader Paul Linnerooth.

"Everybody open your book."

"What page?"

"The front. It's a big book. It's really useful."

As Paul patiently answers a stream of mostly silly questions from his flock of new Scouts, a barrel-chested man in a Scouting uniform watches the proceedings from a comfortable distance, about six feet away. Bob Nelson has witnessed countless scenes like this over the years. He formed Troop 71 back in 1965, when he was 44 years old. Now he's 88. He was the Scoutmaster back then and he's the Scoutmaster now. As far as anyone can tell, he and Dave Moore of Minneapolis troops 33 and 100 are the longest-tenured Scoutmasters in the Northern Star Council and among the longest-tenured in the United States.

Ask Bob Nelson where he gets the energy, at age 88, to keep up with a troop of hyper-energetic Scouts, and he'll tell you he can't imagine not being a Scoutmaster. But a survey of the goings-on at Woodbury Methodist reveals at least one of the secrets behind his Scouting longevity. Troop 71 has 25 assistant Scoutmasters. Nelson knows how to delegate and, more importantly, how to get parents involved.

"What I like is that these people really enjoy each other and doing things together," he says. "Instead of just dropping their kids off, they sit around and talk and slowly get more and more involved. They find things they can do. It doesn't take a lot of training. It mostly takes friendships and relationships. If you've got that, they just enjoy being here. That's the secret behind what you see here. It's a bunch of adults, really enjoying what they're doing."

"Bob has a way of drawing you in," assistant Scoutmaster Maria Westfall explains. "He has a very comfortable style. Bob is a grandfather to the boys. They're very respectful to him."

Most of the troop's adult leaders are parents of Scouts, but a few are former Scouts who grew up in the troop. Troop treasurer Dan Ruda is one of them. Ruda joined Troop 71 in the late 1960s at a time when he wasn't sure what direction his life would take. He says Scouting set him on a course to pursue a career in journalism (he was staff photojournalist at Tomahawk),

but he's not sure he would have stayed with Scouting if Bob Nelson had not been at Tomahawk the summer he tried to pass his First Class swimming requirement.

"I was never a very good swimmer," Ruda says. "There was a point when, if I hadn't been able to make that swimming requirement, I probably would have lost interest in the Scouts and dropped out. . . . Bob got some of the older kids to work with me, to help me with my back float and my strokes. It started a whole sequence of events that have really made a difference in my life. And in part it's the reason I continue to be treasurer, because I want to try to give something back as much as possible and maintain the connection I have with the troop."

"I gave him his First Class," Nelson says with a smile, "That's the reason he stayed with us."

Rules bend with some regularity in Troop 71. "I have a tendency to be a contrarian," Nelson admits. Among the only rules he tries to enforce is a requirement that the troop take at least one camping trip each month, except December. To him, it's a matter of principle. "We've got to get kids off the davenports, off their rear ends, away from the TV, and into the woods," he says. "That's my motto."

Nelson also is a stickler for Scoutmaster conferences. If a Scout wants to advance to the next rank, he has to sit down for a talk with the Scoutmaster first. The same condition applies to boys who are new to the troop. As tonight's meeting winds down, he makes time for short conversations with a few of the boys who were going over the Scout Handbook with Paul Linnerooth earlier in the evening.

"You've been here how many meetings?" Nelson asks a wispy youngster with wire-rim glasses.

"This is my second one."

"I know a number of people who say they really like having you in the troop. So we're enthusiastic about you. It's good to see you. Are you going to stick around and help us?"

"Yeah."

Nelson is unfazed by the boy's reticence. "I need a lot of help running this troop," he confides. "All this doesn't just happen automatically. People get so they really like being around here. We've got a lot of great things happening this year. Do you ever think about the Scout Oath and Law?"

"Yeah." Actually, the young Scout doesn't sound so sure.

"Think about it once in a while. It's kind of like the railing on a bridge. It's nice to have something that says this is right and this is kind of wrong. It guides you in what you're doing."

The boy nods.

"Well, welcome to the troop," Nelson says. "And have fun."

WITHIN MONTHS of the establishment of the councils in Minneapolis and St. Paul, it was clear to nearly everyone involved that the success of the local Boy Scout movement would depend largely on the councils' ability to attract committed adult leaders. In an early recruitment letter, the Ramsey Council asserted that there was "a real demand for men who are living a life of activity to invest part of their time in the conservation of that little developed asset of the community, the boy." Reports from the field indicated that troops with engaged and motivated adult leaders tended to thrive. Those that lacked such leadership often withered.

Over the years the Twin Cities area has produced an impressive roster of adult leaders on the council, regional, and national levels, some of whose names, even today, remain familiar to local Scouts—names like Frank Neibel, Charles Sommers, Fred C. Andersen, and Ron Phillippo. Others, like C. W. Hadden, George Wyckoff, Charles Velie, and Frank Bean, have largely faded from memory despite the considerable contributions they made to Scouting's development in the Upper Midwest.

But beyond the professional Scouters and board members who have guided the Northern Star Council and its predecessors are the thousands of dedicated men, women, and Scout-aged den chiefs who continue to lead the dens, packs, troops, crews, and posts that form Scouting's foundation. For the better part of a century, local volunteers have put in countless hours of training to become effective adult leaders and earn the

coveted "TRAINED" sleeve patch. Today the training continuum is a multilevel process that begins with an introduction to leadership (Fast Start), moves into basic training (New Leader Essentials, Leader-Specific Training, and Introduction to Outdoor Leader Skills), and culminates with ongoing educational opportunities at regularly held leadership extravaganzas (Pow Wows and the University of Scouting) and the internationally recognized Wood Badge advanced training course.

Knot-tying Scoutmasters of St. Paul Troop 17: J. M. "Dad" Drew, 1928; Mark Hanson, 1994.

A rare 25-year Scouter patch awarded to Minneapolis Area Council Scout Executive C. W. Hadden in 1935.

Assistant Scoutmaster Maynard Olsen, Minneapolis Troop 1, at Camp Stearns, 1948.

"Directors in conference" at Camp Rotary, about 1918.

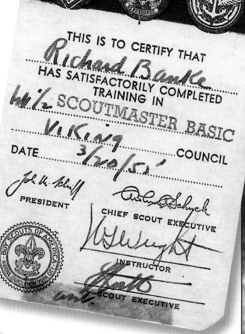

THIS IS TO CERTIFY THAT
Richard Baulke
HAS SATISFACTORILY COMPLETED TRAINING IN
SCOUTMASTER BASIC
VIKING COUNCIL
DATE 3/20/52
PRESIDENT
CHIEF SCOUT EXECUTIVE
INSTRUCTOR
SCOUT EXECUTIVE

The Scoutmaster must be a man who can satisfy a discriminating committee that he is a man to whom parents can safely trust their boys. He must be a man who will take into consideration the physical condition of every boy in his troop, and never give a boy anything to do which is likely to injure him.

— *St. Paul Pioneer Press*, November 20, 1910

The fundamental quality which a Scoutmaster should have is "horse sense," that is, the ability to size up things in a common sense manner and to deal with them without fuss or feathers. . . . No weak, vacillating, inert, back-boneless creature may ever aspire to the leadership of a group of boys.

— "Qualifications of a Scoutmaster," Ramsey County Council No. 1, Boy Scouts of America, 1913

The Viking Council's Jon Pederson makes a suggestion to Scouts gathered for the 2005 National Jamboree at Fort A.P. Hill, Virginia.

Unidentified Scoutmaster, Camp Stearns, 1948.

Scoutmaster Lloyd Grant of St. Paul Troop 9, 1920s.

Each Scoutmaster has his own way of doing things. . . . I believe in discipline. No boy is permitted to have more than $2 with him on a trip, and we permit no radios, comic books, baseballs, footballs, or other athletic equipment. We have our own organized games that keep the boys busy. Everyone goes to bed at 10 p.m., and I personally check each one and say good night. I also personally wake each one at 7 a.m.

— Scoutmaster Les Walther, St. Paul Troop 203, *St. Paul Dispatch,* August 11,1968

TRAINED

Fourth annual Scout Leader's Training Camp at Lake Itasca, 1921.

Cooking tips at the 2009 University of Scouting.

Up to the time of this writing, 75 fine men—troop committeemen, deputy commissioners, Scoutmasters, and assistant Scoutmasters—are enrolled in the University of Minnesota Scout Leadership Training Course. For nine weeks they will Scout in patrols, with patrol leaders selected from their number, just like regular Scouts. They will tie knots, bandage, signal and even Scout-pace, with enthusiasm that would do credit to many Tenderfoot patrols. And as for disporting themselves in Scout games; well, it just can't be described. There will also be hikes. But with all the fun, there is the determined purpose on the part of each one to "do a good job of Scouting better," for the sake of all of us who are the Scouts in the patrols and troops.

— *Be Prepared* (Minneapolis Council newsletter), December 1925

BULLETIN OF
UNIVERSITY OF MINNESOTA

Region Ten
University of Scouting

*Nineteenth Annual Short Course in
Scouting Leadership*

For Local Council Officers and Instructors

JULY 26 TO AUGUST 1, 1937
University of Minnesota Forestry Camp
ITASCA PARK

Itasca Park and the University of Scouting invite you.

SHORT COURSE SERIES

Vol. XL   No. 28   March 24 1937

Entered at the post office in Minneapolis as second-class matter. Accepted for mailing
at special rate of postage provided for in Section 1103, Act of October 3, 1917. Author-
ized July 12, 1918.

By the 1930s, the leadership training course at Lake Itasca was known as the University of Scouting, an official program of the BSA's Region Ten (encompassing councils in Minnesota, North Dakota, South Dakota, and Montana).

St. Paul Council Scout Executive Frank Neibel doubled as the director of the Itasca training camp during its first years of operation.

Pow Wow is not intended to be a total training program but rather it's a day of ideas. Your district has trainers ready to provide you with the sessions you will need to understand and administer the program. Don't deny part of the program for the boys just because you're "untrained" and don't know about them. GET TRAINED. You owe it to the boys and yourself.

— Indianhead Council
"Pow Wow Jungle Book,"
1980

Scouters who successfully complete the Wood Badge training course receive a pair of small wooden beads on a leather thong to wear around their neck.

Although the Itasca program shut down in 1947, the University of Scouting lives on today as an annual one-day leadership academy offering dozens of courses covering a wide range of subjects.

Learning to make neckerchief slides at the Indianhead Council's 1995 Pow Wow for Cub Scout leaders.

Camp Akela, 2007.

In 1977, former St. Paul Area Council President John C. Parish became the only local Scouter to receive the Bronze Wolf, the highest award presented for service to the world Scout movement. Parish's involvement in international Scouting included a six-year term as the BSA's international commissioner.

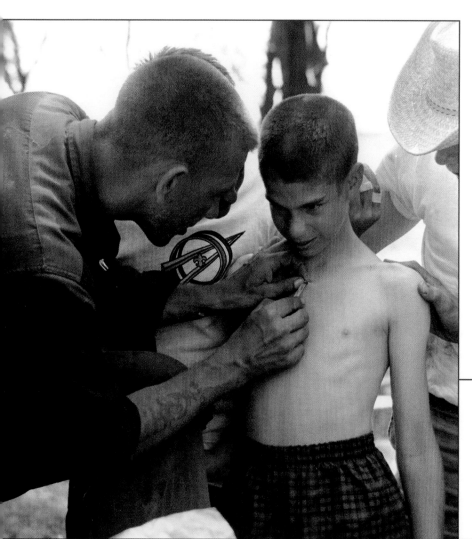

William Koob, advisor of St. Louis Park Explorer Post 369, removes a wood tick from Michael Malter's chest, 1964.

Dear Paul,

Here I have been in the Army for more than a year and I haven't written you a letter yet. I have even managed to miss your birthday. I hope it was a very nice one. . . .

I don't know if I ever thanked you for everything that you have ever done for me but I would like to do it now. Thank you very very much. It is hard for me to write what I want to say. How I feel about you, and how I hope that I have made you proud to know me. . . .

May God bless you,
Jeff

— Letter from unidentified Scout to Scoutmaster Paul Wethern, November 16, 1974

Few adults in the area now served by the Northern Star Council devoted their lives more fully to Scouting than Paul Wethern. Wethern became the Scoutmaster of Champlin Troop 276 (originally known as Troop 176) in 1930 and continued to be active in Scouting until his death in 1992. Shortly after he died, the Viking Council honored his memory by issuing a patch featuring his likeness to Scouts who participated in a Webelos Transition Camp held at the Rum River Camp.

2000s >

OVER THE PREVIOUS NINE DECADES, Scouting in the Twin Cities and surrounding area had undergone a remarkable transformation. From a loosely organized core of several dozen Scouts in 1910, the local Scouting movement had grown exponentially into a still-expanding community serving about 100 thousand young people each year. The two Twin Cities-based councils had expanded their geographic reach as far east as Amery, Wisconsin, and as far west as Canby, Minnesota, near the South Dakota border. Whereas once the two councils had no permanent camps to call their own, they now boasted seven properties offering a dazzling array of camping programs. Over and over again, Scouting in Minnesota and Wisconsin had proved its ability to grow and adapt while remaining true to its core principles. And now, with the coming of the new millennium, that ability and willingness to change was once again on prominent display.

Some of the changes that took place in local Scouting during the 2000s were prompted by decisions made on Scouting's national level. For example, Venturing, the new outdoor adventure program for older youth, which spun off from the Exploring program in 1998, grew significantly in local popularity as the decade progressed. But other changes, including the Viking and Indianhead councils' increasing use of electronic communications technology and their intensified outreach to minority communities, reflected widespread social, economic, demographic, and technological trends. Whatever the case, Scouting's efforts to respond to a changing world often went unnoticed by the public.

But not always.

For nearly a decade, Scouting had been embroiled in a series of legal disputes concerning its membership policies—guidelines that excluded from membership girls, atheists, agnostics, and homosexuals. Now, as the

< Building the future at Camp Akela, 2008.

new millennium got underway, one of those disputes was generating increasingly heated public debate. A long-running case regarding the national Boy Scouts' practice of excluding homosexuals from membership had reached the U.S. Supreme Court, and the justices were due to announce their decision at the end of their term in the summer of 2000. The case involved an assistant Scoutmaster from New Jersey who had been expelled from Scouting after BSA officials learned of his work as a gay rights activist. But the Supreme Court's upcoming decision promised to have ramifications that reached far beyond New Jersey. From Scouting's perspective, the case boiled down to one simple question: Was the BSA a private organization with the right to set its own membership criteria, or a "public accommodation" subject to a wide array of antidiscrimination laws? As the court's term wound down, Scouting leaders from around the country, including those based in the Twin Cities, prepared to respond to the decision, whatever it might be.

Although few people outside of Scouting realized it, the Indianhead Council had been working behind the scenes for several years to have a voice in the BSA's membership practices. In the spring of 1999, it put forward a resolution urging the National Council to reexamine "the relevance and appropriateness of [Scouting's] present membership requirements."[1] The council's main goal was to encourage open discussions within the BSA about a controversial issue that defied simple national—or local—solutions. The BSA's National Executive Board created a task force on membership standards, as proposed by the Indianhead Council, but it put off any action until after the U.S. Supreme Court issued its ruling in the Boy Scout case. (The board ultimately upheld the existing standards.)[2]

On June 28, 2000, the court ruled that the Boy Scouts of America, as a private organization, had wide latitude to set and enforce its own membership standards. The decision constituted a significant legal victory for the BSA, but it did not end the controversy. Critics of the Boy Scouts' membership practices expressed their displeasure, advocates rushed to their aid, and in the Twin Cities the divisiveness that followed the Supreme Court decision was hard to ignore. In St. Paul, the 3M Company significantly reduced its financial contributions to the Indianhead Council after "a major employee uprising" over the BSA's membership standards. Other moves soon followed. The St. Paul United Way considered cutting its funding of the council (it ultimately rejected the idea) and the St. Paul Council of Churches refused to renew its endorsement of Boy Scout programs.[3] In Minneapolis, the foundation of Medtronic, Inc., excluded the Viking Council from sharing its $1 million-plus contribution to the United Way.[4] (That decision prompted many local United Way donors to designate gifts totaling hundreds of thousands of dollars directly to Scouting programs.) At least three Scout leaders in St. Paul and Minneapolis resigned in protest, and a professor at Carleton College in Northfield returned his Eagle badge, sash, and pin to the BSA, explaining that he could "no longer honorably consider himself to be a Scout."[5]

In a guest column for the *St. Paul Pioneer Press,* the chairman of the Indianhead Council's board of directors, Steve Weekes, urged local critics to keep in mind Scouting's many contributions to the community, and alluded to the council's continuing efforts to influence national policy. "The Supreme

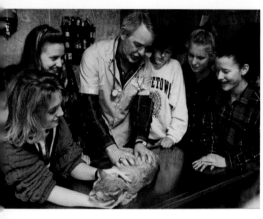

With the introduction of the BSA's Venturing program, Exploring began focusing exclusively on career preparation in fields such as public safety and veterinary medicine.

Chief mission is positive youth development

STEVE WEEKES
COMMENTATOR

In the wake of Wednesday's U.S. Supreme Court ruling, it's important to keep certain things in perspective. We're gratified that the court recognized the Boy Scouts of America's right, as a private organization, to establish its own membership criteria and set its own leadership standards.

At the same time, we're acutely aware that because the case involves a volatile social and political issue — gay rights — public opinion inevitably is going to be divided. In our own "community" — among the Scouts, parents, volunteers, donors and chartered organizations that make up the Indianhead Council — there are disparate views on this issue.

We believe it's important to listen to these differing opinions, but we want to ensure that these differences don't distract any of us from the vital mission of positive youth development. If you fail to support Scouting because of disagreement on this issue, you're walking away from young people who need all the support they can get.

For nearly a century, Scouting has been an important thread in the fabric of American life, serving more than 108 million young people in communities across our country. Studies have confirmed the effectiveness of the Scouting program, showing, for example, that Scouts have an increased willingness to help others, better decision-making skills, greater leadership ability and higher self-esteem.

With the number of at-risk youths increasing, it's more important than ever that Scouting provide a safe and supportive environment that helps young people grow into healthy, productive adults and involved, active citizens.

Indianhead Scouting has been serving youths, families and communities in the East Metro area and western Wisconsin since 1910, and we're committed to doing so into the 21st century.

At the same time, the Supreme Court's decision should not be taken as proof that Scouting does not engage in self-examination. While remaining true to the principles on which it was founded, Scouting has evolved over the years in response to the changing needs of the communities it serves, and it will surely continue to do so.

Fifteen years ago, for example, there was heated debate over whether women should be Scoutmasters. There have been women Scoutmasters since 1986, and Scouting is far richer and far stronger because of their participation. Similarly, hundreds of thousands of young women from 14 to 20 currently participate in Boy Scouts' Venturing and Exploring programs — a development unforeseen just a few decades ago.

The important point is that Scouting does change. But it has never been, and should not be, on the leading edge of social change. There's a very simple reason why this is so: People are trusting us with their children.

One of the things that's not likely to change in the near future is the relative autonomy that chartered organizations (community-based groups that collaborate with us to sponsor Scouting units) and parents have in selecting the leaders of those units. The clearly defined selection criteria include, for example, an interest in youth development, an interest in and appreciation of the outdoors, a willingness to invest time in training and unit leadership, experience in leading group activities and the ability to be a positive role model for young people.

These criteria, however, make no reference to sexual orientation; indeed, Scouting makes no effort to discover any person's sexual preference.

In Scouting, it's your behavior, your motives and the quality of your character that count. That will not change. Over the years, Scouting has been a common denominator, bringing together those of many faiths and viewpoints in an effort to serve our youth.

Although some people undoubtedly were disappointed by Wednesday's Supreme Court decision — as others would have been had the court ruled differently — we hope that our entire community will continue to support Scouting's important work, which is showing positive, measurable outcomes in the lives of thousands of our young people.

Weekes is volunteer chairman of Indianhead Scouting/BSA. Contact him through council information director Kent York at kyork@indianhead.org or call (651) 254-9142.

St. Paul Pioneer Press, June 30, 2000

Court decision should not be taken as proof that that Scouting does not engage in self-examination," he wrote. "While remaining true to the principles on which it was founded, Scouting has evolved over the years in response to the changing needs of the communities it serves, and it will surely continue to do so."[6]

Still, many critics were unwilling to wait for Scouting to change. In October 2000, the Minneapolis School Board voted unanimously to stop chartering after-school Scouting programs and prevent the Viking Council from recruiting in the schools. The meeting in which the decision was made featured passionate arguments on both sides of the issue.

"They're raising our kids to be bigots," one parent said of the Scouts.

"It's programs like [Scouting] that help our kids," countered the gay father of two Minneapolis Scouts. "I'm not here for the Boy Scouts. I'm here for the inner-city kids."[7]

While the Minneapolis public schools engaged in a public and sometimes acrimonious debate over the BSA's membership policies, St. Paul public school officials worked quietly with leaders of the Indianhead Council to insulate students from the controversy. In an e-mail message to the council's new Scout executive, John Andrews, St. Paul School District Area Superintendent Joann Knuth pledged to seek "a middle ground that continues to give our students access to Scouts in schools while also keeping the dialogue going—the education process that says this national position [regarding homosexuals] must change to be inclusive."[8] In the end, the St. Paul district stopped chartering Scout troops, but continued to let Scouts meet in school buildings and distribute recruiting materials. Andrews, for one, was pleased with the result and insisted that the chartering decision would have little practical effect. "St. Paul [schools] will continue to make families aware of Scouting programs," he said.[9]

Still, even with the spirit of cooperation taking root in St. Paul, the controversy surrounding the Supreme Court decision and the BSA's membership standards had a profound effect on recruiting efforts within the combined region served by the Indianhead and Viking Councils. "Join Scouting Nights" attracted fewer and fewer would-be Cubs and Scouts. Andrews lamented that many Cub packs were "shrinking down to nothing" because some schools remained closed to Scouting recruitment.[10] In Minneapolis and the western counties served by the Viking Council, Cub Scout enrollment dropped 20 percent in the decade's first five years.[11] "We can statistically show that when the school refuses to pass promotional material to the parents that local Scouting enrollment sinks like a rock," Andrews explained. "And that all adds up to a pretty nasty future statistic."[12]

Although the BSA's membership policy continued to generate controversy, its effect on enrollment eventually dissipated. In 2005, a little-noticed provision of the federal "No Child Left Behind" education law—a regulation requiring schools to implement consistent policies on recruitment by outside groups—prompted the Minneapolis school district to reopen its doors to Scouting. Opposition to Scouting subsequently declined there, and in other school districts as well.

The blue and yellow lawn signs that popped up in neighborhoods throughout the Twin Cities area in 2006 were a direct outgrowth of the Cub Scout recruiting campaigns conducted jointly by the Indianhead and Viking councils in the early 2000s.

The national controversy surrounding the BSA's membership standards had at least one unanticipated local consequence: the coming together of the Indianhead and Viking councils. In the months following the Supreme Court's decision, leaders from the two councils began meeting regularly to forge a coordinated response to the controversy. Those meetings, in turn, led to a series of joint projects including a high-profile Cub Scout recruiting campaign in the fall of 2001. For nearly 100 years, the two Twin Cities-based councils had proudly maintained their identities as separate and fiercely independent organizations. Now, as they collaborated more and more frequently in the wake of the Supreme Court decision, the question arose: Would there be any benefit in combining the two councils into one?

Representatives from both councils began meeting to explore the possibility in 2003. In the fall of 2004, a task force comprising Viking and Indianhead board members voted unanimously to bring the national organization into the negotiation process. The task force members concluded that the benefits of combining the two councils far outweighed the costs. As they saw it, a consolidation would eliminate fundraising competition between the two councils, increase the number of programs available to young people throughout the region, and save about $800,000 a year. Potential disadvantages such as increased bureaucratization and loss of identity were seen as manageable problems that should not stand in the way of progress.

In the months that followed the task force vote, another group composed of representatives from the two councils began formulating a consolidation plan while striving to keep one question in mind: "What's going to be best for kids, and what's going to be best for Scouting?"[13] The consolidation committee solicited comments from council members, and the responses it received, while mostly supportive, reflected the mixed feelings harbored by many members. Longtime Scouters and leaders from outside the Twin Cities metro area were among the consolidation plan's most vehement critics. They worried that a merger would obliterate the councils' distinct identities and centralize operations in ways that further isolated Scouting programs in small towns and rural areas. The response of one 30-year Scoutmaster was typical. "No merger [is] needed to have 'the best council in America,'" he scribbled on his comment form. "Collaboration yes, but no merger."

On March 30, 2005, 85 percent of voting members of the Indianhead and Viking councils formally approved the consolidation plan. The merger—the largest in BSA history—became official exactly three months later. The Northern Star Council, as the newly created organization was known, now ranked as the fourth-largest Scouting council in the United States, with a membership of 115,000 young people in 21 Minnesota counties and four counties in western Wisconsin. By the end of the summer, Scouts in the Twin Cities and the surrounding region were scrambling to be among the first to sport the new council patches (provided by the consolidation budget at no cost to Scouts) on their left sleeves. "To get the first issue of a new council patch is something of a big deal," explained Jeff Sulzbach, the Northern Star Council's director of development. "Changing council names doesn't happen very often."[14]

Proponents of the merger had long argued that consolidation of the two councils would, above all else, make it possible to pro-

This banner, which was displayed at the 2005 National Jamboree at Fort A.P. Hill, Virginia, expressed the mixed feelings that many people had about the Viking-Indianhead consolidation. It shows a Viking ship—representing the Viking Council—being swamped by a huge Northern Star Council wave.

In one of its first publicity efforts, the newly created Northern Star Council distributed this plush toy to drum up interest in the Tiger Cub program.

vide more Scouting programs for more young people. This benefit was perhaps most noticeable in the camping program. Before the merger, Cubs, Scouts, Explorers, and Venturers in the Indianhead Council attended the four Indianhead camps—Tomahawk, Fred C. Andersen, Phillippo, and Kiwanis—while their counterparts in the Viking Council traveled to Many Point, Stearns, and Rum River. But now, with the consolidation, all Scouts in the new Northern Star Council could participate in a wide variety of camping programs spread across all seven camp properties.

The consolidation of the two councils also expanded opportunities to serve children in communities that Scouting had always struggled to reach. Over the previous decade the Viking and Indianhead councils had each established separate—and in some cases, complementary—programs for underserved youth. Now, thanks to the merger, the best programs developed in either council could be expanded to serve the entire Northern Star territory.

One of the council's most innovative outreach programs was a Viking Council initiative designed to give first-time juvenile offenders an alternative to appearing in court. Juvenile Diversion, as the program was known, was aimed at boys and girls, ages 10 to 17, who had been arrested for misdemeanor crimes such as underage drinking, shoplifting, and property damage. Participants in the program were referred by arresting police officers, judges, or parents, and had to attend 10 weeks of classes and perform at least 16 hours of community service. Juvenile Diversion was part of the Viking Council's—and eventually, the Northern Star Council's—Learning for Life school-based education program.

First implemented in the Minneapolis suburb of Brooklyn Park in 1996, Juvenile Diversion partnered with police and sheriff's departments to give second chances to kids who were willing to admit and learn from their mistakes. Volunteers trained by the council worked with the young offenders to help them understand the seriousness of their actions and the possible consequences if they failed to change their ways. Kids who successfully completed the program had their offenses removed from their records. Although many

Some things never change: Scouts take their accustomed places in the 2007 St. Paul Winter Carnival parade.

were reluctant participants, most were glad to have the chance to stay out of juvenile court.

"They made us feel like we had another chance," said a 16-year-old girl from Andover who had been picked up for underage drinking. "I liked it. I'd rather go this route than the other."

"I see her trying to make better decisions . . . and take responsibility for her actions," her mother added.[15]

Statistics compiled after more than a dozen years of working with youthful offenders showed that Juvenile Diversion was doing exactly what it was designed to do. More than 80 percent of the boys and girls who went through the program kept their records clean. For most of those kids, Juvenile Diversion was their first—and often only—direct experience with the Boy Scouts, but that didn't bother the program's director, Colleen Brazier. "Ultimately [we're] trying to reach 100 percent of the kids (a goal initially set out during the first board retreat of the new, unified council), knowing that not all kids go through Boy Scout programs," she said. "[Juvenile Diversion] is a

A Juvenile Diversion rock climbing adventure helps keep at-risk teens out of trouble.

On June 17, 2009, 16-year-old Anthony Thomas of Lakeville Troop 471 received a singular honor: he was officially recognized as the 2 millionth Eagle Scout in the nearly 100-year history of the Boy Scouts of America. The BSA chose Anthony from a group of nearly 1,400 Scouts who attained Eagle rank during the previous month. As the ceremonial 2 millionth Eagle, Anthony would serve as Scouting's national youth ambassador—riding a float in the Tournament of Roses Parade, ringing the opening bell at the New York Stock Exchange, and delivering the Boy Scouts' annual report to President Barak Obama. "This really gives me the opportunity to use my skills to get people involved in Scouting," he said. "And to be a role model to everyone, especially Eagle Scouts."

In his first official act as the BSA's youth spokesman, Anthony broke ground (using a specially made shovel with a canoe paddle-shaped handle) on the Northern Star Council's latest history-making initiative: the establishment of a new "Base Camp" on the grounds of Historic Fort Snelling. The two events—

the Eagle announcement and the Base Camp groundbreaking—combined to provide a timely preview of the council's upcoming 100th anniversary celebration. "We feel like we won the lottery to a certain degree," the council's marketing director, Kent York said. "Being able to tie the two events together is wonderful."[20]

Anthony Thomas and an Honor Guard of Eagles and other Scouts from Troops 100 and 196.

Scoutreach at work at Camp Akela, 2008.

way of positively affecting their lives without them joining the organization long-term."[16]

But as always, getting more kids to join long-term remained a primary goal, and as the Northern Star Council approached its centennial year, its efforts to reach out to underserved communities intensified. Those efforts began taking solid shape early in the decade when the BSA introduced Scoutreach, a nationwide initiative designed to promote urban and rural Scouting.

In the years leading up to their consolidation, the Viking and Indianhead councils employed distinct strategies to achieve their Scoutreach goals. The Viking Council concentrated much of its urban attention on low-income inner-city Minneapolis neighborhoods while focusing its rural outreach on communities with growing Hispanic populations like Willmar and Bird Island.[17] Meanwhile, the Indianhead Council embarked on a redistricting plan that ultimately led to the creation of four new independent districts based on demographic trends, not geographical lines. The first of the new culturally specific districts—the Silver Maple District—brought together units composed primarily of boys of Asian descent. The second, formed in 2002, was the Zulu District, which served the African American community. After the merger of the Indianhead and Viking councils in 2005, the new Northern Star Council created two more nongeographic districts—the Latino district, El Sol, and the Polaris District, which served children and adults with cognitive and physical disabilities.

With the establishment of nongeographic districts, young people from underserved communities in the Northern Star Council now found it easier to participate in Scouting activities with kids from similar backgrounds. Membership among the area's Asian, African American, Latino, and special needs communities grew substantially, but that didn't mean that Scouts from those groups kept to themselves. The council's intensified commitment to diversity encouraged Scouts and their adult leaders to reach across racial, ethnic, religious, and economic lines, and get to know each other better.[18]

In the winter of 2004–05, Bill Butchee, the Scoutmaster of Troop 96—the Zulu District's most active unit—received an unexpected call from Scoutmaster Bill Hoffmann of Minnetonka Troop 346. Hoffmann suggested to Butchee that their two troops get together for a winter outing over the upcoming Martin Luther King Jr. holiday weekend. The experience would give the white Scouts from Hoffmann's troop and the black Scouts from Butchee's troop a chance to spend time with each other and, ideally, break down a few social

Experiencing a fire hose blast at a 2005 "Join Scouting Night" event.

Crossing over from Cub Scouts at Webelos Experience, 2007.

Top: Troops 96 and 346 spent much of the Martin Luther King Jr. holiday weekend indoors.

Bottom: Temperatures at Lake Minnetonka were not as low as up north, but it was still plenty cold.

barriers. Butchee liked the idea. The two troops began making plans for a high adventure cross-country ski trek in the Boundary Waters Canoe Area Wilderness, including overnight stays in remote round shelters called yurts.

Extreme cold forced the troops to cancel their trip up north, but it couldn't stop the Scouts from finding another way to spend the weekend together. In the end, they wound up at the family "cabin" of Troop 96 Assistant Scoutmaster Byron Jackson—a luxurious vacation home on Lake Minnetonka complete with big-screen television, shuffleboard, and heated indoor pool.

"This isn't exactly a yurt," one Scout observed, "but it will do."

The Scouts broke up into two patrols, Alpha and Bravo, consisting of boys and leaders from both troops. Indoors the boys engaged in spirited competitions of water polo, shuffleboard, and ping pong. Outside they braved below-zero temperatures on a cross-country ski excursion to "Boy Scout Island," the site of the old Minneapolis Area Council's Camp Robinson Crusoe and Camp Wawatasso.

But all along, Scoutmasters Hoffmann and Butchee had hoped to make their troops' time together more than just series of fun activities. On the weekend set aside to honor the nation's greatest civil rights leader, they wanted their Scouts to spend at least some time reflecting on the King legacy. Father Kevin McDonough, the pastor of Troop 96's chartering partner, St. Peter Claver Catholic Church, spoke to the Scouts about King's commitment to nonviolence. Hoffmann described an incident in which he witnessed one brave individual stand up against an act of racial discrimination. Butchee told a story about his eighth grade teacher, who, during the early 1960s, insisted that all his students memorize the Preamble to the U.S. Constitution so they could better appreciate the significance of the civil rights battles that were currently underway. At first, the boys were reluctant to discuss the racial divide that separates American from American, but slowly they opened up. One question led to another. The Scouts were coming to believe that the cancellation of the north woods trip in favor of a weekend on Lake Minnetonka had worked out for the best.

"Living, eating, and sleeping together under the same roof all helped to unite us," explained David Van Sickle of Troop 346. "After this trip, rather than see the differences between us, we realize that [we are a lot alike] and we listen to the same music and play the same sports."

"We all got to know one another better," added Troop 96's Jerome Butchee.

Although the Scouts and leaders of the two troops hoped their weekend together would lead to similar gatherings in the future, they eventually drifted apart. Every once in a while a Scout from one troop would run into one of his counterparts from the weekend on Lake Minnetonka. They would shake hands and exchange fond greetings, but then they would go their separate ways. Still, the two Scoutmasters who arranged the get-together were confident their Scouts had gained something from the experience.

"What [happened] is what we hoped for when we started planning this weekend," Bill Butchee explained. "[It was] the manifestation of Martin Luther King's dream coming true—seeing beyond visible differences."

Bill Hoffmann felt the same way. "Some of the comments that the guys made about being discriminated against because they're black were things that kids like my son would not have heard otherwise," he said. "The kids from our troop came away from that weekend much more sensitive to the importance of being inclusive and thinking about issues of race in a different way."[19]

The emphasis on inclusion was timely. Later that year, at the first board retreat of the newly created Northern Star Council, board members—some from the old Viking Council and some from the old Indianhead Council—set an audacious goal for local Scouting. They declared that the Northern Star Council would seek to have a positive impact on "100 percent" of all youth within its boundaries. As the council approached its 100th anniversary, its inclusive vision took solid form in its plans to create a new urban "Base Camp," open to all young people, at historic Fort Snelling. The new property was a symbol of sorts—a reminder that Scouting in Minnesota and Wisconsin had grown into something much larger than anyone ever imagined when, in the summer of 1910, 86 St. Paul boys gathered at the YMCA's Camp St. Croix to find out just what it meant to be a Scout.

A welcoming sign outside the site of the Northern Star Council's proposed Base Camp at Fort Snelling.

This photograph, identified as "Camp Seton," may have been taken at the mass campout held near Fort Snelling on May 27 and 28, 1911.

ON THE MORNING OF MAY 27, 1911, a procession of streetcars disgorged a steady stream of excited young boys at a regular trolley stop near what local newspapers called the "Riding Lodge" on the grounds of Fort Snelling. The youngsters were all from St. Paul and surrounding communities in Ramsey County. They had come to the bluffs overlooking the Mississippi River to take part in the first mass campout of Boy Scouts ever held in Minnesota. The site of the rally—about halfway between Fort Snelling and Minnehaha Falls—was dubbed "Camp Seton," in honor of Ernest Thompson Seton, one of the founders of the Boy Scouts of America.[1]

The Boy Scout movement had taken root in the Upper Midwest less than a year earlier, and the Scouts of Ramsey County were determined to show just how far they had come during that time. They set up their tents, built campfires, cooked their own meals, and participated in a series of competitions designed to test their knowledge of Scoutcraft. Few councils anywhere in the country had ever organized such an event, and in a letter read aloud to the gathered troops, BSA Field Secretary Preston Orwig praised the Ramsey County contingent for being as "'clean cut' a bunch of Scouts" as he had ever encountered. "I wish I could have been with you today in your sports, and especially as you gather tonight around your campfire," he wrote. "The day has doubtless been filled with real excitement for each Scout."[2]

Now, nearly a hundred years after that first gathering on the Mississippi River bluffs, local Scouting is returning to the site of its first mass gathering. The Northern Star Council of the Boy Scouts of America has purchased what was once known as the "Riding Lodge," the same building that those Ramsey County Scouts saw as they stepped off the streetcar on their way to the rally in 1911. With funds raised through its Centennial Commission—and its largest capital campaign ever—the council is now transforming the building into a "Base Camp" that will offer programs to "all youth" in the area, not just Boy Scouts. "This is a new foray," Scout Executive John Andrews says. "It's an opportunity to make sure we're relevant for our second hundred years."[3]

Where once Boy Scouts hopped off the trolleys of the Snelling-Minnehaha streetcar line, now young people of all stripes will disembark the Hiawatha light-rail line to participate in any number of activities—from rock climbing to geocaching to negotiating a ropes course. And they will do so within sight of Fort Snelling, the old military installation once commanded by the grandfather of Ohiyesa (Charles Eastman), the Dakota physician whose writings influenced the early Boy Scout movement's understanding of American Indian customs and values.

It's tempting to dismiss the cliché of history coming full circle, but in this case the old, moldy saying seems fresh and appropriate. Scouting in the area served by the Northern Star Council has grown in countless ways during the past century, but only, it might be argued, because its roots reach so deep. In his message to the Scouts who attended Camp Seton in 1911, the BSA's Preston Orwig marveled at the progress they had made during the previous few months and predicted only greater things to come. "I have called you 'pace makers,' and I want to use the term again," he wrote in closing. "There is no reason why [you] should not set a pace for the country. You have a good start, so go at it hard."[4]

KEY THREE LEADERSHIP

While the volunteer position of Council Commissioner was not adopted in the earliest years of Council Operations, the positions of volunteer President, Council Commissioner, and the salaried Scout Executive have been long known as the Council Key Three. Following are the Key Three leaders from the two headquarters cities into which various Councils were merged over the years, and that ultimately consolidated as Northern Star Council in 2005.

COUNCIL PRESIDENTS

NAME	YEARS	COUNCIL	NAME	YEARS	COUNCIL
Jesse A. Gregg	1910–11	Ramsey #1	Willis F. Rich	1970–71	Viking
W. F. Webster	1910	Hennepin	Anthony Bechik	1971–72	Indianhead
Louis Koch	1911	Hennepin	James R. Peterson	1972–73	Viking
F. M. Rarig	1911–12	Hennepin	William B. Randall	1973–74	Indianhead
Gov. A. O. Eberhart	1911–15	Ramsey #1	Edward Landes	1974–75	Viking
Louis Koch	1913–17	Hennepin	Roy W. Hawkinson	1975–76	Indianhead
N. R. McLeod	1916	Ramsey #1	Donald W. McCarthy	1976	Viking
Col. George C. Lambert	1917–18	Ramsey #1	Robert S. Davis	1977–78	Indianhead
Charles D. Velie	1918–28	Minneapolis	C. William Briggs	1977–78	Viking
Walter J. Driscoll	1919	Ramsey #1	Roland D. Wilsey	1979–80	Indianhead
Foster Hannaford	1920–27	Ramsey #1	Ted Carlsen	1979–80	Viking
Clarence B. Randall	1928–34	St. Paul Area	John C. Ashton	1981	Indianhead
Frank Gold	1929–33	Minneapolis Area	Edward Landes	1981–82	Viking
J. H. Mitchell	1934–36	Minneapolis Area	Bruce A. Richard	1981–84	Indianhead
Carl W. Cummins	1935	St. Paul Area	Patrick W. Colbert, Jr.	1983–84	Viking
Reuben J. Hagman	1936–43	St. Paul Area	Richard L. Gunderson	1984–85	Indianhead
H. G. Irvine	1937	Minneapolis Area	G. Charles Hann	1985–86	Viking
Andrew B. Dygert	1938–42	Minneapolis Area	Howard M. Guthmann	1985–87	Indianhead
Arthur E. Larkin	1943–46	Minneapolis Area	Paul Curran	1987–88	Viking
Fred A. Waterous	1944–48	St. Paul Area	Jack F. Callaway	1987–89	Indianhead
Whitney H. Eastman	1947–48	Minneapolis Area	Paul A. Taylor	1989–90	Viking
Charles K. Velie	1949–50	Minneapolis Area	George B. Benz	1989–91	Indianhead
Norman H. Nelson	1949–51	St. Paul Area	Charlton Dietz	1991–93	Indianhead
John B. Faegre, Jr.	1951–52	Minneapolis Area	James W. Ladner	1991–94	Viking
John C. Parish	1952–54	Indianhead	Eugene U. Frey	1993–95	Indianhead
Lee A. Potter, Sr.	1953–54	Viking	Lowell C. Anderson	1994–96	Viking
Fred C. Andersen	1955–56	Indianhead	Kay L. Fredericks	1995–97	Indianhead
Sibbald Macdonald	1955–56	Viking	Alan Grove	1996–98	Viking
Robert C. Wood	1957–58	Viking	Winslow H. Buxton	1997–99	Indianhead
Hon. L. C. Shepley	1957–59	Indianhead	Robert Buhrmaster	1998–2000	Viking
Robert W. Dygert	1959	Viking	Steven Weekes	1999–2001	Indianhead
Edward B. Chapin	1960–61	Indianhead	Thomas Morgan	2000–2002	Viking
Raymond N. Beim	1960–61	Viking	James H. Bradshaw	2001–2003	Indianhead
Morrow Peyton	1962–63	Viking	Jo Marie Dancik	2002–2004	Viking
John M. Musser	1962–64	Indianhead	Michael J. Galvin, Jr.	2003–2005	Indianhead
W. N. Dickson	1964–65	Viking	Philip J. Johnson	2004–2005	Viking
Lester J. Asfeld	1965–67	Indianhead	Jon A. Theobald	2005	Indianhead
George McClintock	1966–67	Viking	Philip J. Johnson	2005–2007	Northern Star
Luther Ford	1968–69	Viking	Jon A. Theobald	2007–2009	Northern Star
John M. Budd	1970	Indianhead	Thomas H. Alt, MD	2009–	Northern Star

COUNCIL COMMISSIONERS

NAME	YEARS	COUNCIL	NAME	YEARS	COUNCIL
J. Q. Haas	1915–18*	Ramsey #1	Roland Wilsey	1976–78	Indianhead
Walter Buchanan	1919	Ramsey #1	Thomas H. Alt, MD	1976–77	Viking
George Whitney	1920–21	Ramsey #1	Robert Oldowski	1978–80	Viking
Clarence B. Randall	1922–27	Ramsey #1	J. Robert Stassen	1979–80	Indianhead
William S. Block	1924–39*	Minneapolis	Fred S. Hirsekorn	1981–82	Indianhead
Clifford J. Menz	1928–38	St. Paul Area	Patrick Colbert, Jr.	1981–82	Viking
Harry J. Frost	1939–44	St. Paul Area	Robert W. Rosene	1983–85	Indianhead
David Jones	1939–43	Minneapolis Area	Richard Dohrmann	1983–85	Viking
Howard Hush	1943–49	Minneapolis Area	Chuck Fiebig	1986–88	Viking
John M. Musser	1945–46	St. Paul Area	Thomas A. Holt	1986–88	Indianhead
C. O. Ellsworth	1947–52	St. Paul Area	Paul Wilson	1988–89	Viking
Joseph I. Gitlin	1950–59	Viking	James A. Lee	1989–92	Indianhead
Theodore H. Fenske	1953–54	St. Paul Area	John Stander	1990–91	Viking
Hon. L. C. Shepley	1955–56	Indianhead	Al Holler	1991–94	Viking
J. Clifford Janes	1957–61	Indianhead	Abner H. George Jr.	1993–96	Indianhead
Roger Frey	1960–63	Viking	Rich Dohrmann	1994–98	Viking
Roy W. Hawkinson	1962–68	Indianhead	William E. Rust	1997–2001	Indianhead
John Weaver	1964–68	Viking	J. Scott Woolery	1999–2001	Viking
Earl W. Nystrom	1969–72	Indianhead	Daniel J. Knuth	2002–2004	Indianhead
Ralph R. Lindblad	1969–71	Viking	Daniel T. Segersin	2002–2005	Viking
Loyal W. "Bud" Belk	1972–73	Viking	David L. Wettergren	2004–2005	Indianhead
Fred S. Hirsekorn	1973–75	Indianhead	Daniel T. Segersin	2005–2008	Northern Star
John J. Remes, Jr.	1974–75	Viking	Jon R. Pederson	2008–	Northern Star

First known use of the volunteer position in this council

SCOUT EXECUTIVES

NAME	YEARS	COUNCIL	NAME	YEARS	COUNCIL
J. A. Wauchope	1910–13	Ramsey #1	Judson G. Jusell	1952–60	Viking
C. W. Hadden	1911–17	Hennepin	Maynard Hanson	1960–61	Viking
E. B. Palmer	1913–15	Ramsey #1	L. Robert Killmer	1961–66	Indianhead
H. S. Sorrels	1915	Ramsey #1	Ray Williams	1961–72	Viking
Frank R. Neibel	1915–37	Ramsey #1	Carl M. Martindell	1967–70	Indianhead
Ludwig S. Dale	1918–23	Minneapolis	Norman E. Swails	1970–78	Indianhead
George S. Wyckoff	1923–32	Minneapolis Area	J. Thomas Ford	1972–77	Viking
John L. Tilden	1932–38	Minneapolis Area	Samuel Foust	1977–79	Viking
Elmaar Bakken	1937–40	St. Paul Area	Ronald A. Phillippo	1978–2000	Indianhead
L. D. Cornell	1938–46	Minneapolis Area	Clarence Hammett	1980–90	Viking
Fred Davie	1940	St. Paul Area	Donald Blacker	1990–2005	Viking
Paul L. Hesser, Sr.	1940–60	St. Paul Area	John R. Andrews	2000–2005	Indianhead
Robert Billington	1946–52	Minneapolis Area	John R. Andrews	2005–	Northern Star

COUNCIL NAMES, TERRITORIES, AND OFFICE LOCATIONS

Most people are aware that the council now known as Northern Star Council formed in 2005 when Minneapolis based Viking Council and St. Paul based Indianhead Council consolidated their operations into a single council. It is less widely known that at least a portion of the current geographic area of Northern Star Council was part of seven or more councils over the past one hundred years. In addition, before 2005, the former councils were known by several different names and they maintained offices in many locations.

The councils grew mostly by adding counties not already included in other existing councils. However, in two instances, existing councils were absorbed. In 1927, the newly named St. Paul Area Council added the counties of Dakota, Washington, and Chisago as well as the cities of Hudson and New Richmond in Wisconsin. This expansion apparently included the Stillwater Council (possibly known as the St. Croix Council), which was formed in 1922 when Stillwater broke off from Ramsey Council #1. In 1945, most of the Faribault-based South Central Minnesota Council merged with the St. Paul Area Council. All of the known changes in council names, boundaries and offices are traced below.

COUNCIL NAMES

Prior to 2005, the Minneapolis based council was known by the following names:

1910: Hennepin Council
1918: Minneapolis Council
1927: Minneapolis Area Council (this name was used on council letterhead, but the corporate name was not officially changed until 1937)
1952: Viking Council

Before 2005, the St. Paul-based council was known by the following names:

1910: Ramsey Council #1
1927: St. Paul Area Council
1955: Indianhead Council

CHANGES IN COUNCIL BORDERS

According to national BSA records, both the St. Paul and Minneapolis-based councils adjusted their borders on a regular basis over the years.

ST. PAUL

Between 1927 and 1965, the St. Paul-based council underwent twelve border changes.

1. Started with only Ramsey County on October 1, 1910.
2. Added the city of South St. Paul in 1918.
3. Added Stillwater, White Bear, Mahtomedi, Bald Eagle, Newport and St. Paul Park in 1919.
4. Stillwater withdrew to form its own council in 1922.
5. Added the Minnesota counties of Washington, Chisago, and Dakota and the Wisconsin communities of Hudson and New Richmond on December 28, 1927.
6. Added the rest of St. Croix and Polk Counties in Wisconsin on February 14, 1929.
7. Added Pierce County, Wisconsin on October 28, 1930.
8. Added Rice County, Minnesota from the South Central Minnesota Council on October 26, 1945.
9. Added the southern two-thirds of Scott County, Minnesota from South Central Minnesota Council on October 26, 1945.
10. Added Le Sueur County, Minnesota, except for Kasota, Cleveland, and Washington townships, from the South Central Minnesota Council on October 26, 1945.
11. Added Burnett County, Wisconsin from the Lake Superior Council on April 14, 1960.
12. Gave away Burnsville township of Dakota County, Minnesota to the Viking Council on April 18, 1960.
13. Added Linwood and Columbus township and Lino Lakes and Centerville Villages of Anoka County, Minnesota from the Viking Council on March 23, 1965.

MINNEAPOLIS

Similarly, there were eleven changes in the Minneapolis-based council's borders between 1927 and 1965.

1. Started with Hennepin County, Anoka County and part of Dakota County on October 15, 1910.
2. Added Meeker, McLeod, Isanti, Carver, Anoka, and Wright Counties (except Clearwater and Silver Creek townships) on October 20, 1927.
3. Added Yellow Medicine and Chippewa Counties on June 18, 1928.
4. Added the northern half of Renville County on June 18, 1928.
5. Added Kandiyohi County from the Central Minnesota Council on March 11, 1929.
6. Added the town of Albertville in Wright County from Central Minnesota Council on February 23, 1934.
7. Added the northern third of Scott County from the South Central Minnesota Valley Council on February 13, 1935.
8. Added Monticello and Otsego township of Wright County from the Central Minnesota Council on June 11, 1937.
9. Added Lac Qui Parle County from Pheasant Council on March 26, 1943.
10. Added Eden Valley and Kimball in Stearns County from the Central Minnesota Council on December 31, 1956.
11. Added Burnsville township in Dakota County from the Indianhead Council on April 18, 1960.
12. Gave away Linwood and Columbus townships and Lino Lakes and Centerville Villages of Anoka County to the Indianhead Council on March 23, 1965.

COUNCIL OFFICE LOCATIONS

The growing councils that were based in Minneapolis and St. Paul required sometimes frequent changes of address as they grew in size and staffing, often depending on donated or low-cost offices or homes for their first several decades of operation. The following is a listing of the various council office locations for the two primary councils over the years.

MINNEAPOLIS HEADQUARTERS

BUILDING NAME	LOCATION	DATE
YMCA Boys' House	Tenth St. & Mary Place	1910
Room "N" Main Building YMCA	Tenth St. & LaSalle	1911
Courthouse Basement, Room #26	4th St. & 4th Ave.	1915
414 Plymouth Building	6th St. & Hennepin	1917
Elks Building	210 S. Seventh St.	1921
Abbay Building	806 LaSalle St.	1924
334 Citizens Aid Building	4th Ave. S. & 8th St.	1927
819 Builders Building	15 N. 8th St.	1940
Transportation Building	317-319 2nd Ave. S.	1946
C. D. Velie Home	225 Clifton Ave.	1949
E. L. Carpenter Home	314 Clifton Ave.	1959
Dietrich Building	5300 Glenwood Ave.	1973

ST. PAUL HEADQUARTERS

BUILDING NAME	LOCATION	DATE
Dispatch Building	4th & Minnesota	1910
Endicott Building	4th & Robert Streets	1912
Old Capitol Building	10th & Cedar Streets	1916
Wilder Building	5th & Washington Streets	1926
St. Paul Building	5th & Wabasha Streets	1945
Rudolph Weyerhauser Home	266 Summit Ave.	1953
Charles L. Sommers Service Center/ Hulings Service Center	393 Marshall Ave.	1966

NORTHERN STAR COUNCIL SILVER BEAVERS

The Silver Beaver Award is the highest honor that a council can bestow on a Scouter. The award is conferred for distinguished service to youth upon the nomination of the chartered local Council. In addition to a person's Scouting background, consideration is given to service to community, state and nation—especially that part which concerns youth. This award is given for service "above and beyond normal duty" in keeping with the spirit of the "Daily Good Turn." Nominations are submitted to the local council committee for consideration and approval. Leaders at any level or any program are eligible.

1931: Hugh C. Arey | F.A. Bean | William S. Block | William N. Brown | Frank S. Gold | Samuel A. March | John Mitchell | B.H. Truman | E. F. Waite **1932:** Lester R. Badger | Dr. F. Davis | James Drew | J.O. Edwards | J.Q. Hass | Dietrich Lange | John M. Mason | Shirley Miller | Hon. G.M. Orr | C.B. Randall | J.F. Wrabek | Arthur Zache **1933:** W.A. Reynolds | John Tatam | Henry M.Thompson | F. Gordon Wright **1934:** John C. Bryant | J.W.G. Dunn | David Jones | Dr. R.R. Knight | Carl Peterson | Ralph W. Stanford **1935:** George M. Brack | C.M. Locke | George Oakes | Frank S. Preston | Mendus R. Velve | Edward L. Wilson **1936:** James W. Astle | A.N. Bearman | George Ghizoni | Joseph I. Gitlin | R.J. Hagman| Hon Gustav Loeinger | Arthur J. Sessing **1937:** Kyle G. Cudworth | P.B. Hinds | Dr. H.G. Irving | William Ridley | Charles L. Sommers | T.H. Sweetser **1938:** Dr. Edward R. Cooke | Harry J. Frost | A.H. Houser | D.J.A. Kjelland | C.J. Menz | I.H. Nickels | L.P. Reichmuth | H.L. Rothschild **1939:** C.S. Arnquist | Andrew Dygert | A.M. Endersbee | Lyman Gross | H.K. Scott | C.A. Thomas | H.T. Thornquist | Joseph E. Underwood **1940:** Judge Mathias Baldwin | Leonard M. Elstad | Carl G. Kaeppel | Arthur Kingsbury | Hon. C.F. McNally | A.B. Morgan | A.H. Stokes **1941:** H.A. Anderson | Archie McLane | D.B. Robinson | Frank K. Slaughter | John C. Wells **1942:** V.P. Baumann | Carl Erdman | Howard Hush | Dwight Milliren | Eric Tornstrom | Edward Waters | George S. Wyckoff **1943:** F.L. Lowe | George R. Manning | Rev. H.P. Nordby | W.W. Trenkner **1944:** K.A. Boss | Hon. K.G. Brill | Roy H. Haslund | Rev. W.J. Marks **1945:** Donald Hoffman | Earl Johnson | Arthur A. Kruse **1946:** Joseph A. Bachman | C.O. Ellsworth | Howard Freeman | E.R. Hawley | Arthur E. Larkin | Vern Lennartson | Silas Meckel | Paul Nelson | O.G. Nordlie | Fred Paul | Donald Purrington | C.W.Reid | C.A. Rolloff | Hon. L.C. Shepley | Thomas Tallakson | Charles Velie | W. Glen Wallace **1947:** Ralph Baumholfer | Floyd Davis | Whitney H. Eastman | Charles Eisler | Carl Flink | G.B. Gehrenbeck | T.J. Gibbons | John Hamer, Jr. | Sibbald MacDonald | Marcus Maynard | Milt Nordstrom | D.W. Umbehocker **1948:** Emmett Anderson | Blaine Barker | Henry Deboom | William Esh | Dennis Murphy | O.A. Nelson | Walter Oakes | William Porter | Myron A. Schweizer | Lenno Stelling | Dr. H.E. Stork | Fred. A.Waterous | A.W. Wulf **1949:** Cyrus P. Brown, Jr. | Austin B. Caswell | Frank Drassal | Joseph M. Eheim | Oscar A. Granum | H.D. van Krevelen | Ray Lacknar | Albert Larson | H. Hugh McKinnon | William Nilsen | Arthur Nygaard | A.G. Sirek | H.B. White | H.C. Wygant **1950:** Casper A. Butler | Morris Falk | William Fisher | Malcolm Johnson | Homer Luick | Joseph Morgan | Clyde Robinson | John Sjoquist | George M.R. Smart | William E. Stevens **1951:** William Braddock | John Burlingame | John Faegre | Percy Hopkins | Lloyd Johnson | Marvin Moen | Rolla Peters | Martin Peterson | Dr. Hugh Ritchie | Lester E. Swanberg | Paul Wethern **1952:** Guy Gardner | Walter Haase | Ralph Jacobson | Chas. E. Kneissel | Gustav C. Lohman | Carl Mayer | Max Parslow | Ralph Robinson | Herbert Rose | Lloyd Stivers | Dr. Chas. Tomasek | Alvin H. Weitkamp **1953:** Sam Bender | Alex P. Franke | Harold Gerick | Robert Gustafson | Lloyd Hasz | A. Hawsell Lang | Dr. E.E. Luhring | Donald Miller | John C. Parish | Dr. Lowell L. Rieke | Rudyard Robinson | Irvin F. Smith | Roger Stevens| Gordon Stuart **1954:** Fred C. Andersen | S.N. Bearman | Frederick Bjorklund | Everette W. Chilgren | O. Christopherson | Gerold T. Cotton | A. Donald Haight | Ray S. Hinds | William Kelly | Lee A. Potter | M.C. Rohweder | Reinhart E. Sitzer | Harold Ten Bensel | Oreland Thornsjo | Fritz Weber **1955:** Lincoln Aldritt | Sam Botten | John K. Donohue | G. Forrest Fabel | Boyd Fawkes | Joseph Frey | K.M. LaVine | Oliver A. Lumphrey | Norman H. Nelson | Rolland Packard | William Rilling | Joseph Schecker | Don Tuthill | George Westerlund **1956:** Irving Ames | P. Arthur Clucas | E.O. Dick | Warren E. Dickingson | Theodore H. Fenske | A.W. Fillmore | Luther Ford | Martin Fossum | Roger Frey | Walter R. Holbrook | Willis Johnson | Harry L. Kaye | Frank Moulton | Ralph Peterson | Harold H. Rose | Julian Thompson | Robert Wood **1957:** Virgil L. Anderson | Carl E. Barklind | Kenneth Boots | John M. Budd | Edward B. Chapin | Dr. Clifford Donehower | Leslie Edhlund | Fred Goth | Kenneth Granger | Roy W. Hawkinson | Lyndon S. Holm | Edward J. Huber | Hon. J. Clifford Janes | Eli Levinsohm | Leslie Mason | Theodore Myren | Philip H. Nason | Percy G. Nelson | Forrest R. Schmid | L.D. Shisler | Carroll N. Stenson | Hans Strand | John H. Swesey, Jr. | Stanley Thulin | William Tomlinson | Gabriel Torguson | A. Woolstencroft **1958:** Lester J. Asfeld | Delbert A. Cates | Vernon C. Cooper | Walter W. Flesher | J.K. Foster | Howard Guthmann | William Jaglo | Frederick M. Johnson | Howard Jorgesson | John Kirkvold | Alfred Larson | William E. Lyman | William A. Mahoney | Vincent C. Malmquist | Carl McBride | Gordon Meeker | Harry Moore | Morgan Olson | Harry A. Palm | Algene Peterson | Fred C. Thompson | Walter Ulberg | J. Kim Whitney **1959:** Dr. Louis M. Benepe | Curtis Bennyhoff | Guy B. Chase | Kasmer Dykoski | Stan Eddy | Wayne Foster | F. Patrick Hennessy | James Horner | H.F. Luebke | Robert Mathiason | Frank J. McArthur | Charles Mitchell | Douglas Nooleen | Kenneth Nygaard | John E. Schumm | Kenneth Springer | Edwin E. Stevens, Sr.

| Marcel D. Vax **1960:** Dr. Jack Anderson | William Arnold | Leland Bauck | Louis M. Benepe III | Orville Buehler | Paul M. Burson, Sr. | Dr. Harley Gaustad | George Jonassen | Dr. Mellen A. Knight | Arthur H. Kruse | Walter Larson | Fran Lartch | Alex G. LeVine | Orren F. Lundeen | John Lynch | Hon. Charles D. Madsen | Hugh Munns | Arvid Oas | Robert F. Plante | Robert Scherkenbach | Merton D. Towle | Donald L. Van Engen **1961:** Dr. Arnold S. Anderson | Raymond Beim | Victor Buskirk | Rene Carlson | Dr. Forrest E. Conner | Eugene Hablcht | Peter Heinrich | Jerome J. Jasinske | Harold Neuendorf | Sween O'Neill | Walter Pickens | Lawrence Roberts | Stan Rye | Frank J. Uebel | Gordon Yock | Ewald Otto Zochert **1961–62:** Hon. Elmer L. Andersen | Albert M. Beaunier | Albert G. Bell | Lloyd R. Gust | Hugh F. Gwin | Edwin Halvorsen | Arthur Johannsen | John H. Lloyd | Bernard McCoy | John M. Musser | Robert A. Nichols | Richard Simonson | Robert Smith **1962:** James "Doc" Berry | Carl Morris Carlson | Harold Ericson | Fred Osmer Kittell | Robert Lehman | William Lord | Howard Menter | Daniel Ronning | Melvin Sletten **1963:** Svend Bang | William Deutsche | Gustavas Eglajs | Willard E. Freeman | Garland Hubin | Lester Johnson | Harold Lafayette | Fred Lange | Reynold Clyde Malmquist | Murray McLagen | Leroy Nelson | Howard Nystrom | Carl Odmark | Samuel Parks | Morrow Peyton | Dr. Donald Schultz | Howard W. Schultz | Pershing Swenson | John Weaver **1964:** Kenneth Christiansen | Newell Deutscher | W.N. Dickson | Elmer Fennert | Isamu Higuchi | A.D. Hulings | Chauncey M. Kelsey | Wallace Kopisca | Howard MacMillian | Howard Milbert | Harold Eugene Miller | David P. Nachtsheim | Walter N. Norris | John L. O'Neill, Jr. | Archie Pease | Robert Quigley | Paul Schoberg | Alden Smith | Paul B. Tufte **1965:** Harry C. Anderson | Leonard Benson | John H. Birse | Vernon Bjork | Walter H. Diers | Willard Halldin | Bernard Johnson | Erich Kniebel | Carlton Magnuson | Robert McNeill | Morris E. Nicholson | Raymond M. Nickolay | August Pavel | Alden Russell | Richard Smith | Curtis E. Westerman | Roy Wilds **1966:** Charles Britzius | James L. Brown | Paul Clements | John Conley, Jr. | Ken Conway | James D. Durand | Arthur Elliot | Howard F. Garner | Max Hoemke | Eugene Krause | Joseph Kulbieda | Edwin Magnuson | George McClintock | Loyal T. McFarlane | George S. Mullen | Gilbert L. Peterson | Henry Seifert | Blake Shepard | Gil Snell | Patrick J. Towle | Joseph P. Walsh | Joe Weiser | Donald Wick **1967:** Fred C. Asche | Haldor M. Bly | Henry Boardman | Lucian Brown | Jack Deckenbach | Paul Foss | Albert Holler | Carl W. Homstrom | William A. Jordon | Adolph Kupka | Clifford Mathias | Russell B. McCall | Owen Munkholm | William B. Randall | Stephen Roskos | Raymond Rossbach | Douglas E. Sautbine **1968:** Loyal Belk | Herman Borg | Morry Gale | Roger Halvorsen | Gladstone C. Hill | Clayton Johnson | Dr. Clive Kelsey | Eugene Koch | Ken Luikart | Dwight Marriott | Robert Mullin | James O'Connell | Lloyd Olson | Willis Rich | Duane Scritchfield | Conrad Stai | T.O. Vaala | Duane Van Orsow | Leslie A. Walther **1969:** Paul Adams | Anthony Bechik | Wilmer Boeder | William Eddy | Ben Greer | Ricard Hoglund | George Johnson | Merrill M. Kuller | Harvey W. Leach | Raymond A. Lepsche | John Miller | Carl Peterson | Chester Sahlin | Marvin Simon | Leonard Solum | Bernard M. Troje **1970:** Donald Bloedow | James Burlingame | Willis Butterfield | Verdie Gilbertson | Sherwood Grondin | Robert C. Johnson | Floyd Joynes | Warren Kirk | Kenneth Person | Walter Quast | C. Graham Seymour | Dean Townsend **1971:** Ronald Boles | Fr. John T. Brown | Howard Christiansen | Helen Egberg (Fawn)* | Arnold Erickson | Don Gabbert | Clifton Gustafson, Jr. | Lorna Holm (Fawn) | Richard A. Johnson | Robert W. Johnson | Donald Kees | George Looby | Warren Lynch | Ted Melander | Louis W. Menk | Arthur Morris | Norma Nicholson (Fawn) | Craig L. Parker | William Prentice | Patricia Ross (Fawn) | Leonard Samuelson | Robert Schenkel | Elwin D. Shaner | Arthur Shull | Elaine Weiser (Fawn) **1972:** Albert Barke | Jerry Barthman | Arthur Bauman | Joseph J. Blaha | Richard J. Carroll | Dr. Thaddeus Chao | Ralph Davis | Mark Dewolf | James Dols | Jose Galdiano | Aileen Hookom (Fawn) | Raymond Johnson | William Kirchner | Charles Kramer | Carol Kwiecien (Fawn) | John Kwiecien | Ed Landes | Merle I. Maidin | Loren Ness | Clarence North | Albin Oswood | Milton L. Thompson | Will Tingerthal | Jackie Zahn (Fawn) **1973:** Ralph Albinson | Charles Anderson | Arlene Brattain (Fawn) | Neil Christian | Wilbur Cleveland | Annette Doughty (Fawn) | Bernard Dubois | George Duffy | Virgil Farmer | Sidney Froman | B. Galdiano (Fawn) | Joy Golden (Fawn) | Paul Haney | John Hoffner | Carolyn Johnson (Fawn) | James Kenady | Edwin M. Knight | Shirley Knoll (Fawn) | Martin Koivula | Delores Lehn (Fawn) | Kathryn T. Marquardt (Fawn) | Thomas W. McKeowan | James McKinney | Frederick Miller | Viola Moser (Fawn) | E. Dudley Parsons | Edward R. Peterson | Dr. Theodore Peterson | Edwin Stege | Sylvester Ulsrud | Al Wehr | Howard W. Wilcox | Charles Zahn **1974:** Pat Awold (Fawn) | Rolf Bjelland | Carl Carlson | Rosalie Christensen (Fawn) | Gordon Cleaveland | Rev. Clifford Crook | James Eckberg | Fred S. Hirsekorn | Amelia Hodges | Ken Hookom | Wally Houts | Frederic Irvin | George Jaeger | Robert Jensen | Lester Kelly | Donald Lloyd | Earl Loudon. Dean Mathews | Betty McVey | Dr. Robert Moore | Gerald H. Olson | Robert Parent | Betty Paugh | John F. Proesch | Mariane Rasmussen (Fawn) | John J. Remes | Barbara Shaner | Judie Sorensen (Fawn) | Richard Stromberg | Edmund A. Stuart | James Thomas | Alena Wickland (Fawn) **1975:** Elmer Althaus | Earl J. Bailey | Richard E. Carroll | Pat Colbert | Shirley Dittbrenner | Gray Erick | Al Faulkner | Charles W. Greene | William B. Hershe | Richard Holmberg | Dr. Gordon W. Hovdey | Rev. W.F. Howard | Harold A. Hudachek | Leonard Japs | Roger A. Johnson | Ronald P. Keller | John Kennedy | Marlene Maeser | Howard Mooers | Marvin Nelson | Edward A. O'Mara | John Parker | Marilyn Pulliainen | Lawrence H. Ross | Joseph Sepka | Allen Wiig | George A. Wright **1976:** John C. Ashton | Fay Buss | John Crowther | Eugene L. Dickinson | Fay E. Ehlenfeldt | Bernard J. Eklund | Robert Hansen | Betty Heath | Robert Herbst | Don Hodges | Gary Holstad | Ralph Howe | George Jones | Charles LaVaque | Donald Mackin | Donald McCarthy | Donald McShannock | Lyle Mottinger | Peter Nelton | Earl W. Nystrom | Clyde Ruebel | Joanne Schmidt | Henry W. Schreiber | Martin Thames | Gerald A. Tiger **1977:** John S. Bowers | Donald Breining | Dr. C. Edward Buchwald | Ted Carlsen | Richard Dohrmann | Vernon F. Engebretson | Merle R. Erickson | Harold Hiles | John Jagger | Joseph Kadlec | William Kircher | Elmer McVey | Jerome Peterson | Robert Rosene | Gerald Salsbery | Daniel B. Schultz | William J. Smith | Duncan Steinman | Daniel Walsh **1978:** Robert R. Anderson, Sr. | David J. Apold | Anthony Benkusky | David Bieniasz

| Don Breitenstein | C. William Briggs | Loren Cowden | Robert Dwyer | Russell L. Edhlund | C.R. Ginsburg, Jr. | Donald Hannah | Erling Johnson | Gunnar Kronholm | Darrel Larson | Dennis Lund | Lloyd McAninch | Robert Oldowski | Dexter Pehle | Gary A. Ruud | Lou Schroth | E.H. Stock | Gary Valencour | Donald Wells | Roland D. Wilsey | Elizabeth Ziebarth **1979:** Marianne Anderson | John A. Basinger, Jr. | Marilyn L. Beach | Harry Beardsley, Sr. | Darle Blade | John F. Callaway | Robert S. Davis | Alan Hasse | Richard Johnson | Donald R. Jorgenson | Doran J. Knuth | Fr. Lee Krautkremer | William Lundholm | James Monroe | Lyman Earl Ransom | Oris Rost | Mrs. Harold J. Slawik | Ed Snelgrove | Martin Snoke | Mark Strong | Gib Swanson | Darlo Tetrick | F. Duane Tooley | John C. Torseth **1980:** Valerie Anderson | Tomas A. Holt | Paul Johnson | Richard Johnson | Donald Jorgensen | Charles Kirk | James Ladner | John Lunn | Ralph McLean | Dave Moore | Wallace Mund | Ted Newcomb | George Patterson | William G. Peterson | Robert Pitts | Don Rosvold | David Ryerse | Warren Sanborn | Richard Schaller | Milo Simacek | Clarence Sjodin | Harold Smeby | David Swanson | Frederick E. Wobig **1981:** Thomas E. Anthony | John D. Barry | Arno Dittbrenner | Robert D. Eggert | Donald Esman | Chris Grunke | Duane Haugan | Allan S. Henry | Haakan Henstein | Walter Johnson | Virgil LeBlanc | Donald L. Miller | Gary Morris | John H. Nipp | Carol Oldowski | Don Peterson | John Phillips | Leon L. Pittman | Don Schlaefer | Henry N. Teipel | Terry N. Thompson | Malcolm Van Dyke | Mark Walker **1982:** James A. Anderson | William Baker | Arley Bjella | Elmer Campbell | Toni J. Collins | Elden Eklund | Don Elmquist | Charles Hann | Suzette M. Heinze | Richard Huntley | Dee Jones | Phil Martineau | William Nolan | Norman Peterson | Charles Philpott | Harold Schnarr | Robert Shoush | Richard Silverstein | Oren Steinfeldt | Richard Swanson | Donald R. Swenson | John Twohig **1983:** Edwin Anderson | George Carlson | Bruce Cary | Ed Dressen | John Eckstein | Ruby Farmer | Ron Haase | Gary Hart | Ed Hatlem | Henry Hauer | Ambrose Johnson | Fred Johnson | Lou Kittleson | Boyd Larson | Albert Linder | Mel Lyon | Charles Nelson | Harold Nelson | Roy Nelson | Joan M. Nowlan | James R. Peterson | Ronald Prekker | Joseph Reymann | Wayne Sheridan | Oscar "Pete" Snyder | Dr. David Truaz **1984:** Roy Franklin Anderson | Dale W. Faulds | Rolland D. Giebe | Roger E. Pietsch | David W. Schmidtke | Dennis F. Sherman | Laverne E. Sherman | Daniel J. Smith | Eugene M. Stearns | Doyle L. Strong | Alfred Twist | Ronald E. Werden, Ph.D **1985:** Paul A. Bartyzal | Dennes Borman | Bernard Braun | Richard J. Diedrich | Gustav Erickson | William Feyo | Robert W. Frits | John Gehrman | Bob Haugen | Earl Hobbs | Ana Jean Johnson | Jerry P. Kersten | Robert Leary | Loren Meinke | George Neilsen | Rod Nelson | Walter Oesterreich | Axel E. Olseen, Jr. | Keith Alen Olson | Dennis Pederson | Warren E. Phillips | Verne B. Porter | Elizabeth Reed | Phillip Schorn | Edward Schuster | Edwin "Fred" Snyder | Stephen Sprint | Phillip L. Williams **1986:** Bernard N. Backes | George Baldwin | Gene Clemens | Mike Connor | Paul Curran | Neil Diamond | Fred Dravis | Gene Dufty | Robert Fulton | Barbara Corti Herrmann | Charles Huntley | George Kydd | Paul Lanner | Doug Lees | Captain Michael McGinn | Miles McNiff | LeRoy Nordrum | Teresa O'Neal | Bruce A. Richard | Richard Setter | Bruce Sothern | Gene Steinmetz | Curt Thorfinnson | Art Torseth **1987:** Katherine B. Andersen | Alan Bakke | William Belanger | Al Gitzen | Joseph Glaccum | Richard Green | Jerry Harrington | Ann Herbert | Richard Holden | Marilee Huntley | Kathy Johnson | Carman Keinberger | Michael Lynch | Daryl Moberg | Robert Nelson | Edwin Onstott | Thomas Parker | Fred L. Paul, Jr. | James Pederson | Dorothy Revoir | Fred Riehm | Leo Dennis Roos | Donald Stolz | Gene Temple | Joseph Toone | Virginia Tretter | Douglas Wood **1988:** David N. Bredeson | Don Buck | Edward Bungert | Harvey Golub | John S. Keefe | Prentice Merrill | Woody Numainville | Robert Smith | Joseph B. Steen | Paul Taylor | Paul Wilson | Robert Zeman **1989:** William Boecker | Edward C. Dike, Jr. | Barry Downs | Ellen Dudley | William Duncan | Carol S. Forrest | James H. Forrest | George A. Haun | Lawrence T. Hosch | Will Jass | Susan Ketel | Don Lauver | Barbara J. Leier | Verna Liljenquist | Floyd Miller | Arthur Moen | Gerald Oss | Richard Peterson | Thomas Reyes | Jeanne M. Schadt | Forrest Lee Sexson | William F. Sheffield | Kathleen A. Smith | Tom Sopoci | Thomas B. Wilhelmson | Edward Wink | Joyce Zeman **1990:** Gary Anderson | Barry K. Bain | Robert S. Davis Banks | Burton M. Barber | Ronald Christenson | Darlene M. Collins | Marie E. Cravens | Marge Dillenburg | George A. Graven, Jr. | Keith Howard | Richard L. Johnson | Delorus "Dee" Klawitter | Harold Kleven | David E. Klinkhammer, Sr. | James Lee | Dr. Philip A. Lyon | Roy P. Nauertz, Jr. | Arden Olson | John T. Paprocki | Phillip Popehn | Larry Rich | Robert Sales | Roger M. Schadt | Benjamin Smith | Marvin "Stoney" Stonecipher | Reuben H. Swanson, Sr. | Mary Rosanne Washy **1991:** George B. Benz | John Bergmann | Gary Corpron | Clyde H. Coulter | Henri A. Eisenhauer, Sr. | Will Endsley | Darrell Gagnon | John M. Gerenz | Michael M. Gregory | Nancy Harrington | Arnie Hermanson | Gerald R. Hufman | Robert H. Johnston | Virginia Kagol | Lewis Orans | John Pavik | James Pendergast | Sherwood R. Pomeroy | Linda H. Rawlings | Don Rinkenberger | Gary F. Rogers | R. Lee Runyon | Dennis Schroeder | John Stander | Richard Tyrrell | Robert Ubelhoer, Sr. | Marlys J. Vierling | Thomas Wolter **1992:** Sandra J. Albright | Timothy G. Barrett | Edward Bokusky | Sherman Boraas | Paul E. Cravens | Bill Davies | David R. Denn | Gene Eggleston | Nancy Fairbairn | Graham Ford | Robert Garretson | Charles Gernes | Joseph W. Glenski | Dale Haag | Fred Hack | Richard P. Halverson | Donald Howard | William A. Jones | Lawrence P. Sachi | Marilyn Sobiech | Gene Stobbs | Kathy Stobbs | I. Lamon Thomson **1993:** Kenneth Avery | Daniel L. Bartholic | Bill Bushnell | Pamela (Waterman) Caudy | Don Clough | Maurice Devitt | Lois Dillree | Cherryl A. Evans | Kay L. Fredericks | Al Grove | Dennis E. Hebrink | Elliot Herland | Chuck Hively | Keith D. Hobbie | David Holmberg, Sr. | Richard Koechlein | Terry Kubista | Duane Leier | Bill Lockwood | Anita Miller | Linda H. Popa | Robert Provost | Robert E. Raymond, D.V.M. | Gary P. Salsman | Elaine Sinn | Pete Stibal II | Jim Stillson | Richard Weber **1994:** Tom Brown | John A. Chamberlain | Robert T. Dahl | Mary Degel | Charlton Dietz | Margaret Ann Dravis | Stephen L. Engel | Abner H. George, Jr. | Charles L. Hawley | Soni Horst | Thomas A. Hunter | James H. Jaros | John Kennedy, Jr. | F. Alexandra Klas | James B. Mosner | Jeff Nelson | Pat Noack | Bob O'Fallon | Cole Petersen | Dave Recker | James H. Rupert | Dave Smith | Kim Smith | Ron Taylor | Kent Vesper | Jack Woodhall | Gordon J. Wyman **1995:** Larry Bakken | Daniel Beaudoin | Gary Cayo | Dick Custer | Louis

Dessellier, Jr. | Gregg Grudzinski | David A. Hart | Pete Huber | Don Jacques | Gregory A. Johnson | Brenda Kreuger | Craig Lewis | Lawrence G. Litzkow | Carol Magnuson | Bill Michaelson | Paul Olson | Robert E. Pettitt | Joseph A. Reding | Gary Reisdorph | Dan Segersin | Bob Skogrand | Robert D. Swanson | Merlin Thorn | Steven E. Weekes | Richard Weiss | William Woolever, Jr. **1996:** William Barington | Gary Bebeau | Larry Berg | Stanley M. Berkner | William V. Block | Alfred "Fred" Boulay | Donald Clark | Lloyd Dewey | Scott Howe | Carl "Bill" Ireland | Lee Johnson | Varland Jay Lenz | Stephen Mitton | David R. Novy | Pat Obertin | Jon Pederson | Marie Petersen | Sam Rossi | John Rotert | John "Jack" Rothecker | Bonnie Rowell | Charles Schwoch | J. Kevin Scott | Kenneth Skoglund | Matthew A. Smith | Vern Steppe | Robert W. Strom | Thomas Turba | David Waugh | J. Scott Woolery **1997:** Lowell Anderson | Edward Bunning | Edward Burns | Fred Crawford | Scott Degel | Lindsay Fenwick | Nicholas Heille | Ross House | William Howard | Richard Howe | Fred Hunt | Lynn Johnson | Daniel J. Knuth, Ph.D. | William Larson, Jr. | Michael D. Lund | Donald Manion | Donald McCall | Brian P. McNally | Keith Ottoson | Kenneth Pauley | Thomas Schilling | Joan Schwoch | James Senst | Thomas G. Strom | William L. Sulzbach | Helen Thorn | Donald W. Warhol | Cynthia Wulf | Richard Zaczek | Michael Zastera | Joseph P. Ziskovsky **1998:** Daniel J. Broten | Kenneth Dubois | Galen Erickson | Norbert Gernes | Jerome Hanson | Walter Herbst | Peter Johnson | John Kubicek | Michael Lennon | Donald E. Marose | Dianne Marth | Robert Mathewson | Barbara Matthews | Luverne Moldenhauer | Thomas Morgan | Daniel K. Nelson | David Erland Olson | Joel Ostgaard | Stephen Puetz | William E. Rust | Carol Segersin | Robert Smith | Dean Soderbeck | Jerome Swanson | Joyce Wilson | David G. Wuest **1999:** Michael Joseph Aeling | Bob Wayne Baker | Gerald C. Bird | James Campbell | James Colby | Carole A. Crawford | Bob Dykoski | Lynn Englehorn | Sharon Fertig | Bradford W. Fitzgerald | Marcia L. Gregory | Daniel Hess | Richard M. Johnston | Martha Kasper | Lawrence Krakowski | Larry Lindor | Dan Millenacker | Randy Miller | Dawn (Whiteside) Nelson | Kenneth Porter | Lonna Rahn | Lynne Tellers | Greg Thomes | Clyde Thurston | Bonnie M. Timm | Marvin Williams | Steve Young **2000:** Carole Althoff | Vickie Bakken | Robert Buhrmaster | Jeffery Coleman | Dwight Crisman | Gerald Gagner | Glenn Holmen | Emil "Sonny" Jirik | David Keymer | Mark Kuhl | John Langenbach | Todd S. Levig | Jeffrey Maltby | Linda Miller | Thomas G. Miller | Veidols Muiznieks | Fr. Thomas O'Brien, O.S.C. | Earl Olson | Sophie Pederson | Gregg Peterson | Gary Plantenberg | John Rowell | Mark Joseph Salmen | Ed Sims | Eric Sit | Mike Slobodnik | Todd Tingblad | Roger Wherry | Sandy Zmeskal **2001:** Thomas Allinder | Deborah Baker | Charles Bredeson | Dave Bronson | Lila Caron | Joseph Fitzharris | Loren Fokken | William Fredrick | Thomas Hawkinson | Rodger Hessedal | Richard Howey | Norman Johnson | Robert Koepke | Neil Larsen | James May | George Mueller | Doug Neitzel | Charles Opp | Greg Popehn | James Rice II | Thomas Rossbach | Noel Sagness | Mark Tande | Julie Terpstra | David Thielman | Lloyd Walburn | Joel Wiest | Kurt Zilley **2002:** David L. Borka | Reed Bornholdt | Curtis Brazier | Dr. Kenneth W. Crabb | Joe (Skip) Cunningham | John H. Guthmann | Robert J. Hannah, Sr. | Robert Irish | Keith Kamrath | Steven M. Krech | Beatrice Murphy | Julie A. Nitti | Richard Nylin | Stephen Perry | Raymond H. Ralston | Brett Rasmussen | Craig Reichert | Chris Sandberg | Joseph Showalter | Michael D. Stoddard | Jeffrey Sunderberg | Grant F. Tiefenbruck | John Tinucci | Jeff Walton | Thomas J. Welna | Steven Wilcox **2003:** Dr. Daniel Ahlberg | Michael Althoff | Gurtie Berkner | James Bradshaw | Steve Carpenter | Denice Cousineau | Daniel Engel | Tim Evans | Alan Johnson | Dave Johnson | Mark Johnson | Keith Krause | Ed Morse | Albert Nuness | Craig Paulson | Marie Rice | Mark Sathe | Dennis Selbitschka | James Taylor | Darwin TeBeest | Brenda Tiefenbruck | Dr. John Wahlstrom | Eileen "Mitzi" Welna | Diane Westmoreland | Sam Williamson, Jr. | Philip Zietlow **2004:** John Adamek, Sr. | Allan Boyce | Floyd Caron | Jo Marie Dancik | Maureen Espelien | Robert Gard | Bruce Haverly | Cheryl Heimerl | Carl Hendrickson | Robert "Scotty" Hewitt | Arthur Holle | Ron Jacobson | Paul Klein | Patrick Lombardo | Herb Miller | Jerald Mortensen | Dave Roberts | Kevin Schwarzbauer | John Severance | Curtis Stoltz | Karen Theisen | Rae Ann Trinka | Thomas Tweit | Robert Walsh | Mary Wangerin | Mary Zalazar **2005:** Richard Baer | Judy Bedor | Jerry Brokaw | John Caldwell | George Cusick | John Czech | Barbara Engel | Steven Erickson | Michael Galvin, Jr. | Randall Greenly | Jeanne Holland | Barbara Jirik | Phil Johnson | David Kasper | Daniel Lenort | James Letourneau, Sr. | William Matthews, Sr. | Tim Morris | Richard Oehmke | Chris Sellner | Rich Sperry | Lynn Swon | Beth Toutges | Duane (Joe) Wherry | Steven Wojan | Ralph Zalazar **2006:** Faith Anderson | Dave Baden | Margaret Brunner | Kim Brynildson | Gary Chapman | Chad Claude | Laurie Johnson | Pam Kiley | Allen Kupka | Walter Lange | Cheryl Leifermann | Jerome Malmquist | Roger McCabe | Cal Miner | David Misemer | Mark Neuman | Karl Nordberg | Terry Peterson | Tom Polzin | Tom Rockne | Kay Stewart | Dave Wettergren | Raymond Wood **2007:** George Abide | Steven Ackerman | Judy Christensen | Rebecca Englehart | William Falconer | Kelly Glover | Phillip Goodrich | Mark Hansen | Mel Hoagland | Daniel Hurley | Pam Jerve | David Jungkunz | Edward Kadlec | Doug King | Corey Kline | Gary Kwong | Carl Meincke | John Mills | Jamie Niss Dunn | Greg Nonweiler | John Olson | Joan Smith | Charles Wangerin | Peter Wickert **2008:** Stephen Anderson | Todd Bollig | William Butchee | John Capecchi | James Corniea | Lee Corti | Lewis Ely | Kurt Fischer | Michael Gardner | John Hanson | Elizabeth Hoffmann | Curtis LaClaire | Kenneth Lillemo | Miranda Oliver | Don Peterson | Charles Podominick | John Raymond | Twyla Sietsema | Tony Smith | Christopher Tashjian | Jon Theobald | William Trinka | Daniel Valentine | Steven Vasey **2009:** Brian Bullock | J. Peter Devine | Doug Farmer | James Fitch | Robert Gavigan | Debbie Greiner | Roger Hagerman | Scott Harvey | Randy Johnson | Rusty Johnson | Maggie Knuteson | Steve Larson | Deb Lyons | Ted McLaughlin | Randy Miller | Richard Neuner | Bruce Paulson | Jack Piepel | Craig Reid | Joanne Robbins | Dave Roehler | Richard Thomalla | Steve Weber

* The Silver Fawn was the first award for women Cub Scouters (women were not accepted in the Boy Scout program at that time). The Silver Fawn was introduced in 1971 and discontinued in 1974 when women began receiving the same award as men, the Silver Beaver.

CAMPS OF THE NORTHERN STAR COUNCIL AND PREDECESSORS

	NAME	COUNCIL	LOCATION	DATES OF OPERATION
1	Camp St. Croix	St. Paul	South of Hudson, WI	1910; 1917 (established by St. Paul YMCA in 1909)
2	Crocker's Point	Minneapolis	Harrison Bay, Lake Minnetonka	1911–1912
3	Maxwell's Bay AKA Camp Rotary (1918)	Minneapolis	Maxwell's Bay, Lake Minnetonka	1913–1920
4	Silver Lake Camp	St. Paul	Silver Lake, North St. Paul	1913–1915
5	Lake Charlotte Camp	St. Paul	6 miles NW of Rockford	1916
6	Lake Emily Camp	St. Paul	4 miles north of Como Park	1917
7	Square Lake Camp AKA Oak Point Camp	St. Paul	8 miles north of Stillwater	1918–1937
8	Camp Tonkawa	Minneapolis	North Arm, Lake Minnetonka	1921–1965
9	Camp Pa-Hu-Ca	Faribault, St. Paul (obtained through merger with South Central Minnesota Council in 1945)	Fish Lake near Lydia	1921–1952
10	Rice Creek Camp AKA Camp Manomin (1931)	Minneapolis	Confluence of Mississippi River and Rice Creek, near Fridley	1927–1965
11	St. Croix River Camp AKA Fred C. Andersen Scout Camp (1965)	St. Paul, Indianhead, Northern Star	4 miles above Stillwater on the Wisconsin side of the river	1928–Present
12	Camp Robinson Crusoe AKA Camp Wawatasso (1936)	Minneapolis	Dunlap (AKA Wawatasso) Island, Lake Minnetonka	1928–1942
13	Isle of Pines AKA Camp Iyota (1935)	Minneapolis	Bay Lake near Deerwood	1929–1946
14	Nest Lake Camp	Minneapolis	Eastern shore of Nest Lake, north of Spicer	1935–1946
15	Camp Sylvia AKA Camp Stearns (1942)	Minneapolis	Lake Sylvia, west of Annandale	1936–1983
16	Camp Neibel	St. Paul	Balsam Lake, Polk County, WI	1937–1954
17	Many Point Scout Camp	Minneapolis, Viking, Northern Star	Near Ponsford	1946–Present
18	Cedar Camp	Minneapolis	South Cedar Avenue, Minneapolis	1947–1968
19	Long Lake Camp AKA Tomahawk Scout Reservation (1955)	St. Paul, Indianhead, Northern Star	Long Lake near Rice Lake, WI	1953–Present
20	Rum River Scout Camp	Viking	Ramsey	1957–Present
21	Cannon River Scout Reservation AKA Phillippo Scout Reservation (2000)	Indianhead, Northern Star	Byllesby Reservoir between Randolph and Cannon Falls	1965–Present
22	Camp Heritage AKA Camp Stearns (1984)	Viking, Northern Star	Near Annandale	1966–Present
23	Kiwanis Scout Camp	Indianhead, Northern Star	Marine on St. Croix	1989–Present (established by St. Paul Kiwanis Club in 1922)
24	Eagle Landing	Indianhead, Northern Star	St. Croix River, across from Marine on St. Croix	2003–Present
25	Base Camp	Northern Star	Fort Snelling	2008–Present

TABLE OF CONTENTS FOR CENTENNIAL HISTORY DVD

As a supplement to the centennial history book, Northern Star Council has produced a commemorative DVD. The DVD contains numerous items of historical interest for which there was simply no room in the book. The DVD is included in the purchase price of the hardcover edition or it may be separately purchased. What follows is the DVD Table of Contents.

I. Introduction – "100 Years of Northern Star Council" video

II. Centennial Commission Members

III. Important Contributors to the First Century of Northern Star Council

    A. Youth Recognitions
1. Eagle Scouts
2. Outstanding Eagle Scout Award Recipients
3. Young American Award Recipients
4. Venturing Silver Award Recipients
5. Life Saving Award Recipients
6. National and Regional Venturing Leadership

    B. Adult Recognitions
1. Council Key Three (Presidents, Scout Executives, Council Commissioners)
2. Camp Rangers
3. Silver Beaver/Silver Fawn Award Recipients
4. Silver Antelope Award Recipients
5. Silver Buffalo Award Recipients
6. Distinguished Eagle Scout Award Recipients
7. Eagle-to-Eagle Award Recipients
8. Distinguished Citizen Award Recipients
9. Distinguished Community Builder Award Recipients
10. Scoutmaster of Philanthropy Recipients
11. William D. Boyce Award Recipients
12. F. Alexandra Klas and Max Hoempke Special Needs Scouting Award Recipients
13. Spurgeon Award Recipients
14. International Scouting Recognition

    C. Institutional Recognition
1. Northern Star Council Chartered Partners as of December 31, 2008
2. Chartered Partners with 25 or more years of continuous tenure

IV. Totanhan Nakaha Lodge, Order of the Arrow

    A. History of Totanhan Nakaha, Agaming, and Tonkawampus Lodges

    B. Important Contributors to our Order of the Arrow Lodges
1. National Vice Chiefs and Section/Region Chiefs
2. Lodge Chiefs and Lodge Advisers
3. Vigil Honor Award Recipients
4. Distinguished Service Award Recipients
5. Founder's Award Recipients
6. Red Arrow Award Recipient
7. E. Urner Goodman Camping Award

V. History Book Supplemental Material/Photographs Organized by the Subject Chapters

    A. Troop
    B. Achievement
    C. Outing
    D. Camp
    E. Gathering
    F. Jamboree
    G. Service
    H. Scouter

VI. Information on Independent Local Organizations that Provide Scouting Support

    A. Tomahawk Alumni Association
    B. Many Point Staff Alumni Association
    C. North Star Museum of Boy Scouting and Girl Scouting
    D. Order of the Odor/Skunks
    E. Bunny Bearman Museum
    F. Troop 39
    G. Pine Bend Scouters Association

VII. Council Identities, Geography, and Properties 1910–2010

    A. Map of current Council boundaries
    B. Map of Council boundaries—1927
    C. Map listing camp names and showing camp locations 1910–2010
    D. Council names, territories, and office locations 1910–2010

VIII. Locally Produced Scouting Advertising

IX. Excerpts from Historical Films/Videos

NOTES

Abbreviations Used in Notes:

AH   *Anoka Herald*

AU   *Anoka County Union*

BP   *Be Prepared* (Minneapolis Area Council Newsletter)

CC   *Council Close-ups* (Indianhead Council Newsletter)

CE   *Cokato Enterprise*

CRH   *Coon Rapids Herald*

DT   *Dakota County Tribune*

FDN   *Faribault Daily News*

MHS   Minnesota Historical Society

MJ   *Minneapolis Journal*

MS   *Minneapolis Star*

MSJ   *Minneapolis Star Journal*

MST   *Minneapolis Star Tribune*

MT   *Minneapolis Tribune*

NYT   *New York Times*

SD   *St. Paul Dispatch*

SDN   *St. Paul Daily News*

SPD   *St. Paul Pioneer Press/Dispatch*

SPP   *St. Paul Pioneer Press*

All council documents from Northern Star Council Archives unless otherwise noted.

INTRODUCTION

1. *SPP,* August 28, 1910.
2. Robert W. Peterson, *The Boy Scouts: An American Adventure* (New York: American Heritage, 1984), 20-32; 58.
3. R.D. Bezucha, *The Golden Anniversary Book of Scouting* (New York: Golden Press, 1959), 27.
4. *SPP,* March 24, 1912.
5. Elvin Heiberg, "Northfield Early Scout History" speech, Carleton College, Northfield, MN, March 27, 2009.
6. *SPP,* August 28, 1910.

1910s

1. Peterson, *Boy Scouts,* 51.
2. *SPP,* September 4, 1910.
3. Ibid.
4. Ibid., September 19, 1910.
5. Ibid., October 2, 1910.
6. *MT,* October 2, 1910; Hennepin Council minutes, October 15, 1910; *MJ,* August 18, 1935.
7. "The Founding of Ramsey Council #1 BSA," 1935.
8. C.D. Lundin, "Recollections of the Origin of Scouting in St. Paul," 1927.
9. Hennepin Council minutes, April 5, 1911.
10. *SPP,* April 16, 1911.
11. Ibid., April 23, 1911.
12. B.M Bailey to "The Chief Scout Master," March 27, 1911, St. Paul-Ramsey County War History Committee, Box 103.K.7.6F, MHS.
13. *SPP,* November 6, 1910.

14. *MJ,* May 6, 1911; *SPP,* May 7, 1911.
15. *SPP,* March 3, 1912.
16. *MJ,* June 3, 1911.
17. Hennepin Council minutes, April 11, 1912.
18. Ibid., October 21, 1912.
19. Ibid.
20. "Boy Scouts of Hennepin Council Registered at National Headquarters," December 24, 1915.
21. F. R. Neibel to "Gentlemen," October 17, 1916, St. Paul-Ramsey County War History Committee, Box 103.K.7.7B, MHS.
22. H.S. Sorrels to National Headquarters, B.S. of A., April 9, 1914, St. Paul-Ramsey County War History Committee, Box 103.K.7.7B, MHS.
23. Frank Neibel to Walter P. McGuire, December 19, 1917, St. Paul-Ramsey County War History Committee, Box 103.K.7.7B, MHS.
24. *MT,* November 4, 1917.
25. Frank Neibel to Walter P. McGuire, December 19, 1917, St. Paul-Ramsey County War History Committee, Box 103.K.7.7B, MHS.
26. *MJ,* February 28, 1918.
27. *MT,* May 5, 1918.
28. *SDN,* April 18, 1918.
29. *MT,* November 10, 1918.
30. Ibid., April 29, 1918.
31. Ibid., November 10, 1918.
32. Ramsey Council, "Semi-Annual Report, Scout Commissioner," 1919.
33. *MT,* June 14, 1919.
34. David Martinez, *Dakota Philosopher: Charles Eastman and American Indian Thought* (St. Paul: Minnesota Historical Society Press, 2009), 7; Karin Luisa Badt, *Charles Eastman: Sioux Physician and Author* (New York: Chelsea House, 1995), 106; Charles Alexander Eastman, Michael Fitzgerald, ed., *The Essential Charles Eastman* (Bloomington, IN: World Wisdom, 2007), 154; Raymond Wilson, *Ohiyesa: Charles Eastman, Santee Sioux* (Urbana, IL: University of Illinois Press, 1983), 151.

NOW & THEN: TROOP

1. "Sixth Annual Report: Archdiocesan Committee on Scouting, Archdiocese of St. Paul, 1941.
2. Ramsey Council, "Information Concerning Scouting in St. Paul," 1917, St. Paul-Ramsey County War History Committee, Box 103.K.7.6F, MHS.

1920s

1. Peterson, *Boy Scouts,* 98.
2. *MT,* May 21, 1926.
3. Ibid.
4. Ibid., August 28, 1927; December 30, 1928.
5. Ibid., January 1, 1928.
6. Minneapolis Area Council minutes, August 15, 1928.
7. *MT,* November 4, 1930.
8. *CE,* June 28, 1923.

9. Ibid., March 1, 1928.

10. Cokato High School Yearbook, 1938.

11. *St. Paul Scout,* December 1924.

12. *MJ,* December 3, 1930.

13. Minneapolis Area Council Executive Committee minutes, March 3, 1925.

14. Minneapolis Area Council minutes, January 17, 1924.

15. *DT,* April 4, 1947.

NOW & THEN: ACHIEVEMENT

1. Orwig to Scouts of Ramsey County, May 23, 1911, St. Paul-Ramsey County War History Committee Records, 103.K.7.6F, MHS.

2. *SPP,* March 10, 1912; September 1, 1912.

1930s

1. 1929 St. Paul Area Council Annual Report.

2. Dave Kenney, Northern Lights: *The Stories of Minnesota's Past* (St. Paul: Minnesota Historical Society Press, 2003), 237.

3. *MJ,* November 26, 1930.

4. *MJ,* December 5, 1930.

5. "Report of the Field Executive," Minneapolis Area Council, October 1, 1930.

6. Minneapolis Area Council Administrative Committee minutes, January 31, 1934.

7. Minneapolis Area Council Troop Organization Committee minutes, September 21, 1933.

8. Minneapolis Area Council Board of Directors minutes, January 6, 1932; Minneapolis Area Council Administrative Committee minutes, January 4, 1933.

9. Minneapolis Area Council uniform exchange meeting minutes, April 20, 1938.

10. *DT,* January 20, 1939.

11. Peterson, *Boy Scouts,* 97.

12. Magnus Johnson, "'Skipper's' Report of the Covered Wagon Expedition," 1932.

13. Minneapolis Area Council East Section Area minutes, October 15, 1931.

14. Boy Scouts of America, *Handbook for Scout Masters* (New York: Boy Scouts of America, 1914), 88.

15. *BP,* February 1924.

16. Minneapolis Area Council, "Report of Sea Scout Division," August 22, 1931.

17. *NYT,* July 17, 1938.

18. Peterson, *Boy Scouts,* 107-109.

19. Carl G. Kaeppel to Julian J. Kuhn, February 10, 1955.

20. Minneapolis Area Council, "Brief Outline of the Cubbing Program," 1934.

21. Minneapolis Area Council minutes, December 1, 1930.

22. *SPP,* March 16, 1932.

23. R. J. Hagman, "Our Modern Scouts," source and date unknown, reprinted in "Pine Bend, 1932-1955: 60th Anniversary," 1992.

24. http://pinebend.org/history.htm, accessed March 21, 2009.

NOW & THEN: OUTING

1. *SPP,* August 28, 1910.

2. Ibid., July 2, 1911.

1940s

1. Minneapolis Area Council Board of Directors minutes, January 3, 1941.

2. *MSJ,* February 19, 1941.

3. L.D. Cornell, "Preview of the Annual Report of the Scout Executive for the Year 1941," December 4, 1941.

4. St. Paul Area Council, "Part II: What the St. Paul Area Council, Inc., Boy Scouts of America Has Done and Plans to Do with the Scouting Program," Summer 1942, 36.

5. *SPP,* February 2, 1944.

6. St. Paul Area Council, "What the St. Paul Area Council," 36.

7. *SPP,* October 19, 1942.

8. *MT,* April 12, 1943.

9. Ibid., November 30, 1942.

10. Ibid., April 3, 1943.

11. Minneapolis Area Council annual meeting minutes, January 8, 1945. 6.

12. SP, May 7, 1944.

13. Minneapolis Area Council annual meeting minutes, January 10, 1944, 4.

14. Minneapolis Area Council Board of Directors minutes, March 4, 1943.

15. Elbert Fretwell to Arthur Larkin, March 1943.

16. Minneapolis Area Council Health and Safety Committee, Camp Inspection 1943.

17. Minneapolis Area Council Board of Directors minutes, October 7, 1943.

18. St. Paul Area Council, "Report of the Scout Executive," May 23, 1946.

19. Minneapolis Area Council Board of Directors minutes, September 5, 1946.

20. Minneapolis Area Council Senior Scout Committee minutes, December 5, 1946.

21. John Earl Davis, "Prepared for Peace," *Shell Progress,* May-June 1946.

22. Willis V. Elliott, *Men of Paul Bunyan Stature* (St. Paul: Region Ten, Boy Scouts of America, 1968), 133-134.

NOW & THEN: CAMP (PART 1)

1. Hennepin Council minutes, June 19, 1911.

2. Arvid H. Edwards, "Slices of My Life" (unpublished monograph), 1995, MHS.

3. Bonn Clayton, "The Scalp Program," n.d.

1950s

1. Dave Kenney, *Minnesota Goes to War: The Home Front during World War II* (St. Paul: Minnesota Historical Society Press, 2005), 234.

2. "Scout Executive's Report," St. Paul Area Council, November 1950.

1. "Ibid., November 28, 1951.

4. Mike McCollor, *Always There's a Fire Bright: Fifty Years of Scouting at Many Point Scout Camp* (self-published, 1996), 58.

5. "Strengthen the Arm of Liberty: 40th Anniversary Crusade, Boy Scouts of America," BSA, 1949.

6. Leslie A. Stratton, "The Statue of Liberty," *The Scout Executive,* July 1950.

7. http://troop101.thescouts.com/liberty, accessed November 4, 2008.

8. "Onward for God and My Country: A Guide for the Four-Year Program," Boy Scouts of America, 1956.

9. "Activities," from remarks at Indianhead Council 1956 annual meeting.

10. Edwin E. Stevens to Executive Board, St. Paul Area Council, December 2, 1954.

11. Viking Council Health and Safety Committee minutes, September 16, 1953.

12. Ibid., December 15, 1953.

13. Minneapolis Area Council Executive Board minutes, January 3, 1952; Viking Council Business Planning Committee minutes, June 7, 1952.

14. St. Paul Area Council Executive Committee minutes, January 13, 1955; Indianhead Council Executive Committee minutes, February 4, 1955.

15. *CC,* March 1959.

NOW & THEN: CAMP (PART 2)

1. *MJ,* August 7, 1921.

2. Tom Wilson to Tomahawk Alumni Association, January 20, 2004, in untitled 50th anniversary booklet, 2004.

1960s

1. "50th Anniversary Viking Council Boy Scout Circus" program.

2. *CC* ("Golden Show Edition), undated.

3. Viking Council Executive Board minutes, February 24, 1960.

4. *MT,* February 7, 1960.

5. Indianhead Council, 1960 Annual Report.

6. *SPP,* June 18, 1964.

7. Ibid., January 6, 1971.

8. Ibid., November 12, 1961.

9. Viking Council Executive Board minutes, March 25, 1964.

10. Viking Council Executive Board minutes, April 24, 1968.

11. Indianhead Council, "Statement on Present Agency Program to Greater St. Paul United Fund and Council, Inc.," October 23, 1967.

12. *MT,* March 29, 1965.

13. Indianhead Council Executive Board minutes, December 9, 1968.

14. *SPP,* September 27, 1969.

15. Membership statistics compiled by the author.

16. *MT,* October 2, 1966; AU, November 18, 1966.

17. *MT,* October 2, 1966; June 6, 1967.

18. Ibid., October 29, 1967.

19. Ibid., January 28, 1967; http://www.worldofportraitpainting.com/adventures/section1/calendarartist.htm, accessed July 6, 2009.

NOW & THEN: GATHERING

1. Bob Cary, "Twin Cities SCOUTEXPO '83," *Scouting,* September 1983, 91.

2. Linda Irmen, untitled research paper, Macalester College, 1987, Troop 17 Archives.

1970s

1. *MT,* April 19, 1970.

2. Ibid., undated.

3. Dave Kenney, *Twin Cities Album* (St. Paul: Minnesota Historical Society, 2005), 230-36.

4. Indianhead Council, "A Statement on Community Priority Problems," April 13, 1970.

5. Ibid.

6. *SPP,* October 26, 1971.

7. Chuck Wills, *Boy Scouts of America: A Centennial History* (New York: DK Publishing, 2009), 183.

8. *SPP,* May 27, 1973.

9. Wills, *Boy Scouts of America,* 184.

10. *SPP,* May 27, 1973.

11. *MS,* June 10, 1974.

12. Ibid.

13. *MT,* April 28, 1974.

14. *MS,* June 10, 1974.

15. Ibid.

16. *SPP,* January 6, 1971.

17. Indianhead Council, "Special Report: Target Area Penetration and Scouting in Housing Areas in St. Paul," November 1974.

18. *MT,* March 16, 1971; SD, June 28, 1971.

19. Indianhead Council, 1974 Annual Report.

20. *SPP,* April 18, 1971.

21. *MS,* November 29, 1973.

22. SPD, May 6, 1978.

23. Indianhead Council, 1979 Annual Report; Viking Council Handicapped Scouting Operation Committee, "Handicapped Units," September 1979.

24. Viking Council Handicapped Scouting Operation Committee, "Handicapped Scouting Division," September 1979: "Where possible, prospective Cubs, Scouts and Explorers who are handicapped, should be maintained into normal units, depending on the extent of their limitations."

25. Actual numbers: 52,115 at the end of 1969; 51,940 at the end of 1975. Statistics compiled by the author.

26. Indianhead Council, 1976 Annual Report.

27. Indianhead Council, "Major Market Communications for Scouting in the Twin Cities Area," undated (autumn 1978).

28. *SPP,* May 27, 1973.

29. *SD,* November 12, 1979.

30. Wills, *Boy Scouts of America,* 214.

31. *SPP,* February 4, 1979.

NOW & THEN: JAMBOREE

1. *CRH,* September 12, 2007.

2. Chad Heise, interview by the author, March 5, 2009.

3. *Navigator,* January 2008.

4. Heise interview.

5. *Navigator,* January 2008.

6. Chad Heise, "2007 World Scout Jamboree" (unpublished monograph), 2009.

7. *Navigator,* January 2008.

8. Elliott, *Men of Paul Bunyan,* 19-20.

9. Ibid., 21.

10. *AH,* July 14, 1937.

11. Newspaper clipping of unknown origin.

12. Alan A. Clothier, "Finding a Home for the Ideal Boy Scout Statue (unpublished monograph), 2008.

13. *CRH,* September 3, 1971.

14. Ibid.

1980s

1. David L. Moore, *Dark Sky Dark Land: Stories of the Hmong Boy Scouts of Troop 100* (Eden Prairie, MN: Tessera Publishing, 1989), 29.
2. Kenney, *Twin Cities Album,* 2005.
3. Moore, *Dark Sky Dark Land,* 42.
4. Ibid., 42.
5. Ibid., 130.
6. *SPP,* August 31, 1989.
7. *MST,* June 4, 1989.
8. *MT,* March 1, 1980; *SPP,* March 27, 1980; *MT,* November 26, 1980.
9. *MT,* June 16, 1980.
10. Viking Council, "A Look at Inner-City Scouting," 1982.
11. *MST,* August 11, 1988.
12. *SPP,* July 10, 1984.
13. Indianhead Council 1987 Annual Report; Indianhead Council, Update on Outreach to Special Youth," December 14, 1988; Indianhead Council, "Special Needs Division Report," December 13, 1989.
14. Tim Hunt, "What Freedom Means to Me," Indianhead Executive Board minutes, November 18, 1987.
15. *SPP,* September 22, 1981; Indianhead Council Executive Council minutes, September 16, 1982; Wills, Boy Scouts of America, 218.
16. *MST,* February 14, 1988.
17. *FDN,* April 8, 1988.
18. *SPP,* April 5, 1988.
19. Indianhead Council, "The Case for Serious Action in '83," February 16, 1983; Executive Board minutes, July 27, 1983.
20. Indianhead Council Executive Board minutes, April 20, 1981.
21. Betty Heath to Board Member, undated (Fall 1982).
22. Indianhead Council, "1987 Fall Product Sale," undated.
23. *SPP,* April 11, 1980.

NOW & THEN: SERVICE

1. *St. Paul Pioneer Press,* March 5, 1911.
2. Minneapolis Area Council Board minutes, January 5, 1927.
3. *MJ,* April 7, 1920.
4. Minneapolis Area Council Bulletin, March 14, 1939; *MT,* October 23, 1920.
5. *CC,* February 1980.

1990s

1. Suzanne Wilson, "Fun, Games, and a Lot More," *Scouting,* November-December 1991, 26-27.
2. Judith B. Erickson, *D.E.L.V.: An Activity Program for Cub Scouts to Encourage Ethical Decision-Making* (Minneapolis: Viking Council, Boy Scouts of America, 1988), iii.
3. Erickson, *D.E.L.V.,* 2.
4. Wilson, "Fun, Games," 50.
5. Terry Wolkerstorfer, "A Winning Formula for Junior Leader Training," *Scouting,* January-February 1993, 43.
6. Terry Wolkerstorfer, interview by the author, February 20, 2009.
7. Terry Wolkerstorfer, "Rescuing Costa Rica's Endangered Sea Turtles," *Scouting,* October 1992, 44-45.
8. Mike Hughes, interview by the author, March 18, 2009.
9. Ibid.

10. *CC,* February 1999
11. *MST,* August 21, 1992.
12. *SPP,* June 4, 1999.
13. *SPP,* June 13, 2001.
14. *CC,* March 1994; Indianhead Council, "Executive Summary: Long Range Plan Strategic Positioning: Diversity Strategies," September 28, 1996.
15. *MST,* January 9, 1992.
16. *SPP,* August 7, 1992.
17. *MST,* January 9, 1992.
18. Ibid., August 7, 1992.
19. *SPP,* August 7, 1992.
20. Ibid., August 13, 1990.
21. Ibid., February 9, 1995.
22. *CC,* August 2000.

NOW & THEN: SCOUTER

1. Elmer B. Palmer to "Volunteers," June 16, 1913.

2000s

1. Indianhead Council, "Proposed Resolution," February 16, 1999.
2. J. Carey Keane to John Andrews, November 2, 2000.
3. John Andrews to Bob Denlinger, June 16, 2000.
4. *MST,* September 28, 2000.
5. Ibid., August 4, 2000.
6. *SPP,* September 30, 2000.
7. *MST,* October 11, 2000.
8. Joann Knuth to John Andrews, October 9, 2000.
9. *SPP,* December 8, 2001.
10. John Andrews to All Commissioners, September 22, 2003; *CC,* February 2002.
11. *Business Journal* (Minneapolis/St. Paul), October 18, 2004.
12. *CC,* February 2002.
13. Indianhead Council and Viking Council, "Council Consolidation Update," February 23, 2005.
14. *SPP,* June 22, 2005.
15. *MST,* November 21, 2007.
16. Ibid.
17. Viking Council Executive Committee minutes, March 19, 2003.
18. Here and below: Cindy Ross, "Sharing Winter Adventure, Honoring a Great American," *Scouting,* January/February 2006.
19. Bill Hoffmann, interview with the author, April 17, 2009.
20. *MST,* June 18, 2009; *SPP,* June 18, 2009.

CONCLUSION

1. *SPP,* May 21, 1911; May 28, 1911.
2. Preston G. Orwig to Scouts of Ramsey County, May 23, 1911, St. Paul-Ramsey County War History Committee, Box 103.K.7.6F, MHS.
3. *MST,* September 25, 2008.
4. Orwig to Scouts of Ramsey County.

ILLUSTRATION CREDITS

Northern Star Council: 4; 7 (constitution); 27; 28 (bean feed photo); 35; 41; 45 (announcement); 56; 66 (North Wind); 67 (bed roll; painting); 75 (report); 76 (music); 77 (both); 88 (race); 89 (diving); 91 (inspection); 99 (photo); 100 (cartoon); 101 (color photo; Squadron 424); 102-103; 108 (dining hall); 110 (Kiwanis); 111 (Stearns); 112 (pajama; Lone Ranger); 116 (circus); 122 (Clancy); 124-125; 129; 130 (plans; program; both towers); 131 (posters; Brookdale); 132 (signaling; Wasli-Ga-Zhu); 133 (2008 Pinewood); 134 (Ripley photo; 1921 encampment); 143 (invitation); 144 (Rixmann); 146-147; 151 (photos); 152 (Pierson); 154 (1955 Jamboree); 155 (nap); 156 (announcement; broken arm); 157 (candle); 158; 160 (Troop 100); 162; 167; 168-169; 173; 174 (signs); 176 (toys; food); 177 (Goodwill; ushers; pass); 178 (before/after; Pack 283); 180; 182 (DELV; Pinewood); 183 (photo); 186; 187 (three photos); 188; 189; 196 (Rotary); 197 (Pederson; shave); 198 (cooking); 199 (brochure; University; Pow Wow); 200 (Akela; Bronze Wolf); 202; 204 (both); 205; 206; 207 (banner); 208; 209 (both); 210 (four photos); 211 (both); 213.

NORTHERN STAR COUNCIL TROOPS

Troop 1: 16; 17; 18.

Troop 17: 21 (banner; Roundup); 68 (Troop 17); 98 (Troop 17); 121; 132 (banner); 195 (Hanson).

Troop 89: 82; 83; 84; 104; 105; 106.

Troop 197: 19 (both).

Troop 224: 25 (Troop 224).

Troop 226: 23.

Troop 246: 63 (Troop 246); 120 (Hutchinson); 179 (highway); 196 (certificate).

Troop 345: 25 (Troop 345).

Troop 411: 67 (Troop 411).

AFFILIATED MUSEUMS

North Star Museum of Boy Scouting and Girl Scouting (Claudia Nicholson): Cover; iii (handbook); 5; 12 (medallion); 20 (neckerchief); 21 (Troop 18); 22 (Troop 87); 23 (neckerchief; Pack 44); 24 (neckerchief; patch); 25 (drum); 32 (potatoes); 34 (both); 36-37; 44 (badges); 48; 50; 51 (Miller); 53 (patch); 55 (sign); 58-59; 64 (Troop 17); 65 (Troop 96); 66 (patches); 69 (both); 74 (patch); 75 (ribbon); 76 (photo); 78 (Troop 118; "Monitor"); 80-81; 86 (both); 88 (patch; Neibel; neckerchief); 89 (Iyota); 90 (River Camp); 91 (tent; beanies); 92; 97; 99 (strips);

100 (strips; neckerchief; slide); 101 (patch; "Savage"); 107 (both); 108 (patches); 109 (patches); 110 (canoe; patches); 111 (Pa-Hu-Ca photos; Cannon River patch); 113 (Yetty); 116 (button; photo); 117 (both); 122 (Pack 118); 130 (patches); 131 (ribbon); 133 (patches); 134 (patch); 135 (patch; oven); 139 (handbook; Schmidtke); 145 (handbook); 151 (pack); 153 (Cudworth); 154 (1991 Jamboree; slide; shoes); 155 (neckerchief; train; swapping); 156 (neckerchief); 163 (patches); 165 (shirt); 166 (neckerchief); 176 (patch); 177 (patch); 183 (booklet); 195 (Drew); 196 (Grant); 198 (patch)

Bearman Museum (Hank Seifert): 28 (ticket); 33; 43 (Eagles Nest); 53 (photo); 54 ("Santa Maria"); 64 (Troop 176); 66 (Troop 342); 78 ("Santa Maria"); 79; 96 (bell); 98 (truck; badge); 132 (Beard); 154 (1953 Jamboree); 201 (Wethern).

Many Point Scout Camp Museum: 47 (patch); 87 (letter); 95; 108 (plans; trading post); 112 (lumberjack); 113 (photo).

UNAFFILIATED MUSEUMS AND HISTORICAL SOCIETIES

Anoka Historical Society (Maria King): 14-15.

Cokato Museum (Mike Worcester): 24 (Troop 249); 32 (charter); 44 (certificate); 120 (Cokato).

Jewish Historical Society of the Upper Midwest (Susan Hoffman): 22 (Troop 86); 174 (Krischner).

Minnesota Historical Society: 2; 6; 8; 9 (three photos); 10 (both); 11; 12 (fruit pits); 13 (Ohiyesa); 20 (both photos); 25 (Pack 181); 28; 42 (both); 44 (Square Lake); 45 (Temple Israel; award); 52; 54 (cave); 55 (photo); 57; 66 (Battle Creek); 90 (Square Lake); 94 (Pack 67); 101 (color photo); 164; 175 (hydrants; Lakewood); 176 (Troop 62); 179 (tornado); 190-191; 214.

Minnesota Historical Society, *Pioneer Press* photo collection: 46 (Christensen); 133 (1972 Klondike); 135 (barbeque); 136; 142 (both); 156 (Knutson); 160 (Troop 273); 163 (photo); 165 (photo).

Minnesota Historical Society, *Star Tribune* photo collection: 24; 68 (taste test); 70; 72 (photo); 73 (both); 74 (photo); 114; 118; 123 (both); 130 (auditorium); 132 (Troop 132); 133 (1964 Pinewood); 134 (Bicentennial); 135 (Camporee); 138; 139 (uniforms); 140 (both); 141; 143 (photo); 144 (Pack 215); 145 (photo); 157 (souvenirs); 161; 177 (Williams); 179 (Isaak); 200 (Koob).

Minnesota State Fair Archives (Steve Granger): 30 (both); 51 (State Fair); 131 (State Fair); 135 (flapjacks; encampment).

Scouting Memories Museum (Bob Hannah): 21 (button); 87 (patch); 111 (Pa-Hu-Ca patch); 152 (Collins; medal); 153 (certificate); 196 (patch); 198 (Itasca); 199 (Neibel); 207 (toy).

PUBLICATIONS

Boys' Life: 46.

Scouting: 131 (Troop 327); 182 (ladder).

INDIVIDUALS

John Andrews: 7 (parlor); 13 (book).

Reid Christopherson: 29.

Jim Frost: 47 (color photo); 109 (three photos).

John Guthmann: 157 (typhoon).

Howard Guthmann: iii (songbook); 1.

Barb Herrmann: 63 (bus); 166 (photo).

Bill Hoffmann: 212 (both).

Tim Jopek: 44-45 (Jopek).

Dave Kenney: 39; 60; 61; 62; 96 (statue); 126; 127; 128; 170; 171; 172; 193.

Charlie Opp: 44 (Tunseth); 175 (Fort Snelling).

David Pearson: 133 (2009 Klondike).

Jon Pederson: 94 (Many Point); 149.

David Pettiford: 119.

Dave Roberts: 178 (Troop 319).

Norma Spicer: 65 (San Francisco-bound Scouts).

Terry Wolkerstorfer: 43 (Troop 96); 184; 185.

Steve Young: 47 (b&w photo); 72 (telegram); 89 (Manomin); 201 (troop; patch).

ORIGINAL PHOTOGRAPHY

Doug Knutson: 4–5, 26–27, 48–49, 70–71, 92–93, 114–115, 136–137, 158–159, 180–181, 202–203 (hands holding books); 26–27, 92–93 (background photos).

Hand models: Dex Beckman, 5; Marques H. Jones, 27; Felicity Smith, 49; Henry Seifert, 71; Lucia & Danny Ayala, 93; Isaac Her, 115; Steve Granger, 137; Zack Schuster, 159; Joseph Jopek, 181; Marty Klein, 203

INDEX

A

Abbott Hospital, Troop 199, 120
adult leaders, 72–73, 77–78, 188–189,
    191–202
African American Scouts, 43, 119, 141,
    162, 211
Afton
    Klondike Derby, 133
    Troop 226, 23
Aids to Scouting (Baden-Powell), 1
Air Explorer Squadron 424, 101
Air Force Association, Ray S. Miller
    Squadron, 101
Air Scouting, 78
Alderman, Grady, 123
American Indian Scouts, 8, 13, 141, 162
American Legion
    Troop 134, 31–32
    Troop 249, 24, 32
Andersen, Fred C., 195
Andrews, John, 38–39, 205–206, 215
anniversary celebrations, 33
    40th anniversary, 95–96
    47th anniversary, 101
    50th anniversary, 115–116
    50th Anniversary, Cub Scouting,
      163
    Golden Anniversary Show,
      Indianhead Council, 115
Anoka
    Troop 124, 14–16
    Troop 204, 79
    Troop 276, 79
    Troop 631, 183
Anoka County, Scouting in, 30–31
Antonini, Debbie, 142
Archer Daniels Midland Company,
    123
Asian American Scouts, 211

B

Baden-Powell, Robert S. S., 1, 5, 9
Barber, Alden, 138
Bartelt, Harry, 76
Bartyzal, David, 136–137
Bean, Frank, 195
Beard, Daniel Carter, 3
Beard, John, 162
Bennett, Dan, 126–127
Benson, O. H., 28
Bernstein, Max, 65
Beth El Synagogue, Troop 86, 22
Bethlehem Lutheran Church,
    Cub Scout Pack, 56

Bevan, Bill, 177
The Birch Bark Roll (Seton), 13
Blackfoot Troop, 42
Blackmun, Harry, 21
Blaeser, Mark, 162
Blaine, Troop 513, 24
Blakey, Brandi, 163
Blakey, Sheila, 163
Blakey, Tony, 163
Blazejack, Edward, 123
Blehert, Leon, 65
Bloomington, Scouting in, 99
Boehm, Toni, 142
Bonacci, Shaun, 189
Boy Pioneers, 3
Boy Scouts of America (BSA),
    1–3, 7, 166
Boyce, William Dickson, 1, 27
Boys' Brigade, Northfield, 3
Boys' Life magazine, 13, 46, 188
Braley, Duane, 123
Bray, Mrs. Philip, 137
Brazier, Colleen, 209
Bronze Wolf award, 200
Brown, Richard, 140
Brown & Bigelow Company, St. Paul,
    115, 118, 143
BSA. *See* Boy Scouts of America
Burger, Warren, 21
Burton, Edwin, 79
Burton, Kenneth, 79
Bustamante, Jonathon, 178
Bustamante, Robert, 178
Butchee, Bill, 211–213
Butchee, Jerome, 213

C

calendars, 79, 115
camping and camps, 57–60, 80–92,
    103–114. *See also specific camps*
    Agaming Lodge, 41
    Base Camp, Fort Snelling, 209,
      213–214
    Birch Bend, Round Lake, Onamia,
      55
    Camp Ajawah, Linwood Lake,
      Anoka County, 85
    Camp Akela, 165, 200, 202–203, 210
    Camp Fire Girls, 13
    Camp Heritage, Annandale, 107,
      165 (*See also* Camp Stearns)
    Camp Iyota, Deerwood, 89

camping and camps *(continued)*
    Camp Kiwanis, Marine on St. Croix,
      12, 165
    Camp Manomin, Fridley, 89, 107
    Camp Neibel, Balsam Lake, WI,
      85–86, 88–89, 94
    Camp Pa-Hu-Ca, Lydia, 111
    Camp Robinson Crusoe, Lake
      Minnetonka, 54
    Camp Rotary, Lake Minnetonka,
      12, 85, 91, 196
    Camp Seton, 129, 214–215
    Camp St. Croix, Hudson, WI, 5–6
    Camp Stearns, Annandale, 60–62,
      66, 107, 111–112, 181, 196–197
      (*See also* Camp Heritage)
    Camp Tonkawa, Lake Minnetonka,
      12, 47, 63, 76–77, 85, 87–91, 95
    Cannon River Scout Reservation,
      Cannon Falls, 107, 136–137, 165
      (*See also* Phillippo Scout
      Reservation)
    cave camping, 67
    Charles L. Sommers Wilderness
      Canoe Base, Moose Lake, 63
    Crocker's Point, Lake Minnetonka,
      85
    depicted, 57–60
    dressing up, 112
    food, cooking, and meals, 68–69,
      82–84, 90, 104–105, 135
    Fred C. Andersen Scout Camp,
      Stillwater, 85, 165 (*See also*
      St. Croix River Camp)
    Kiwanis Scout Camp, Marine
      on St. Croix, 107, 110
    Lake Itasca leadership training
      camp, 198–199
    list of, 224
    Many Point Scout Camp, Ponsford,
      47, 67, 77, 91, 94–95, 107–108,
      112–113, 184
    map, 85
    Phillippo Scout Reservation, Can-
      non Falls, 107 (*See also* Cannon
      River Scout Reservation)
    quinzee building, 61–62
    Rum River Scout Camp, Ramsey,
      107, 110
    St. Croix River Camp, Stillwater,
      12, 34, 52, 85–86, 90, 107, 122
      (*See also* Fred C. Andersen
      Scout Camp)

camping and camps *(continued)*
Sky Camp, 161
Square Lake Camp, Stillwater,
44–45, 63, 80–82, 85–86, 90–91
Stearns Scout Camp (*See* Camp
Stearns, Annandale)
Tomahawk Scout Reservation,
Rice Lake, WI, 47, 60, 82–84,
104–107, 109, 162, 188–189
Tonkawampus Lodge, 41, 47
Totanhan Nakaha Lodge, 41
Victory Camp, 76–77
Webelos, 165
winter camping, 60–62, 66
candy sales, 167
Capitol District, 119
Carlos, Juan, 178
Carlson, Renne, 28
Carver County, Scouting in, 30–31
Caswell, Arthur, 8
Caswell, Dwight, 8
Caswell, Leigh, 8
Centennial Commission membership,
vi–vii
Center for Victims of Torture, 186
Center for Youth Development and
Research (CYDR), U of MN, 181
Champlin
Troop 176, 64, 201
Troop 276, 45, 89, 201
charter partners, 15–26, 204–206
Chase, Parker, 179
Chippewa County, Scouting in, 30–31
Chisago County, Scouting in, 31
Christen, Dominic, 38
Christensen, Brian, 46
Ciresi, Kevin, 118
Clothier, Alan A., 156
Coder, Ben, 148–150
Cokato
Explorer Post, 120
Troop 134, 31–32
Troop 249, 24, 32
Colbert, Pat, 131
College of Wilderness Knowledge, 55
Collins, Harvey, 151–152
Community Chest, St. Paul, 51–52, 166
Community Fund, Minneapolis, 51–52
community service, 169–180. *See also
specific programs*
care packages for military troops,
170–172
civil defense training, 97–99
clothing and supplies collections,
50–51, 176
conservation programs, 96, 142–143
emergency messengers, 74–75

community service *(continued)*
emergency services program, 98
food drives, 168–170, 173, 176
food production during WWII,
76–77
at Fort Snelling cemetery, 175
Good Turns, 98–99, 173–174
at Lakewood Cemetery, 175
natural disaster relief response,
178–179
paper drive, 92–93
patriotic programs, 95–96
political campaign sign cleanup,
174
Project SOAR, 142–143
recycling projects, 142–143, 178–179
Safe Rides, 167
snow removal around fire hydrants,
175
in state parks, 50
toy repair, 176
trash cleanup, 178–179
ushering at U of M football games,
173, 177
during World War I, 12
during World War II, 70–71, 73–77
Coon Rapids
Troop 406, 148
Troop 513, 24
Cornell, L. D., 71–72
Costa Rica, sea turtle rescue project,
185
Court of Honor. *See* Eagle Scout
Courts of Honor
Craig, Hamilton, 43
Craig, Mary, 188–189
Crocker, Neal, 43
Cub Scouting (Cubbing). *See also
entries beginning with* "Pack";
Webelos
30 millionth member, 163
50th Anniversary, 163
day camps, 110
den mothers, 72–73, 166
Edina Pack, 118
establishment, 41, 55–56
expansion during 1950s, 93–100
membership statistics, 121
Minneapolis packs, 24, 56
recruitment campaigns, 206
St. Paul packs, 56
Tiger Cub program, 164–165,
182–183
TV promotions, 122
Cudworth, Kyle, 153

D
Dale, L. S., 143
Dale, Ludwig, 8, 12
Dan Beard Trophy, 132
Dan Patch district, 99
Dean, Edwin B., 3
Delgado, Humberto, 178
DELTA program, 182
DELV program, 182
Diamond, Corwin, 60–62
disabilities, Scouts with, 143–144,
162–164, 187, 211
diversity issues, 180–189
Donaldson, Robert, 153
Drew, James "Dad," iii, 195
drum and bugle corps, 33–34
DuBois, Sam, 127–128
Duncan, Bill, 166
Dutch Troop 21, 150

E
Eagan, Troop 345, 25
Eagle Bluff District, 135
Eagle Cave, La Crosse, WI, 67
Eagle Scout Courts of Honor,
3, 36–40, 45
Eagle Scouts, 41–43, 143–144,
160–161, 170–172, 179, 209
Eason, Jim, 123
Eastlund, Kenneth, 44
Eastman, Charles (Ohiyesa), 13, 215
Eastman, Seth, 13
Eddy, Stan, 132
Edina, Cub Scout Pack, 118
Edwards, Arvid H., 86
El Sol District, 211
Eliot, Frederick May, 35
Elizabeth Kenny Polio Institute,
Cub Scout Pack, 24
Elk River, Troop 90, 156
Emigh, Joel, 179
Erickson, Jordan, 104
Erlandson, Bill, 162
Ersfield, Ronald, 78
Ethics in Action initiative, 182–184
Excelsior, Troop 40, 66
Explorer Emergency Service Unit, 98
Explorer Post 9, 101
Explorer Post 17, 121
Explorer Post 369, 114–115, 200
Explorer Post 467, 122–123
Explorer Post 707, 123
Explorers program, 55, 78–79
emergency services program, 98
girls accepted, 123, 142, 188–189
membership statistics, 122
specialty posts, 101, 122

F

Fagenstrom, Ernest, 5–7
Faribault State School and Hospital,
	Troop 330, 164
Farmington
	Pack 118, 122, 139
	S.S.S. "Monitor," 78
	Troop 118, 52, 69, 78, 139
Federal Aviation Administration,
	Explorer Post 707, 123
Fehring, Gary, 101
First National Bank of St. Paul, 116
Foede, Zach, 178
Fond du Lac Reservation, 8
Forest Lake
	first troop, 41
	Troop 733, 38–40
Fredericks, Kay, 189
Freeburg, J. W., 79
Freer, James, 78
Fretwell, Elbert, 77
Frost, Gale, 132

G

Gagnor, Nate, 158–159
Garaghty, Max, 179
Gardner, Dick, 154
gatherings and events, 125–136.
	See also anniversary
	celebrations; Jamborees;
	State Fair gatherings
	1932 Scout Roundup, 21
	1941 Camporee, 134
	1947 National Scout Executives
		Conference, 76
	1964 Adventure Exposition, 135
	1964 Scoutcapades, 133
	1965 Scouting Exposition, 122
	1970 Camperall, 132
	1970 Scout-O-Rama, 137–138
	1972 Camporee, 135
	1974 Camporee, 141
	1976 Bicentennial Camporee, Fort
		Snelling State Park, 134, 145
	1991 Camperall, 181–182
	Agaming Lodge, 47
	Boy Scout Circuses, 115, 129
	Boypower '76, 120
	Centen-O-Rama, 100
	Chili Cookoff, 135
	Expositions, 129
	Klondike Derbies, 129, 133
	Martin Luther King Jr. holiday
		weekend, 211–213
	National Round-Up, 78
	parades, 10, 208

gatherings and events *(continued)*
	Pinewood Derbies, 126–129,
		133, 182
	Reviews, 129
	Ripley Rendevous, Camp Ripley,
		134
	Roundups, 33, 129
	Scout Expo '81, 167
	Scout Expo '83, 131
	Scout-O-Ramas, 129–130, 137–138
	Wali-Ga-Zhus, 33, 129, 132
	Wali-Ga-Zips, 129
George Washington Troop 1, 16
Gerster, James, 78
Gerster, Paul, 78
Gethsemane Lutheran Church, Troop
	197, 19
Gilligan, F. J., 16
girls in Scouting. *See* women and girls
Godwin, Frank, 140
Goodrich, John, 45
Goodwill Industries, 177
Grant, Lloyd, 196–197
Great Depression era, 49–57
Greater St. Paul United Fund, 119
Grey Wolf leadership program, 184
Grim, George, 120
Guthmann, John, 157

H

Haag, Dale, 167
Hadden, C. W., 195–196
Haney, Dennis, 139
Hansken, Terry, 114–115
Hanson, "Boots," 94
Hanson, Mark, 195
Har Mar Mall, ScoutExpo '83, 131
Harris, Larry, 118–119
Hartman, Wint, 95
Hastings State Hospital, Pack 215, 144
Hawley, David, 110
Heath, Betty, 167
Hedtke, Scott, 189
Heiberg, Fredrick, 3
Heinze, Suzette, 163
Heise, Chad, 148–150
Hennepin Council, 7, 85
Henrichs, Ted, 38, 40
Hesser, Paul, 77, 93, 115
Hewitt, Leland, 43
Hiawatha District, 162
Hillcourt, William "Green Bar Bill,"
	145
Hillstrom, Donald A., 108
Hintermeister, Hy, 67
Hinton, John, 140

Hispanic Scouts, 162, 210
history of Scouting
	1910s era, 5–14
	1920s era, 27–36
	1930s era, 49–58
	1940s era, 71–80
	1950s era, 93–102
	1960s era, 115–124
	1970s era, 137–146
	1980s era, 159–168
	1990s era, 181–190
	2000s era, 203–213
Hmong Scouts, 159–161, 186
Hoel, Robert, 115
Hoffman, Bill, 211–213
Hoffman, Louis, 69
Holt, Luther, 141, 161
Holy Redeemer Catholic Church,
	Troop 87, 22
Homecroft Elementary School,
	Cub Scout Pack 181, 24
homosexuals, antidiscrimination
	lawsuits, 203–206
Hopkins, Troop 396, 179
Hosanna Lutheran Church, Forest
	Lake, 38–40
Hughes, Mike, 185–186
Humphrey, Hubert H., 52
Hunt, Tim, 163–164
Hussman, Ben, 162
Hutchinson
	Eagle Scouts, 120–121
	Troop 245, 63
	Troop 246, 179
	Troop 319, 178

I

Improved Scouting Program,
	138–140, 145
Indian Scout Talks (Ohiyesa), 13
Indianhead Council. *See also* St. Paul
	Area Council
	consolidation with Viking Council,
		41, 206–208
	Drum and Bugle Corps, 115–117
	exchange program, 186
	first woman president, 189
	fundraising efforts, 166–167,
		186–187
	gatherings and events, 129–136
	Golden Anniversary Show, 115
	name change, 100
	sea turtle rescue project in Costa
		Rica, 184–186
	special needs Scouts, 143–144, 163,
		187

Isaak, Matthew, 179
Isanti County, Scouting in, 30–31
Italian American Scouts, 22
Izaak Walton League, 123

J
Jackson, Byron, 212
Jamborees, 147–158
    1920 World Scout Jamboree,
      England, 151
    1924 World Scout Jamboree,
      Denmark, 151–153
    1929 World Scout Jamboree,
      England, 151
    1937 National Jamboree,
      Washington DC, 151
    1937 World Jamboree,
      Netherlands, 153
    1947 World Scout Jamboree,
      France, 151, 154
    1950 National Jamboree,
      Valley Forge, PA, 155–156
    1953 National Jamboree,
      Irvine Ranch, CA, 154, 156
    1955 World Jamboree, Canada, 154
    1971 World Jamboree, Japan, 157
    1973 National Jamboree, Idaho, 156
    1991 World Jamboree, South Korea,
      154
    2005 National Jamboree, Fort A.P.
      Hill, VA, 146–148, 155–157, 197
    2007 World Scout Jamboree,
      England, 148–150
Jamison, Mark, 187
Johnson, C. Rudolph, 79
Johnson, Dan, 38
Johnson, Elam L., 176
Johnson, Gregory, 145
Johnson, Herb, 116
Johnson, Magnus, 53
Johnson, Newton, 121
Johnson, Paul, 157
Jones, David, 53
Jopek, Tim, 44
Juvenile Diversion program, 208–210

K
Kammerlohr, Frank, 28
Kamrath, Josh, 179
Kancans, Robert, 105
Kane, Thomas, 165
Kasmi, Rahman, 186
Keller, Roger, 141, 161
Keller, Zane, 178
Kissell, James, 139
Kiwanis Foundation of St. Paul, 12

Klas, Sandy, 163
Kline, Corey, 184
Kniebel, Charlie, 122–123
Kniebel, Frank, 122–123
Knox, J. Mason, 49
Knuth, Joann, 205
Knuth, Kate, 189
Knutson, David, 156
Kodletz, Adolph, 28
Kohl, Linda, 166
Koob, william, 200
Kravik, Rick, 157
Krischner, Hy, 174
Kvidera, MaryJo, 142

L
Lake Elmo, Troop 224, 25
Lakeville, Troop 471, 209
Lange, D., 67
Lape, Steve, 162
Larkin, Arthur, 77
Larson, Doug, 105
Last, Kenny, 177
Latino Scouts, 211
lawsuits, membership policies,
    187–188, 203–206
leadership roles for women, 72–73,
    188–189
leadership training programs, 184,
    198–199
Learning for Life program, 208
Lee, Robert, 43
Lefevre, Dakota, 127–128
Lessary, Bob, 188
Levan, Charlie, 183
Liberty Loan campaigns, 11–12
Likens, Robert, 132
Linner, Eric, 104
Linnerooth, Paul, 192, 194
Lions Clubs
    Troop 224, 25
    Troop 733, 25
Lone Scouts of America, 27, 29–30
Lucas, Kenneth, 43
Lund, Willis, 73
Lutheran Brotherhood, 123

M
Magnuson, Adam, 188
Mahtomedi, Troop 89, 82–84, 104–106
Malter, Michael, 200
"Many Point Ballad," 107
Maplewood, Troop 197, 19
Marcellus, Fred, 65
Marcellus, Harry, 65
Marrone, Mark, 16–18
Martindale, Carl, 120

Matta, Mildred, 73
McCoy, Bernie, 144
McDonough, Father Kevin, 212
McDonough Homes, St. Paul
    Pack 274, 141
    Troop 274, 116–117, 141–142, 160
McKay, Gerry Jr., 121
McKinney, Professor, 101
McLeod County, Scouting in, 30–31
McQueen, Bob, 151
Medtronic, Inc., funding, 204
Meeker County, Scouting in, 30–31
Melcher, Bernie, 140
membership standards in 2000s, 204
membership statistics, 10–12, 115,
    121–122, 142
    1920s, 27, 30–31, 34
    1940s, 79
    1950s, 93
    1970s, 145
    1980s, 162
    2000s, 206
    Cub Scouts, 56
Memorial Lutheran Church,
    Troop 226, 23
Menichini, Simone, 150
merit badges, 28–29, 41–47, 139
Metzger, Evan, 179
Meyers, C. J., 178
Miller, Hadley, 51
Minneapolis
    Cub Scout Packs, 24, 56
    Sea Scout Ship 1, 54
    Sea Scout Ship Santa Maria, 54
    Sea Scouting, 54
    S.S.S. "Admiral Byrd," 54
    S.S.S. "Minnehaha," 54
    S.S.S. "Santa Maria," 78
    Troop 1, 196
    Troop 9, 28
    Troop 17, 124–126
    Troop 33, 73, 85, 153, 192
    Troop 61, 178–179
    Troop 89, 60–62
    Troop 91, 140
    Troop 96, 65
    Troop 100, 160–161, 186, 192, 209
    Troop 195, 92–93
    Troop 196, 44
    Troop 342, 66
    Troop 375, 177
    Troop 789, 141
    Troop K, 20
Minneapolis Area Council. *See also*
    Viking Council
    adult leaders during WWII, 72–73
    budget issues in 1930s, 51

Minneapolis Area Council (continued)
   camps, 85
   community service, 50–51
   gatherings and events, 129–136
   membership statistics, 56
   name change, 99
   office and administrative
      organization, 31
   scrap drive during WWII, 73–75
   territory expansion, 30–31, 99
   uniform exchange, 52
Minneapolis Elks Club, 12
Minneapolis Rotary Club, 12
Minneapolis School Board, 205
Minnehaha Lutheran Church, S.S.S.
   "Minnehaha," 54
Minnesota Vikings, Explorer Post 467,
   122–123
Minnetonka, Troop 346, 211–213
Monkey Patrols, 7
Moore, Dave, 159–160, 192
Morris, Charles, 91, 107
Murray, John G., 20
Mustang Patrol, Northfield, 3

N
Nacy, Chris, 162
Nacy, Curtis, 162
National Court of Honor, 3
National Youth Leadership Training,
   184
Neibel, Frank, 11–12, 191–192, 195,
   199
Nelson, Bob, 192–194
Nelson, Carroll, 143
Nelson, Fred, 69
Nelson, O. A., 112
New Brighton
   Troop 106, 170–172
   Troop 132, 132
   Troop 299, 23
   Venturing Crew 367, 189
New Prague, Troop 323, 24
Nicholson, Blake, 104
Nieszner, Tom, 18
North Branch, Troop 411, 67
North Star Museum of Boy Scouting
   and Girl Scouting, 25, 34
North Star Scouting Memorabilia,
   Inc., 34
North Wind Winter Adventure
   program, 60–62, 66
Northern Star Council, 206–213
   Base Camp, Fort Snelling, 209,
      213–214
   camps, 224
   establishment, 41

Northern Star Council (continued)
   Grey Wolf leadership training
      program, 184
   Key Three Leadership, 216–217
   Learning for Life program, 208
   oldest troops, 19
   Pinewood Derby, 133
   Silver Beavers, 220–223
Northfield, Boy Scout troops, 2–3
Northwest Airlines, 101

O
O'Donnell, Kim, 166
Ohiyesa (Charles Eastman), 13, 215
Ohman, Joel, 38–40
"older boy" programs. See Air
      Scouting; Explorers program;
      Rover Scouts; Sea Scouting;
      Senior Scouting; Venturing
Olivet Congregational church,
   St. Paul, 6
Olsen, Maynard, 196
Olson, Floyd B., 51
Olson, Jacob, 38–40
Olson, Joshua, 38–40
Olson, Steve, 38, 40
"On My Honor" (Bartelt), 76
Operation Minnesota Nice, 171–172
Order of the Arrow, 41, 47
Order of the Odor, 34
Orwig, Preston G., 41, 215
Osseo, Troop 219, 89
outdoor activities, 59–70. See also
      camping and camps
   competitions, 132
   food, cooking, and meals, 68–69,
      82–84, 90, 104–105, 135
   generally, 4–5, 63–69
   hiking, 63–66
   picking grapes, 9
   swimming, 67, 103–104
   water polo, 105
   wireless radios, 28

P
Pack 7, 163
Pack 9, 101
Pack 25, 143
Pack 44, 23
Pack 67, 94
Pack 118, 122, 139
Pack 120, 69
Pack 133, 126–128
Pack 181, 24
Pack 215, 144
Pack 274, 141
Pack 283, 178–179

Pack 356, 182
Palmer, Bryce, 170–172
Palmer, Elmer, 11
Palmer, Flora, 171–172
Parish, John C., 200
Parker, Craig, 113
Paul Bunyan Troop 21, 151
Pearson Candy Company, 167
Pederson, Jon, 197
Peria, Joseph, 118
Peterson, Jim, 132
Peterson, Robert, 78
Phillippo, Ron, 145, 166, 186, 189, 195
Philmont Ranch, NM, 63
Pickett, Daniel, 28
Piekarski, Jake, 83
Pierson, Edgar, 66, 151–152
Pillsbury Settlement House, Troop K,
   20
Pine Bend Association, 55
Pine Bend Scout Club, 55, 101
Pine Tree junior leadership program,
   184
Pine Tree Troop 9, Minneapolis, 28
Plante, Bob, 116–118, 141–142, 162
Plymouth Congregational Church,
   Troop K, 20
Polaris District, 211
Polk County, WI, Scouting in, 31
popcorn sales, 186–187
Pow Wow leadership training, 199
Prescott, WI, Cub Scout Pack 133,
   126–128
Primeau, Marcel, 84, 106
Pringle, Mike, 18
Proctor, C. J., 7

R
Ramsey Council No. 1, 7, 11, 42, 67,
   129, 214–215
Rasmussen, Earl, 157
Ray S. Miller Squadron, 101
recruitment efforts
   in 1930s, 53
   in 2000s, 210
   Cub Scouts, 206
   inner cities, 119–120, 140–142,
      161–167
   rural areas, 27–35, 53
Reisewitz, Michael, 178
Renville County, Scouting in, 30–31
Report to the Nation (BSA), 115
Richfield, Scouting in, 99
Rixmann, Warren, 143–144
Robinson, Edgar, 1, 3
Rochat, Harold, 113
Rockwell, Norman, 79, 115, 118, 143

Rogalla, Duwayne, 162
Rotary Clubs, Troop 345, 25
Rover Scouts, 55
Ruda, Dan, 192, 194
rural Scouting organizations, 8, 27–36

S

St. Anthony Park
    Troop 17, iii, 19, 21, 42, 51, 64, 68,
        86, 98, 132, 195
    Twilight Troop, 41–42
St. Anthony Park Congregational
    Church. *See* Troop 17
St. Anthony Park United Church
    of Christ. *See* Troop 17
St. Casmir's Catholic Church,
    Cub Scout Pack 44, 23
St. Cloud, Ripley Rendevous, 134
St. Croix County, WI, Scouting in, 31
St. James AME Church, Troop 405, 119
St. Louis Park
    Explorer Post 369, 114–115, 200
    Troop 86, 22
St. Mark's Church
    George Washington Troop 1, 16
    Troop 1, 16–18
    Troop 68, 16
    Troop 69, 16
St. Paul
    Air Explorer Squadron 424, 101
    Cub Scout Pack 7, 163
    Cub Scout Pack 9, 101
    Cub Scout Pack 25, 143
    Cub Scout Pack 44, 23
    Cub Scout Pack 67, 94
    Cub Scout Pack 181, 24
    Cub Scout Pack 274, 141
    Cub Scout Pack 356, 182
    Cub Scout Packs, 56
    Explorer Post 9, 101
    Explorer Post 17, 121
    S.S.S. "Savage," 101
    Troop 1, 16–18, 185
    Troop 5, 113
    Troop 9, 58–60, 101, 196–197
    Troop 11, 156
    Troop 18, 21
    Troop 38, 86, 90
    Troop 87, 22
    Troop 96, 43, 211–213
    Troop 99, 136–137
    Troop 184, 161
    Troop 195, 69
    Troop 203, 197
    Troop 274, 116–117, 141–142, 160
    Troop 356, 182
    Troop 477, 139

St. Paul Area Council. *See also*
    Indianhead Council
    adult leaders during WWII, 72–73
    camps, 85
    gatherings and events, 129–136
    Liberty Loan campaign, 12
    name change, 100
    office and administrative
        organization, 31
    San Francisco hiking expedition, 65
    scrap drive during WWII, 73–75
    territory expansion, 31, 99
St. Paul Commercial Club, 7
St. Paul Council of Churches, 204
St. Paul Rotary Club, 12
St. Peter Claver Church, Troop 96,
    43, 211–213
Sallow, Howard, 46
Salt, John, 28
Samways, Thomas, 114–115
Sanden, Howard, 118
Savage, Scouting in, 99
Schara, Ron, 145
Schmidtke, David, 139
Schroeder, Sam, 105
Schultz, John, 133
Schuster, Andy, 157
Schuster, Jim, 82, 104
Scout Handbook, iii, 3, 5, 139, 145
"Scout Vesper," iii
Scouter, 191–202
Scouting for Boys (Baden-Powell), 1, 5
"Scouting in Church" Sundays, 33
Scoutreach, 210
Sea Scout Ships. *See entries beginning*
    "S.S.S."
Sea Scouting, 53–54, 73, 78
sea turtle rescue project in Costa
    Rica, 184–186
Senior Outfits, 78–79
Senior Scouting, 55, 78
Seton, Ernest Thompson, 1, 3, 8–9,
    13, 214
Shakopee, Troop 218, 137–138
Sheldon, John, 121
Shoop, Jim, 68
Silver Maple District, 211
Silver Pathfinder leadership
    program, 184
Solomson, Chester, 43
Sommers, Charles, 195
Sons of Daniel Boone, 3
Sorrells, H. S., 11, 65
space exploration, 100
Spearhead program, 60
special needs Scouts, 143–144,
    162–164, 187, 211

Spider Island, 60–61
Spohn, Frankie, 29
sponsoring organizations, 15–26,
    204–206
Sproat, John, 157
S.S.S. 1, 54
S.S.S. "Admiral Byrd," 54
S.S.S. "Minnehaha," 54
S.S.S. "Monitor," 78
S.S.S. "Santa Maria," 54, 78
S.S.S. "Savage," 101
State Academy for the Blind,
    Faribault, Troop 335, 166
State Fair gatherings, 129–131,
    134–135
    1910s, 129–130
    1920s, 26–27, 30, 32, 35, 134
    1930s, 21, 51, 135
    1940s, 135
    1950s, 131
    Boy Scout Expositions, 47–49, 55,
        129–130
    Court of Honor, 36–38
    Golden Anniversary Show, 115
Steen, Joe, 120
Steiner, Tyson, 178
Sulzbach, Jeff, 207
Sumner Branch Library, Troop K, 20
Sunshine Society, Minneapolis, 50–51
Svien, Larry, 140
Swails, Norman, 139
Swallow, Matt, 60–62

T

Talbot, Donald, 79
Tatam, Willard A., 132
Tengdin, Dave, 157
Thao, Su, 160
Thomas, Anthony, 209
3M Company funding, 204
"Tomahawk Camp Song," 107
Tomahawk Yetty, 113
Tretter, Patrick, 46
Trinity Episcopal church, St. Paul, 6
Troop 1 (Minneapolis), 196
Troop 1 (St. Paul), 16–18, 185
Troop 5, 113
Troop 7, 43
Troop 9 (Minneapolis), 28
Troop 9 (St. Paul), 58–60, 101, 196–197
Troop 11, 156
Troop 17 (Minneapolis), 124–126
Troop 17 (St. Anthony Park), iii, 19,
    21, 42, 51, 64, 68, 86, 98, 132, 195
Troop 18, 21
Troop 21 (Dutch), 150
Troop 21 (Paul Bunyan), 151

Troop 27, 140
Troop 33, 73, 85, 153, 159–160, 192
Troop 38, 86, 90
Troop 40, 20, 66
Troop 61, 178–179
Troop 68, 16
Troop 69, 16
Troop 71, 192–194
Troop 72, 43
Troop 86, 23
Troop 87, 22
Troop 88, 43
Troop 89 (Mahtomedi), 82–84, 104–106
Troop 89 (Minneapolis), 60–62
Troop 90, 156
Troop 91, 140
Troop 96 (Minneapolis), 65
Troop 96 (St. Paul), 43, 211–213
Troop 98, 43
Troop 99, 136–137
Troop 100, 160–161, 186, 192, 209
Troop 106, 170–172
Troop 110, 43
Troop 118, 52, 69, 78, 139
Troop 124, 14–16
Troop 132, 132
Troop 176, 201
Troop 184, 161
Troop 195, 69, 92–93
Troop 196, 44, 209
Troop 197, 19
Troop 199, 120
Troop 203, 197
Troop 204, 79
Troop 218, 137–138
Troop 219, 89
Troop 224, 25
Troop 245, 63
Troop 246, 179
Troop 249, 24
Troop 274, 116–117, 141–142, 160
Troop 276, 45, 79, 89, 201
Troop 283, 19
Troop 299, 23
Troop 301, 148–150
Troop 319, 178
Troop 323, 24
Troop 327, 131
Troop 330, 164
Troop 334, 113
Troop 335, 166
Troop 342, 66
Troop 345, 25
Troop 346, 211–213
Troop 356, 182
Troop 396, 179

Troop 405, 119
Troop 406, 148
Troop 411, 67
Troop 431, 145
Troop 471, 209
Troop 477, 139
Troop 513, 24
Troop 631, 183
Troop 700, 140
Troop 733, 38–40
Troop 789, 140–141
Troop K, 20
Tunseth, Devin, 44
Twilight Troop, 41–42
Twin Cities Scouting
    achievements, 37–48
    diversity initiatives, 180–181
    early activities, 8–9
    Ethics in Action initiative, 182–184
    founding, 7
    patriotic activities in 1950s, 95–96
    urban focus in 1960s, 116–123
    World War I, activities during,
        11–12

U

uniforms, 52, 139, 141
United Fund, 166
United Way funding, 161–162, 166, 204
University of Scouting, 198–199

V

Van Sickle, David, 213
Vang, Xe, 160
Vegdahl, Roger, 112
Velie, Charles, 77, 195
Venturing Crew 367, 189
Venturing program, 189, 203–204
Victory Gardens, 76
Viking Council. See also Minneapolis
    Area Council
    consolidation with Indianhead
        Council, 41, 206–208
    fundraising efforts, 166–167,
        186–187
    gatherings and events, 129–136
    name change, 99
    special needs Scouts, 143–144
Volling, James, 188
Voytovich, Alex, 83

W

Waconia, Troop 327, 131
Walsh, Gerald, 69, 78
Walther, Les, 197
Wauchope, Commissioner, 20
Wayzata, Pack 283, 178–179

Wayzata Community Church,
    Troop 283, 19
Wayzata Congregational Church,
    Troop 283, 19
Webelos, 100, 111, 165, 201, 211. See
    also Cub Scouting (Cubbing)
Webelos Woods, Faribault, 165–166
Weekes, Steve, 204–205
West, James E., 3, 9, 11, 31, 55, 153
Westad, Alex, 82, 104, 106
Westad, Tom, 105
Westfall, Maria, 192
Westminster Presbyterian Church
    S.S.S. "Admiral Byrd," 54
    Troop 33, 73, 159–160
Westmoreland, William, 121
Wethern, Paul, 45, 79, 201
Whalen, William, 101
White Bear Lake, Troop 431, 145
Wild River District, 133
Williams, Dave, 177
Wilson, Tom, 109
Winkel, Ray, 79
Winkler, Zach, 105–106
Wisconsin, Scouting in, 99
women and girls
    antidiscrimination lawsuits,
        187–188
    girls accepted into Explorer
        program, 123, 142
    in leadership positions, 72–73, 166,
        188–189
Woodbury United Methodist Church,
    Troop 71, 192–194
Woodcraft Indians, 1, 3
Wright County, Scouting in, 30–31
Wyckoff, George, 31, 33, 51, 195

Y

Yang, Xia, 161
Yellow Medicine County, Scouting in,
    30–31
YMCA
    Boy Scouts and, 1, 5
    Indian reservation chapters, 13
York, Kent, 209
Young, Roy, 41–42
Young, Warren, 188

Z

Zahn, Jamey, 139
Zamberletti, Fred, 123
Zielinski, Gary, 127
Zulu District, 211

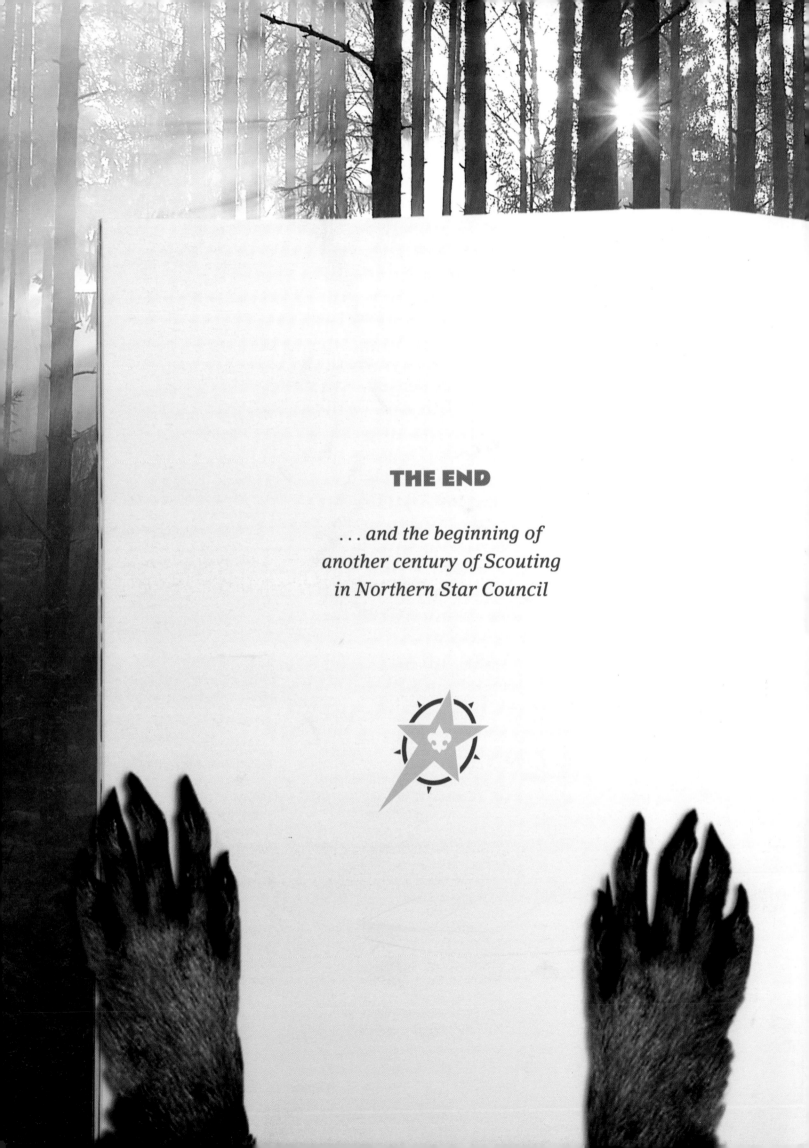

THE END

*... and the beginning of
another century of Scouting
in Northern Star Council*